THE RIGHT KIND OF HEROES

THE
RIGHT KIND
OF
HEROES

COACH BOB SHANNON AND
THE EAST ST. LOUIS FLYERS

KEVIN HORRIGAN

ALGONQUIN BOOKS OF CHAPEL HILL

1992

Published by
ALGONQUIN BOOKS OF CHAPEL HILL
Post Office Box 2225
Chapel Hill, North Carolina 27515-2225
a division of
WORKMAN PUBLISHING COMPANY, INC.
708 Broadway
New York, New York 10003

LIBRARY OF CONGRESS CATALOGING-IN-PUBLICATION DATA

Horrigan, Kevin.
The right kind of heroes : Coach Bob Shannon and
the East St. Louis Flyers / by Kevin Horrigan.
p.   cm.
ISBN 0-945575-70-X
1. Shannon, Bob, 1945– .   2. Football—United
States—Coaches—Biography.   3. East St. Louis
Flyers (Football team)   I. Title.
GV939.S42H67   1992
796.332'092—dc20
[B]   92-13723 CIP

10 9 8 7 6 5 4 3 2 1
First Edition

I say Eastside, you say Flyers.

Eastside!

Flyers!

I say who's that, you say Flyers.

Who's that?

Flyers!

I say what side? You say Eastside.

What side?

Eastside!

> *—Pregame cheer*
> *East St. Louis High School*

ACKNOWLEDGMENTS

East St. Louis, Illinois, is an accident of geography. So is this book. From 1986 to 1990, during a time when I was writing newspaper columns in St. Louis—first for the St. Louis Post-Dispatch *and then for the short-lived* St. Louis Sun—*I lived next door to Shannon Ravenel. Ms. Ravenel was then, and is now, an editor at Algonquin Books of Chapel Hill.*

From time to time I would write a newspaper column about Bob Shannon and the East St. Louis Flyers football team. Shannon Ravenel was fascinated by Shannon, Robert. She would drop broad hints. "You know, Bob Shannon would make a terrific subject for a book," she would say.

"I know, I know," I would answer. "Maybe someone will write one. I'm much too busy now."

In April of 1990 the newspaper I was working for dropped dead in its tracks. Ms. Ravenel, a Carolinian who embodies the best of southern sensitivities, waited for a decent mourning period to pass—two or three days—and then she approached me again. "Well," she drawled, "you're not too busy now."

I first met Bob Shannon at a sports banquet in early 1986. His team had just won its third state championship in a row and had been ranked as the top high school football team in the country. Though I had been a sports columnist for the St. Louis Post-Dispatch *for three years by then, I'd never seen the Flyers play. I had admired them condescendingly from my lofty perch where I wrote mostly about professional and college sports. What I admired most about Bob Shannon was his record; I had very little idea about what had gone into compiling that record. Bob and I talked for a long time at that banquet, and I began to get the idea that he might be a very special man.*

In 1989 Peter Hernon, a feature writer for the Post-Dispatch, *wrote a marvelous five-part series about Shannon and his team, based on reporting Peter had done throughout the 1988 football season. I am indebted to him for revealing more of the potential in Shannon's story and for graciously putting aside his own hopes to expand his series into a book.*

I am also indebted to Mike Eisenbath, high school sports editor of the Post-Dispatch, *for his reporting on the Flyers over the years and for sharing his impressions of Coach Shannon. Mike, too, had wanted to write a book about the Flyers, but it's hard to do that working sixty hours a week for a newspaper.*

I had no such obligations after April 1990, when the St. Louis Sun *went out of business. I became a radio broadcaster instead, stealing hours from that job to work on this project. My KMOX Radio colleagues, Charles Brennan and Fred Zielonko, patiently endured my lack of total concentration. I am grateful to the late Robert F. Hyland, regional vice president of CBS Radio in St. Louis, for my new career, as well as for his encouragement of this*

project. I owe thanks, too, to Thomas E. Rice and Ed Hines of the
Suburban Newspapers of St. Louis, to whom I still contribute a
weekly column.

I spent many happy hours in the Mercantile Library in St.
Louis, poring over old newspaper clippings from the Post-
Dispatch, *the* St. Louis Globe-Democrat, *the* Metro-East Journal,
and the Belleville News-Democrat. *I practically memorized cer-*
tain parts of Robert Mendelson's The Politics of Urban Planning
(University of Illinois Press, 1973*), which was central to under-*
standing the way East St. Louis developed; Ellen Schoen's Tales
of an All-Night Town *(Harcourt Brace Jovanovich,* 1979*) helped*
explain the bizarre flavor of East St. Louis. Rube Yelvington, an
old shoe-leather newspaperman who is now the Charles Foster
Kane of Mascoutah, Illinois, sent me a copy of his privately
published East St. Louis, The Way It Was *(*1990*), which I read as*
a Michelin's Guide *to East St. Louis.*

I must thank my family for enduring my absences and for
explaining to friends why the old man was so obsessed with a high
school football team. My sons, Dan and Casey, kept me company
at a lot of games and practices. My wife, Kate, is always my first
and best editor. I daresay my daughter, Sally, is the only four-
year-old in St. Louis who knows that the proper response to the
question "What side?" is "Eastside!"

Above all, I must thank the players, coaches, staff, and fans of
the 1990 *and* 1991 *East St. Louis Flyers football team. They let me*
hang around and get in the way for the better part of two years. I
went to their practices. I went to their off-season workouts. I lurked
behind the bench at their games. I rode their buses. I even cadged

an old broken Flyers helmet to mount in my office. They shared their triumphs and disappointments, their thoughts and their confidences, their hopes and fears. To the extent that it's possible for a fortyish white klutz who grew up in Texas to feel like a part of the East St. Louis football tradition, I do.

I thank them for their cooperation, and more than that for their dedication. As they slowly learned Bob Shannon's creed, I relearned it: No matter what stands in your way, success is possible if only you work hard enough. They are the future of East St. Louis, and it is to them and to that future that this book is dedicated.

THE RIGHT KIND OF HEROES

CHAPTER

1

High school football season in the state of Illinois begins in the middle of August, two weeks before the first day of classes. It ends in late November, on the Saturday after Thanksgiving, when the Class 6-A championship game is played at Hancock Stadium on the campus of Illinois State University in Normal. These are just the formal dates. For some people football season runs 365 days a year. There is always something to do. Never enough time.

July 11, 1990, for example. It is 94 degrees and stiflingly humid. The air in East St. Louis, Illinois, is almost yellow. This is a city edged with chemical plants. Their effluents hang over the city and mix with the smoke from the fires its citizens set to burn their trash. It's been three years since the city ran out of money for trash pickups. When the trash piles up high enough, someone torches it. Old tires, too. They pile up on vacant lots, steel-belted mountains, until someone with nothing better to do pours gasoline on them and touches them off. Tire fires are the devil to put out. Black smoke rises for days, mixing with chemical goo and the sweet-pungent aroma of burning trash. On days like today, when the breeze doesn't blow, the air can make you gag.

Bob Shannon, head football coach at East St. Louis Senior High School, is spending the afternoon with a can of Ortho weed killer. He is trying to turn a weedy lot into something resembling a football field. He paces back and forth across the field, squirting weed killer onto the crabgrass, trying to burn yard lines into it so his quarterbacks and receivers will have boundaries when they practice pass patterns. He laughs when it is suggested that chalk dust might do the job better and look a little more professional.

"Chalk," he scoffs, as if chalk dust were gold dust. He squeezes the can of Ortho. "Chalk," he scoffs again, squirt, squirt, squirt. "Who's going to put chalk down? I can't get them to cut the grass, so how am I ever going to get them to put down chalk?"

He's not only the head football coach, he's the de-facto groundskeeper as well. He is also the head equipment man and chief equipment scrounger, not to mention the head security guard for his domain. The domain includes the huge, weary-looking gym at the high school, a dingy locker room, a dank little weight room, and two weedy practice fields. It's not much of a domain, but it's all his. He has made quite a bit out of it.

He shakes his head. "Chalk. Do it this way, at least it stays down for a while. Who cares how it looks as long as it gets the job done?"

He doesn't mark the entire field, just some sidelines and four or five ten-yard yardstripes. Weed killer is not included in Illinois

School District No. 189's budget, so he's bought his own supply. Four quarts. Enough to set up at least a few boundaries. Shannon believes in boundaries. You've got to have boundaries if you're going to play football, got to have some idea of where you are and where you're trying to go. Boundaries are especially important to the passing game, and Shannon loves the passing game. Likes to talk about it, too, as he lines his field. He likes its precision, squirt, he likes its discipline, squirt, he likes its element of the unexpected. He likes upsetting the idea that black high school football teams are supposed to be too helter-skelter to run a precision passing game. Squirt. He likes doing what folks tell him he can't do. Squirt. The passing game is perfect for that, but you've got to have boundaries. Ten yards down and square in. Twelve down and square out. Go nine when you're supposed to go ten and you miss the first down or you have to run it up the gut. Squirt. He doesn't like running it up the gut, though he coaches that, too. Far better to go up top, read the situation and adjust, as long as you're disciplined and precise about it. Squirt. If the quarterback reads the coverage and throws the twelve-yard out, the receiver better make his cut after eleven steps and turn with his hands ready, fingers down. You can't do it without boundaries. Squirt.

The field is no great shakes. If you don't look close enough to see the yard lines–by-Ortho, you'd swear it was just another weedy vacant lot in a city that specializes in weedy vacant lots. The field stretches north behind the pale red brick blockhouse that is East St. Louis Senior High School, and on out toward more vacant lots where houses and small businesses used to stand.

Forty thousand people live in East St. Louis. In 1950 there were twice that number. The houses where those folks used to live have been torn down or left vacant, the lots allowed to grow back to forest primeval. The factories and businesses where those people used to work are mostly vacant now, too. They're locked and abandoned, FOR SALE signs faded from lack of hope.

To the east of the high school are a couple of streets of small white houses and then more vacant lots. West down State Street are strip shopping malls that are mostly abandoned. Forty blocks farther west you come to what's left of downtown East St. Louis. If the air wasn't so bad, you could climb to the top of the gym at the high school, look west, and see the gleaming Gateway Arch and the skyline of St. Louis, Missouri.

"Eastside" is what St. Louisans call East St. Louis High School. It lies toward the eastern edge of East St. Louis, forty-nine blocks east of the Mississippi River along State Street, out toward where the floodplain rises to meet wooded bluffs, along the route white folks migrated just as soon as they could scrape up enough money to leave town. West of the river, in St. Louis, "Eastside" is a slightly pejorative term, negative enough to have been banned from the pages of the newspapers along with "ghetto" and "slum." Over there, "Eastside" carries hints of ghettoes and slums and poverty and sin. The word isn't broad enough to encompass the burgeoning—and mostly white—Illinois suburbs of St. Louis. The name "Eastside" is left to the boys who practice on this field, the Eastside Flyers.

The grass on the field is trampled weeds, grown up high around the edges. The team found a body with bullet holes in it in the high grass once, but this is a city that specializes in bodies with bullet holes. The police were called, and practice went on as scheduled. There are ruts in the middle of the field where bulldozers and dump trucks have used it as a shortcut to the site five hundred yards behind the school where a new football stadium has been under construction for the last three years. "Look at this, man," Shannon says, digging the toe of a shoe into a rut. "Guys building a new stadium for the football team and they drive a truck across the field so a guy on the team can break an ankle and maybe never play again. Makes you wonder. I don't say nothing about it. Doesn't do any good. They're going to do what they want, anywise. Just got to go on and get it done anyhow."

"Get it done" is his favorite phrase. See a job, get it done. Need a first down, get it done. No money from the school board to buy new uniforms, wear the old ones, scrounge new ones. Get it done. Don't have fancy equipment, improvise. Make a weight sled, throw some two-by-twelves on the ground, use them for footwork drills. Get it done. Can't get a ride to practice, walk. Take a bus. Get it done. Eighty guys don't come out for football anymore because so many families have left town, deal with the forty or fifty who do come out. Work them like a chain gang. If they quit, deal with the ones who stay. Get it done.

In his fourteen seasons as head coach at Eastside, Bob Shannon's Flyers have won 144 games and lost only 20. Four of those losses have come by forfeit, 2 when a teacher's strike halted the season and 2 others when he discovered that one of his players was too old to be eligible. He's been beaten on a football field only sixteen times. Over the previous seven years, he's lost only 4 games. In fourteen seasons, he's taken his Flyers to the state championship game seven times and won five of them. He won 44 straight games at one stretch. Four times *The Sporting News* has named him High School Coach of the Year. And still here he is, on a hot day in July 1990, assassinating crabgrass.

He runs out of weed killer somewhere beyond the thirty-yard stripe and screws the lid back on the can. "It's hot," he says, running his arm across his forehead. "Going to be hotter in August, too. Might as well get ready. I tell the fellas, get your work in now, don't mind the weather. Going to be hot in August and you're going to work harder then. August, I'm in charge."

He walks back across the field and then across his main practice field, which is actually the back yard of the school, to a door in the corner of the rear of the gymnasium. The heavy steel door leads to the football locker room. It's deadbolted, as is his office door just inside. He locks his office every time he leaves it, even if he's only going to be gone for two minutes. This corner of the gym is the seat of Bob Shannon's kingdom, such as it is.

On this day in July, the showers don't work, but nobody expects the showers to work. Shannon's players must shower at home. The real problem is that none of the rest of the plumbing works either. No sinks, no toilets, no urinals. The floor is covered with water from the leaky plumbing. Only one bank of fluorescent lights is working, which gives the locker room the feeling of a cave. The buff-and-dark-green lockers are battered, some of them missing doors. A training room contains an examination table, some cabinets, and a stainless-steel whirlpool tub. The training room is filthy, too, but it will get a good cleaning before fall practice begins. "George will take care of that," Shannon says, speaking of his volunteer trainer,

George Walsh. "The rest of it, the school district is supposed to take care of. Been waiting on the plumber all summer. Maybe he'll be here, maybe he won't."

He pulls a jammed key ring out of his pocket and unlocks his office. It is actually a storage room, a messy storage room, a windowless room with walls of two-tone beige cinder block, lined with metal lockers. One end is piled high with boxes full of football shoes and T-shirts, hand-me-downs from the Phoenix Cardinals of the National Football League. The T-shirts all say ST. LOUIS CARDI-NALS, a reminder of the days when the football Cardinals made their home across the Mississippi. The shoes are all white and trimmed in Cardinal red, but each pair saves Shannon fifty dollars, so he doesn't care that they don't match his team's blue and orange colors. .

Shannon's own clothes hang from the exposed water pipes. He wears dress jeans and a golf shirt when he teaches his physical education classes or takes his turn as study-hall or lunchroom monitor. When it's time for practice, he usually wears leftovers himself—coach's shorts or sweatpants with St. Louis Cardinal shirts, or blue-and-orange coaches shirts he gets at football clinics at the University of Illinois, or one of the blue T-shirts that he finds someone to buy for his team. Today he has on a blue shirt that says, EAST ST. LOUIS FLYERS, NATIONAL CHAMPIONS, 1985–89. He believes in motivation by T-shirt. In some of the beat-up metal lockers lining his office walls are boxes of T-shirts. If a player excels in the weight room or in the forty-yard dash, he gets a T-shirt. T-shirts are one of the few tangible rewards Shannon has to offer a kid. Sometimes a kid will do something for a T-shirt that he wouldn't do for a twenty-thousand-dollar college scholarship.

There's a well-used television set and a VCR on a rolling metal stand in the middle of the room, an old student's desk, a wobbly orange plastic chair, and a brown corduroy sofa that looks like it was scrounged from a muffler repair shop. The arms of the sofa are upholstered in towels secured by adhesive tape. The sofa is piled high with notebooks and football manuals and a pile of letters from various colleges and universities. The letters are addressed to various players on Shannon's team, standard bulk mailings from college recruiters. In fourteen years, he has sent well over a hundred players on to college with football scholarships. He doesn't know exactly how many. He says he's never bothered to count.

The corners of the room are piled high with old newspapers and boxes full of equipment that needs repair. Shannon used to share this office with a couple of rats, but when a feature writer for the *St. Louis Post-Dispatch* put that in the newspaper, an exterminator showed up the next day. There is no telephone in the office, even though the coach gets a dozen calls a day from reporters, college recruiters, and other coaches. To reach him on the phone, one must first call the high school switchboard, which routes the call to the athletic director's office at the other end of the gym, where a student will be given a message for the coach. Sometimes the messages get delivered. The system suits Shannon. He does not like interruptions. Besides, he says, if he had a phone in his office, other teachers would complain that they didn't have phones, too.

Many of the teachers at the high school, as well as many people around town, feel about Shannon the same way that the Russian peasant in the old story feels about his neighbor who buys a goat. "I do not want to buy my own goat," the peasant says. "I wish my neighbor's goat were dead."

Despite his successes, or perhaps because of them, he is not universally admired around town. Part of that comes from the insidious rivalry between the two East St. Louis high schools. Part of it comes from the intensely political atmosphere in East St. Louis. And no small part of it stems from his own personality, blunt and aloof—some see him as arrogant. The few people who know him well speak of his sense of humor, his gift for mimicry. Shannon doesn't show that side of himself to many people.

He walks into his office, puts the weed killer cans in an overflowing trash can and takes a deep pull from a blue-and-white water jug. He keeps his own water supply because the fountains don't work either, although there is a water pipe on his wall with a valve he can open. The drain is in the floor. He puts the jug on his wooden desk, next to a brown ceramic football clock he got as a gift a few years earlier. The clock doesn't work, but it's the only decorative touch in the room, so it stands out. He sits behind his desk, puts his hands behind his head and stretches. He is a big man, six-three, a shade over two hundred pounds. In two weeks he will be forty-five years old, and he worries about his weight and his cholesterol count. He worries incessantly about his health. He has sworn off red meat and usually eats only one full meal a day, at night. In the off-season he jogs five miles a day; during the season he is too preoccupied to exercise. His cheekbones are high and well cut, his eyes are deep brown and cautious. His hairline is receding slightly, and he wears his hair cropped very short, leaving his sideburns long. His jaw is usually set firm, but when he smiles, the smile is wide and genuine and shows off a slight gap between his front teeth. His arms are long and his hands huge and graceful. When he speaks, he waves his arms as if he's conducting an orchestra.

"You know how he stretches out his arms and starts talking in that preacher's voice he's got?" Terry Hill, who played for Shannon in the late 1970s and is now an assistant coach, once said. "I tell you, it's scary, man. But when he speaks, you listen. He's got that voice, like a preacher, and you listen."

He looks less like a preacher than he does a retired NFL wide receiver, jogging gracefully into middle age. Twenty years earlier, he tried being an NFL receiver, but was cut after one summer's training camp with the Washington Redskins. "Guys always tell you they were the last guy cut," Shannon says. "Not me. I was the second-to-last guy cut. No speed. You know how they say all black guys are fast? I'm the exception that proves the rule."

He came to East St. Louis the year after his Lombardi summer of 1970, to seek work as an assistant football coach. "I remember the first time I saw East St. Louis," he says. "I thought I'd landed on the moon. It was the summer of 1971, and I'd come to town for an interview. I came in State Street and I remember thinking, man, I've never seen anything like this, and it wasn't as bad then as it is now. Boarded-up buildings, burned buildings. It didn't dawn on me then, but that was all the stuff left over from the riots of 1968. All I knew then was that I needed a job. I didn't pay as much attention to it as I should have.

"I went to the board of education building, and the first guy I saw coming out of the building was a guy in a hot pink outfit. Someone told me it was one of the principals. That was a shock to me, too, because where I came from the principals all wore blue suits, white shirts, and ties. I went in anyway, and they hired me and gave me my first assignment, down at the Hughes-Quinn

Junior High School. I went down to look for it. I found where it was supposed to be, but all I saw was this old building that looked like a factory, all boards on the windows and wire around it. I knew that couldn't be it, but I asked a guy and he said, yeah, that's it. I said, man, what am I doing out of Tennessee?''

But twenty years later he was still there in East St. Louis, lord of the corduroy couch and the cardboard boxes and the ceramic football clock that doesn't work. Asked if he wouldn't be more comfortable in an office that didn't look like a tornado had just struck, he says, "I haven't got time for that. There's never enough time in a football season and I've got to get ready for that."

The year before had been spectacular. His team had gone unbeaten and had won his fifth state championship. The two previous years, his teams had taken 13-0 records into the championship game, only to be beaten both times. Around town his detractors were saying he'd lost his touch, that he'd gotten soft. By winning it all in 1989, and by winning the championship game 55-8, he had laid that talk to rest. But now it was time to do it again, and he was not happy with his prospects. Too many good players had been lost to graduation, twenty-one in all—including three all-state players and five others who'd made the All St. Louis Metro team. Among them were his team leaders, linebacker Dana Howard, who'd won a scholarship to the University of Illinois, and wide receiver Kenneth Dunn, who had received a scholarship to play football at the University of Missouri. And he'd lost his quarterback, Rollie Nevilles, a brilliant sprint-out passer and scrambler. Shannon knew he'd miss Dunn and Howard, great players and intense, vocal team leaders. But he worried most about replacing his quarterback. He could spend all day spraying weed killer on his practice field, but unless he found a quarterback who could execute within the boundaries he drew, his summer would be a waste. There would be no time to find one once the season began.

"I've got to have a leader at quarterback," he said, sitting behind his desk, arms folded behind his head. "He's got to have the ability, but he's got to be a leader first and foremost. A kid can have the greatest arm in the world, but you never know how he's going to react when his helmet has been spun around and there's nobody blocking and he's eighty yards away with the wind blowing in his face."

He took another swig of water, then turned and spat half of it into the drain in the floor behind his desk. "I'm very hard on my quarterbacks for that reason," he continued. "I tell 'em if they can put up with me, they can put up with anything. Why they do it, I don't know. Some of 'em do it to get girls, some of them do it to make their dads proud. But they've got to have a reason to put up with me, a need to belong to something or the feeling of the challenge. That's the best reason, the need for a challenge. I tell all the kids that. If you come out for football, and you stay, then you'll know there is some reward in doing that. The reward is that I teach them to succeed."

Football, he said, is but a means to an end. For these kids the end is finding a way out of East St. Louis, or a way to stay in East St. Louis on their own terms. "The key is that they get to choose," he said, stretching his arms wide. "They gain the determination, the knowledge that if they work hard in a team setting and pull their share of the load, they can be successful in life. Heck, I don't want to win just so I can say I won, but to change attitudes and values, especially in a situation like the one around here.''

The best quarterback prospect he'd ever had was a young man named James Harris. He was six feet, eight inches tall and weighed well over two hundred pounds. He was big and strong and smart and fast. As a sophomore in 1984, Harris was a backup on an unbeaten state championship team. In the normal progression, Shannon expected him to challenge for a starting job in 1985. But when James Harris showed up for practice in the summer of 1985, he was sporting an earring. Bob Shannon hates earrings. He permits some of his players to wear them, but he will not abide them on a quarterback.

"To me, an earring says a guy's a follower, not a leader," he explains. "It means a guy is following a style, trying to impress somebody he shouldn't be trying to impress. That's not what I'm looking for in a quarterback. They want to be wearing an earring, they can play defensive back or split end.''

James Harris had a strong will; that's one of the things Shannon liked about him. Harris refused to take off the earring, so Shannon told him to start learning to catch a football instead of throw it. Harris walked out instead and transferred across town to Lincoln High. Under the school district's open enrollment policy, a student can attend either high school, regardless of where in the district he lives.

Harris got a measure of revenge. He started at quarterback for Lincoln for two years, and he played on a state championship basketball team there. But Shannon found other, earringless quarterbacks, and won two more state championships in those years, clobbering Lincoln 61–7 and 40–0 along the way. James Harris won a football scholarship to Temple University, where he played linebacker, and later recalled the earring incident. "When I got to college, it became much clearer to me. I sat back and said, 'Damn, so *that's* what he was talking about.' He was right about the label I was putting on myself."

No one among the four quarterback prospects in the summer of 1990 possesses James Harris's physical skills. The would-be quarterbacks, like all kids who hope to play for the Flyers, are required to show up at the gymnasium three or four days a week during the summer if they have any hope of making the team. Shannon calls this his "summer camp," and to comply with state athletic association rules, it is open to any kid who wants to play football, not just Flyers players. Unlike many coaches who run summer camps, he charges no fees. Campers lift weights, run, and go through informal drills. Shannon gets to the gym early, all by himself, and walks up and down the basketball court pushing a wide, ragged dust mop. He is there early in the morning, for kids who must get to summer jobs; and late in the afternoon, for those who prefer to work out then. "I figure if I'm going to ask them to put in the time, they've got to see that I'm doing it, too," he says. "I tell them this is the time when you make the team. If you're not in here getting better, some other guy is, and when August rolls around, it'll be too late. I don't cut anybody. They cut themselves. If you put in the work, you make the team. If you don't, you don't."

Would-be quarterbacks get special attention, an hour or two of intense instruction from Shannon. Of the four candidates this summer, only two are on hand this day in July. One is a stocky sophomore named Ben Williams, open and likable, but very raw. He played line in junior high school but wants desperately to be a quarterback. Ben Williams rides a bus across town every afternoon for practice, and Shannon likes that attitude. Ben Williams can't throw a football very well, but Shannon figures he can teach him that. His attitude and persistence are more important.

The other candidate today is a junior named Deondre Singleton, a boy with a long, sad face and a body that looks like it has been designed specifically not to play football. He has long, skinny legs; high, wide hips; and an upper body that is less a trunk than an attaché case. Singleton spent the previous season running Shannon's offensive scout team in practice. Scout teams are made up of young players and second-stringers who mimic the next week's opponent. Singleton spent a year being clobbered by the first-team defense. He impressed Shannon by never complaining, getting up each time he was knocked down, and coming back for more. Another thing impressed the coach:

"I was sitting over there in the bleachers one day with some of the kids and I heard one of the seniors, Jerry Creer, teasing Deondre. Jerry's a fullback, a good kid, but he was saying stuff like, 'I guess I'm going to have to play quarterback this year because you won't be able to handle it.' And Deondre said, 'We'll see about that.' "

Singleton has been showing up every day this summer to lift weights and work on his passing technique. Bit by bit, he's slowly tamed his awkward body. Under Shannon's instruction, he's learned to drop back quickly and avoid tripping over his long legs. He's learned to rotate his upper body, keeping the football held high, and to deliver the ball crisply, straight over the top of his head, without cocking his wrist. His passes are getting sharper and more accurate.

On this day, Singleton and Williams are splitting time throwing to would-be receivers. The receivers line up and run the patterns Shannon orders. Shannon stands off to the side and screams.

"You've got to rotate your body!" he yells in the hot, dusty gym. "Get your shoulders back around."

"Ben! Don't cock your wrist!"

"Quicker now, look him off! Come over the top!"

"Catch the ball with your hands, son, don't wait for it to hit your chest!"

"Fingers down when you catch the ball!"

He stalks onto the floor, waving his arms, walking a receiver through a pattern, then stalks back to his seat on the bleachers.

"Do it again."

"Catch the ball!"

"Don't cock your wrist!"

"Rotate, get your shoulders around!"

"Get your body into it! You ain't that strong."

"What you do wrong? What?"

"Do it again."

"Do it again."

"Not bad."

"Not bad" is his highest compliment. The receivers are

getting tired, running out of gas. The quarterbacks are having trouble getting their arms up.

"Do it again."

Finally he lets them quit. Linemen are up on the balcony of the gym, practicing technique with an assistant coach. He ignores them. Their most important work is done in the weight room, getting stronger. He will coach line technique later or leave it to an assistant. Right now he has to find a quarterback.

Under the normal progression, the choice would be easy. He has a returning senior quarterback, a bright and cocky young man named Darren Eubanks. Only his family calls him Darren. To everyone else he is "Stick." Stick Eubanks is bright enough to know that under Shannon, quarterbacks are cannon fodder as sophomores, backups as juniors, and starters as seniors. Stick reasoned this meant this year's cannon fodder would be Ben Williams and Kenvir Dixon, another sophomore. Deondre Singleton would be the backup, and he, Stick Eubanks, would be the starter. He'd paid his dues and was cocky enough to believe the job was already his. He hadn't been particularly diligent about summer workouts.

"And that's bad, because right now, Singleton's already as good as he is," Shannon said. "I got a sophomore out there and a junior, but where's my senior? Where's my senior leadership? He ain't here, and that's not good. By the time a boy is a senior, he ought to be a whole lot better than the junior or the sophomore because he's had two full years of work. But if you've got a junior who's as good as the senior, then the junior is going to start, because the junior is going to get better."

A couple of weeks ago, Shannon took both Singleton and Eubanks with him to a passing camp run by the University of Missouri coaching staff. The trip was a reward for the hardest-working players and a chance for Shannon to see them competing against players from around Missouri's recruiting area. The players were exposed to college-level coaching and had a chance for an overnight trip, the first time some of them have been out of the St. Louis area. There were two days of drills and eight-on-eight, pass-only games.

"Deondre was very impressive," Shannon said. "It was the first time I've really been impressed by him, and the Missouri staff was impressed, too. He just stood out in the eight-on-eight games. Eubanks just can't get his mechanics right. He keeps cocking his wrist when he throws, and everything sails high. Deondre just keeps getting better. I told Stick he'd better look out, but I don't think he believes me."

As he is saying this, he is locking his office and preparing to go home for the day. An assistant coach will supervise the late-afternoon weight lifters. Shannon makes a last check of the weight room to see who's there. Only one kid is left. Deondre Singleton.

Bob Shannon has been coaching in East St. Louis long enough that the city's 33 percent teenage pregnancy rate has begun to work to his advantage. He discovered this inadvertently one afternoon as he was telling stories about former players.

"We had this one player, the first couple of years I was coaching, he was built like a prehistoric monster," he said.

The line drew a laugh from the coaches and the players who were sitting around a water cooler listening to him. "Yeah," Shannon continued, "he had these long old arms and this skinny upper body. He looked like one of those flying monsters you see in dinosaur movies. He dislocated his shoulder and never did play much for us. What was his name? I want to say Pruitt. Yeah, that was it. Wendell Pruitt."

Suddenly he stopped and turned to Deondre Singleton. "Wait a minute. Didn't you tell me your dad's name was Pruitt?"

Singleton was blushing and laughing. "Yeah, that was my dad," he said.

"Don't tell him I said he looked like a prehistoric monster," Shannon said.

Wendell Pruitt had indeed tried out for the Flyers football team. He didn't win a letter and he didn't play, but he remembered. His greatest contribution to Eastside football came sixteen years later, when the son he fathered as a high school student became the Flyers' quarterback. Deondre had been given his mother's name, but had stayed close to both his parents. "I think one of the reasons he works so hard is he wants to please his dad," Shannon said. "And that's good. In this town, so many of the kids don't have the father around, but at least he's got a relationship with him."

Singleton was raised by his mother in a house a few blocks away from East St. Louis High. Sports, particularly baseball, dominated his life. "I figured on playing baseball, going to college if I could, then on to the pros if I could," he said.

His mother wasn't as enamored of East St. Louis as her son, so she moved him and his sister a few miles east to Belleville when Deondre was in junior high. He attended Belleville West High School as a freshman. "I kind of felt lost there," he said. "I didn't think I was going to get a chance to play very much."

Besides, his friends were all going to Eastside, and they all planned to go out for football. "I hadn't intended to play football, but Dennis Stallings, he told me the sophomore team needed a quarterback," he said. "I asked my mom, and she moved back here so I could play."

Not that he played very much, except to get creamed as the scout team quarterback. "It teaches you poise," he said. "You just got to keep getting up and doing it again. I'd stick around the huddle when the first team offense was practicing and stick my head in to hear Coach Shannon call the play, and then I'd watch. I got to learning the offense that way. Then over the winter, I decided if I was going to do this, I might as well try to be the best I could. I wanted to see how far I could take it. I knew people were looking at me, trying to see if I could do it, and I wanted to surprise them."

Singleton's best friend, a boy named Homer Bush, lived just up the street. Bush was a splendid athlete, a split end on the football team, and Singleton liked throwing the ball to him. "Homer and me started coming over here real early, my mom would bring me, and we'd throw for forty-five minutes every morning and then come back in the afternoon. Coach Shannon'd see us, and then he started giving me and Stick these papers with the offense on them, manuals to read and that kind of stuff. We'd have to study them and then he'd give us tests. He'd take us to the blackboard and then we'd have to teach him, like. We'd be the teacher and we'd have to diagram stuff and explain it all to him.

"The thing about him is he's not too bad in the off-season, but once practice begins, he's in your face all the time, lecturing you about the books. That wasn't new to me; my mother and father were on me all the time about getting my books, telling me if I wanted to play baseball I was going to have to hit the books, but he never lets up.

"It doesn't bother me. It's not like I'm a guy who wants to do the wrong thing, anyway, hang with the wrong guys. I'm not that kind of person. I want to do the right thing. I like to work hard, prove other people wrong. I'm a determined kind of person. If there's something I want to do, I'll do anything to reach that goal. I like to work hard. I don't need people all the time telling me to do it. I'm the kind of guy who knows what it takes to be a successful person."

Bob Shannon hardly knows what to think about the summertime. Some days he thinks it moves too quickly. Other days it seems to last forever. Fall practice starts August 13, and between now and then there's so much to do. And yet he can't wait to get started, really started, find out who shows up and who was just blowing smoke. You can only supervise so many passing drills, watch so much weight lifting, attend so many clinics, diagram so many plays, make so many plans, before you have to put your hands on the thing and see if it works.

Some days this summer, when there's time on his hands, he

walks out behind the school to where the new football stadium is under construction. When completed, the stadium will seat seven thousand fans in aluminum bleachers. It will have an all-weather track, a three-tiered press box, a lighted walkway from a front parking lot surrounded by wrought-iron fencing and stately brick columns. Shannon is alternately vastly amused and vastly irritated by the $5 million project.

He has a professional interest in it, and his team's success was chiefly responsible for the inspiration to build it, but he has been among the stadium's most vocal critics. Sometimes when he shows up to check on its progress, he's asked to leave the premises. "Sometimes I go over there just to see if I can find anybody working on the thing," he says.

In the early 1980s, Shannon was a strong advocate for a new stadium to replace the city's sixty-year-old high school stadium, Parsons Field. Parsons is one hundred yards of ragged grass surrounded by a worn-out cinder track. One rusty brown grand-stand stands at its edge. A busy set of railroad tracks runs behind the bleachers on the visitors' side. A chemical plant, one of the few remaining private industries in town, is located across the street. Edging the field are some of the most decrepit and dilapidated houses in East St. Louis, a neighborhood so tough that many people in town won't go near it, not even to see some of the best young athletes in the country.

When the new stadium was first proposed, the city's two public high schools were each producing top-flight athletes. Shannon's football team had won its first state championship, and Nino Fennoy, the track coach at Lincoln High School, was coaching athletes like Jackie and Al Joyner, the sister-and-brother combination that went on to become multiple gold medalists at the Olympics. Shannon and others argued that pride in the young athletes should be manifested in a new stadium. "The kids deserve better than that," he had said at the time. "The nice clean locker rooms that other kids take for granted. The good facilities. The field that doesn't look like the site of a gang killing."

On the other side of the argument had been Clyde C. Jordan, publisher of an influential city newspaper, the *East St. Louis Monitor*, and a powerful figure in local Democratic party politics. Jordan argued that the "mystique" of Parsons Field was part of a home-field advantage that shouldn't be wasted.

Then, in the mid-1980s, Jordan was elected president of the East St. Louis school board. Suddenly he became the stadium's biggest booster. Jordan's political clout helped convince voters to approve its construction as part of a $12 million capital-improvement bond issue passed in 1986. The stadium was to be completed in time for the 1988 season. But in April 1987 Clyde Jordan died of lung cancer. For two years the only decision made on the stadium was that it would be named the Clyde C. Jordan Memorial Stadium.

Finally specifications were drawn up and a contractor chosen. But the contractor found trouble getting an insurance company to underwrite the project, partly because the insurance firm originally chosen had run into legal troubles in two other states. All of this delay caused costs to rise, and design changes had to be made to bring the stadium in at the contractor's bid of $4.3 million. Electrical and mechanical contracts pushed the total cost to more than $5 million. Ground wasn't broken until April of 1989, with completion scheduled in time for the 1990 season.

But as Shannon makes his visits to the project site in the summer of 1990, it is apparent that the deadline will not be met. The grass on the field has been planted, but not watered, and heavy equipment is still parked on it. The track still isn't laid. Light standards haven't been raised yet. Nobody will let him in to inspect the locker rooms, but he's sure he'll be unhappy with what he finds. He says nobody checked with him when the architects designed the stadium, and as a result it is a little short on football amenities.

For example, while it will have a huge luxury viewing box for VIPs below the press box, it will have a home locker room only twelve feet square. While it will have fancy brickwork and wrought-iron fencing, it will have a nineteen-by-twenty-eight-foot meeting room that won't be big enough to squeeze in all the players and coaches. The team facilities have been shrunk because of the cost overruns caused by construction delays.

He was told early on that his team wouldn't be able to practice in the stadium, even though it was right behind the school and had lights that would permit evening workouts in the late fall, when darkness closes in early. He was told no, because that would give the Flyers an advantage over Lincoln High, which would also play its home games there. He then asked if bulldozers could level the ground just east of the stadium, which might be sodded for a new practice field. He figured he could have an assistant video-tape his practice sessions from the top of the bleachers. He was denied that request, too. It wouldn't be fair to Lincoln.

Also eliminated from the budget were the concession stands

and rest rooms planned for the visitors' side of the field. Portable toilets would be brought in for the visitors and their fans if attendance exceeded the thirty-five hundred seats on the home side of the field.

"Five million bucks and it'll have Porta-Johns," Shannon says. Friends tease him that the Porta-Johns will be stored in his office at the school when they aren't in use. "Might as well," he laughs. "It's the only place they won't get stolen."

The stadium has come to symbolize his frustrations with getting things done in East St. Louis, where nearly everything has a political ramification. With an independence born of a tenured teaching position and five state championships, he rarely misses an opportunity to criticize the city and school district's political structure. The politicians, he says, get even with him in small ways and large, and the stadium is the biggest one of all. Shannon responds by criticizing the stadium every time a newspaper reporter asks him about it.

Friends have urged him to be more tactful, to try to get along with the city's power brokers. "They tell me I should try to deal with them, go around to them when they're sitting in the bars, drinking and talking, try to bullshit with them," he says. "I won't do that. I don't hang in bars and I don't hang with the guys who do. They'll pat you on the back today and stab you in the back tomorrow. I'd rather go home and be with my wife."

This is perhaps the biggest sore point with the power brokers— not that he goes home to his wife, but that the home he goes home to is in Ferguson, Missouri, which lies near the St. Louis airport some twenty-five miles from East St. Louis High School.

"They tell me I'm selfish for criticizing the city when I don't even live here," he says. "I figure it this way. You only have one life to live, and I say you ought to live it as comfortably as you can. Hey, I come from poverty. I want to live in a place where they pick up the trash, where if you call the police you can be sure they're going to come. I don't think it's selfish to want to go home and be secure.

"People say, 'You don't come out enough, they don't see you enough.' I say, 'Hey, you don't need to see me, you need to see what I'm doing.' "

His boss, Samuel Morgan, principal of East St. Louis High, winds up catching a lot of the political flak about the coach. "I wish the hell he'd shut up sometimes," sighed Morgan, a blocky, balding man who has to be a political tap dancer himself to maintain his job as principal. "I told him one time, 'Coach Shannon, sometimes as you get older, you get wiser, and sometimes it's wise to learn how to bite your tongue.' He's getting worse as he gets older. His remarks about the stadium in the paper brought the wrath of God down on me."

Shannon can't seem to help himself, and most days he doesn't even try. He spends his summer days squirting weed killer on a rutted practice field, or trying to find enough practice jerseys for his players, and he looks out the door to see a $5 million stadium that's three years behind schedule, and who knows how many hundred thousand dollars over budget, and he just seethes. If you try to calm him down by pointing out that at least they're building him a decent place to play, he just smiles grimly and says, "Shoot. They'd build me a pyramid if they thought there was any money in it for them."

In the last week before the official start of practice, Shannon begins a series of meetings with his assistant coaches. "We have to get together on what we're going to do this year," he explains, though it quickly becomes clear that the coaches are going to do precisely what Shannon wants to do. The assistants are there to listen, to sit on bleachers in a corner of the gym and watch him scribble plays on a portable blackboard and to write down what he says in their spiral notebooks. Very few questions are asked, and nobody expresses a dissenting opinion. Shannon is the only professional coach on the staff. The rest are either teachers who coach other sports and coach football on a part-time basis, or volunteers who are paid out of Shannon's pockets or by donations he gets, or volunteers who aren't paid at all. None of them is on a career path to be a head coach elsewhere.

This is not by Shannon's choice, but by economic necessity. School district rules give preference to teachers in the district and limit to five the number of paid assistants, not that the pay is all that great. For coaching, Shannon earns about $2,500 a year over the $36,500 annual salary he earns for teaching two physical education classes a day and performing his other school duties. Each assistant is paid $1,700 above his teacher's salary for coaching, and nobody ever knows when the checks will arrive. It works out to about $4 an hour over four months of work. Shannon would like his assistants to do what he does, spend time in the off-season attending coaching clinics and seminars, reviewing films and books and technical manuals. But he doesn't think for $1,700 he can insist on that.

His five paid assistants this year are John Davis, a short, lithe

man with a perpetual smile on his face, the Flyers' track coach;
Terry Hill, who is built like the star running back he was for the
Flyers in the 1970s, now a teacher's aide and assistant track
coach; Art Robinson, a burly junior high school teacher known as
"Coach Rob"; Ken Goss, tall and intense, also a junior high
teacher; and Lenzie Stewart, stocky and quiet, whose coaching
duties are limited by his regular job as a police officer.

Also on the staff, hoping to be paid by some source or another,
are Wendell Smith, a lean and scowling man, a loner who sits
apart from the others; Morris Hunt, a large, barrel-chested
businessman whose hobby is the team; James Rucker, a blocky,
balding ball of fire, a school district employee who works
miracles as Shannon's aide-de-camp and equipment manager; and
George Walsh, a sixty-eight-year-old Illinois Transportation Department official who is the team's volunteer trainer and kicking
coach.

The men never refer to one another by first or last names. It's
always "Coach Shannon" or "Coach Hunt" or "Coach Davis."
The only exception is Rucker, who answers only to "Ruck" or
"Coach Ruck," and then answers mainly to Shannon. When
Shannon convenes his coaches meeting, Rucker stays in the
equipment room, taking inventory and trying to arrange for the
return of the team's missing helmets and pads. The equipment
was sent out for refurbishing over the summer, but the firm doing
the work has refused to return it. "They say the school board's
got a past-due bill of $40,000," Shannon noted. "I wouldn't be
surprised."

Shannon starts with a lecture on defense, which is tough for him because he regards defense as a necessary evil, something you do only to get the ball back for the offense. Defense plays to the strength of the players who come to East St. Louis—tough, fast kids who aren't afraid to hit someone. The key to defense is making sure the kids are in the right position to make a hit. It's a philosophy that has worked well for him in the past. His 1985 national championship team gave up only fifty-three points in fourteen games. Only once in the last ten years has a Flyers team given up as many as four touchdowns in a game.

"On defense, gentlemen, I would like you to stress form tackling. Last year we couldn't tackle worth a darn," he says by way of introduction, ignoring the fact that the 1989 team gave up only twenty touchdowns in fourteen games. "Tell 'em to make contact, then roll off and go make the tackle. Tell them never to hit with their heads down. Tell 'em over and over again, 'Heads up and butt down and drive through the man.' "

Shannon does not come from a family that regularly attended church, but you can't tell it by listening to him. He has the cadence and the pacing and the lilting pitch of a country preacher. From time to time he will stress a single word, drawing it out and pronouncing it slowly and carefully, as if teaching the word to a three-year-old.

"On defense, we play *read* defense," he says, as if teaching that three-year-old the word "read." "*Read* defense. Tell them to *read* what their guy is doing and adjust to the *read*. Making the *reads* on the line tells you where the ball is going. We want to play *sound*. Everything must be *sound* and have a relationship to everything else.

"Another thing. On the defensive line, I went to a clinic a year or so ago and had the opportunity to hear Barry Alvarez, who was coaching defensive line at Notre Dame. He said you want to find a guy who wants to get a lick in. Get a *lick* in. We want to build pride on the defense, want those guys who are *proud* to get a *lick* in. Our philosophy must be the opponents don't move the ball on us, and if they catch the ball, they *pay* for it with a *lick* and limp back to the huddle. You have to get it into their *heads* that we won't accept a *subpar* performance. And the way you teach them that is to keep them out there and do a little extra *running*. *Running* is how we discipline these guys, gentlemen. We do not hit them."

This last statement represents a change from Shannon's early years as head coach. Former players who drop by the school to watch practice tell him he's gotten soft. "Back then I used to be a whole lot tougher," he admitted one day. "At least I acted tougher. I used to whack kids with what I called the 'motivation board' if they messed up in practice. I got to thinking about that, and in 1983, I told the coaches we weren't going to do that anymore. They told me we won't win, the kids will take advantage of us. I said, well, we're going to try. We have to have the courage to try things a different way, try it before someone comes in and tells us we can't do it. We did it, and we won three state championships in a row. The kids appreciated it, and it showed them we can become different people, too."

The motivation board, an old cricket bat with adhesive tape on the handle, is still around. It goes along on all road trips and is used to handle cases of nonfield-rules violations, like skipping class, losing equipment, or wild behavior on the team bus or in a team hotel. Shannon has very few such problems with his players, mostly because the rigors of his program weed out troublemakers. Occasionally, though, a nonplayer will confront him in a school hallway or the gym or in the parking lot outside.

"There's been a few times I've had to challenge a kid, tell him to meet me in the back room," he said. "You tell him, 'If you think you're a man, well come on. We'll go head up. You take that pistol out of your pocket and we'll see how good you are.' Most of them just want to be talked out of it, so they back down and shut up. You tell them to hit you first so you won't get into trouble, but very few of them will take you on. Nobody has ever done it on me, though I've challenged a few. I knew a guy here, a teacher, who used to do it all the time. He stopped after one time when he took a kid back there and got his ass kicked."

East St. Louis is a violent town, and there are plenty of fights and, Shannon assumes, plenty of guns around the high school. But the violence on the football team is limited to the field, where Shannon controls it absolutely. Players guilty of personal fouls or flagrant cheap shots are removed from games or sent home from practice, and they don't play until reparations have been made, usually by *running*.

The question of disciplining players settled, Shannon continues his lecture on defense, calling out line calls, or code words, he wants used for certain defensive alignments. He loves football terminology, likes the way it sounds, likes the way it all fits neatly into the boundaries of his system. The players must all learn the line calls, learn to recognize and react to them when they hear them, learn to yell them out when they recognize an offensive formation. There's the "shade" call for the strong-side defense, focusing on the offense's tight end. There's "jayhawk," meaning the weak-side defensive end will slant on the pass rush. Or "shade tough," moving out of the "jayhawk" and holding position. "Eagle" tells the strong-side tight end to slant and the strong safety to flow to the hole he leaves. "Hawk" and "buzz" tell defensive ends to drop off the line, and "tango" tells the defensive end he must contain the outside play. "Easy" is the call from the defensive end to the defensive tackle, telling him to take the quarterback on the option while the end watches the running back for a pitch.

It's all ungodly complicated, and the new coaches are scribbling furiously into their notebooks. Shannon then moves into his defensive secondary, which can roll into any of four different pass coverages, not to mention the options given by the "press" or "loose" calls on the defensive line, which can turn a defensive end into a fifth defensive back. There are line stunts, signaled by "bingo" or "ram" or "jet," where players roll off their blocker and open a hole for a blitzing linebacker or a stunting lineman. There are "sky" and "cloud" calls between safeties and cornerbacks to determine who's in deep coverage and who's forcing the run.

It is too much for a grown man to absorb in a single sitting, and he hasn't even gotten into his offense, which is even more complicated. He leaves most of the offensive discussion for another day, knowing that it's really not that critical for his assistants to understand his offensive system, since he doesn't trust the offense to anyone but himself and the quarterback he will choose to execute it.

He dismisses "class" for the day, answering a few questions, watching the assistants huddle with one another like college students reviewing notes. He still has some coaching to do. Deondre Singleton has shown up for quarterback drills.

A few days later Shannon is sitting in his office talking about why his offensive and defensive systems are so complicated, about how he can expect sixteen-year-old kids in an inner-city high school to absorb tangos and bingos and jayhawks, arrows and slants and double-breasted plays like 22-23 pro-right 1. He gets the look on his face that former players, like Terry Hill, call "The Glare."

"You've seen that glare, man," Hill says. "You'd do anything not to have that glare in your face."

"Let me tell you something," Shannon says slowly, switching into his preacher's voice. "As long as I've been here, East St. Louis has been suspect, because black inner-city coaches are always suspect. The perception is they can't coach, and they've got all these good players, so they must be cheating. What they say about black inner-city coaches is they just get all that great talent and then let 'em play. That's not what I'm about. My philosophy is get good kids who may be great athletes, but they've got to be good kids first. Then you take them and make them execute well, understand what they're doing.

"A kid may come in here and have that quickness and have that breakaway speed that a lot of good black athletes have. But what good is it if he can't understand what he's doing? We try to do three things. Number one, I understand how to do it. Number two, I teach him how to do it. And number three, we do it. We execute. You know what they say about my teams? We make very few mistakes. We don't beat ourselves."

He rocks back in his chair, locking his long fingers behind his head, looking into the distance, and choosing his words carefully. "I know people don't think inner-city coaches understand the game," he said. "I love to play people who think like that, we'll lay fifty on them right quick. You see that there? It's a tape recorder. Every coach that comes in here to recruit a kid, and there are a lot of them, I make him sit here and talk football with me first. If he's the defensive line coach, we talk about what he does where he coaches. Then I take the tapes and play them in my car when I drive around. Some people listen to music, I listen to football. We have a whole system. Audibles. All my quarterbacks learn to call audibles and read defenses. We're noted for something and that's good skill people and good quarterbacks.

"The number-one problem with high school coaches is they don't know how to deal with kids. I get on my kids out there, but I tell 'em when they're doing it right, too. Dealing with people is one thing, and technical knowledge is another. Around here, we do both. It's tougher that way, but that's the way I am.

"All over America, we're losing that pioneer edge, the drive to tackle something tough and see it through. I hate the idea that black inner-city coaches can't coach. It's the driving force behind my work. My whole life is dedicated to showing people that if you put in the time, do the work, ask for help when you need it, you can succeed. I never want to add to a stereotype. I want to break it down."

CHAPTER

2

When the morning sun hits it just right, the parking lot at East St. Louis High School can be a dazzling sight. It's nearly three acres in size, and every square yard of it is sprinkled with broken glass. Hanging out in the parking lot and drinking is a time-honored recreational activity in town. The fun is punctuated by shattering the empties on the asphalt. Over the years, the glass has broken and rebroken until most of it has been ground down to the size of BBs. The parking lot can glitter in the morning sun and look almost beautiful.

The back corner of the parking lot borders the gymnasium and the back yard of the school, and it is there that Bob Shannon assembles his football team early on the morning of August 13, 1990, the first day of fall practice. Someone once drove a car around the light poles that stand in the lot and clocked the distance on an odometer at precisely one-quarter mile. Since the high school has no track, and won't be allowed to use the one in the new stadium when it's complete, Shannon uses the parking lot as a substitute. Four laps around the light poles to a mile. One mile before practice, and then speed work during practice and punishment laps afterward. A boy can learn to hate this parking lot long before he has a car to park on it.

There is no welcoming speech to start the fall practice, no laying down of the rules, no sign-up sheets, no induction ceremonies. In the season that never ends, this is just the beginning of a phase. A kid doesn't come out for football in the fall at East St. Louis. He has to be out all year long, out where the coach can see him. Fall practice just formalizes the control Shannon has all year long.

"I want you to enjoy this, fellas," he tells the players by way of introduction. "This is the easiest part of the year. You don't have to hit, you don't have to wear that heavy equipment. You just have to run and get into shape, and you should have been running all year long. It's not even hot today, so I don't want to hear anyone complaining. Go on and give me four."

The kids take off, dressed in a bizarre assortment of shorts and T-shirts. Most wear gym shorts, some wear sweatpants or the bottoms of nylon warm-up suits, some wear cut-off jeans or cut-off sweatpants. The shirts are old football jerseys or college or pro-team T-shirts. Missouri. Illinois. Duke. Chicago Bulls. Miami Dolphins. Miami Hurricanes. The shoes are a different story. Athletic shoes are important status symbols in East St. Louis, as they are in most American cities. Today's shoes are the expensive brands, Nikes and Reeboks for the most part, though most of them are very worn.

Shannon watches the players closely as they run their laps,

looking for kids who aren't going all out. If a boy who should be running close to the front of the pack is running close to the back, he'll get an extra lap tacked on this first day. It won't be a problem on subsequent days. He also takes note of the kids who arrive late, juniors and seniors mostly, who are trying to arrive in time to avoid the prepractice running. They'll get a chance to make it up, with interest, later in the day. Over the eighteen days that remain until the first game of the season, the team will build to two miles before practice and then run sprints after practice. "I like 'em to practice when they're already tired," Shannon says. "Some time down the road, they're going to have to win a game in the fourth quarter, when they're tired, and they better be ready for that."

Only about two dozen kids are on hand for the first day of practice, some eighteen to twenty fewer than the number who will make the team. Some have excuses, summer jobs that haven't finished yet. Others are unexcused. These unfortunate souls will drift in later, out of condition, and their days will be brutal until they get into shape. "Sure I wish there were more people here," Shannon says. "But I can't worry about the kids who ain't here. My job is with the ones who are. I've changed over the years. Used to be I didn't cut no slack for summer jobs. When I said be here, you'd better be here. But times are too tough for that now. Some of these guys have to work to make enough to buy their clothes and school stuff, and summer is the only time they can do it. I can't have them working when school starts, so they have to do it now."

The players finish their running in various states of exhaustion.

A few wander to the bushes that edge the parking lot, where they lose their breakfasts. "Gotta eat that breakfast, son, or you'll be sick," Shannon tells one boy. "Can't eat too much, though, 'cause that'll make you sick, too. Gotta get into shape. Those Bulldogs are in shape."

Those Bulldogs are from Sumner High School in St. Louis, a perennial Missouri high school powerhouse. In eighteen days the Flyers will open the season against those Bulldogs. A year ago East St. Louis beat Sumner 39-0, but Sumner went on to win the Missouri Class 4-A championship. Shannon is worried about revenge. "Those Bulldogs know we had a bunch of seniors last year," he says to his gasping troops. "Those Bulldogs think they can beat you guys."

To prepare for those Bulldogs and the teams that will come after them, Shannon will work his team three times a day. Most high school coaches are content with two-a-day workouts, but Shannon always goes three times. If he hears that another team on his schedule is working three times a day, he will schedule a fourth practice. "Nobody is going to outwork us," he says.

Actually the practices are more or less continuous: running at 8:30 A.M., followed by a short break and then drills from 10:30 to 11:00, the kids have from 11:30 to 2:00 P.M. for lunch and rest, but at 2:00 P.M. the offense takes the field for drills, followed by the defense at 4:00 P.M. Practice doesn't usually conclude until after 6:00 P.M.

It will go on like this for two weeks, when school starts with a week of half-day classes. Shannon will gear down reluctantly to a once-a-day practice schedule, but that once a day lasts from

2:30 P.M. until almost sunset. There is never enough time, especially this year, because he still has no idea when or if his helmets and pads will get here. State rules say he can't practice in helmets and pads until two weeks before the first game, but he plays in just eighteen days. If the equipment isn't back by the weekend, he'll fall farther behind. "Can't do nothing about that, so I try not to be bothered," he says. "Over the years, you get used to it, and you just have to go on and get it done anyway. But it's aggravating. Sometimes I wonder what it'd be like to work somewhere where you didn't have to put up with stuff like that."

On the positive side, he has stopped worrying so much about the quarterback position. A summer spent working with Deondre Singleton has caused him to do something he hardly ever does, which is talk in superlatives about players who are still on his team. He will use words like "best" and "greatest" when talking about a Kellen Winslow or a Dana Howard, young men who have graduated, but he always holds back with current players. Too many of them have disappointed him. But now, as he watches Singleton throwing outside on a practice field, for the first time, he can't help himself. "He could be the best we've ever had," he says.

Certainly Singleton is unlike any quarterback he's ever had. The tall, awkward boy can still barely run without tripping over his feet. He won't make any Flyer fans forget great scrambling quarterbacks like Vernon Powell, who went to Nebraska, or Ronnie Cameron, who went to Missouri. Singleton's gifts are his intelligence and his work habits and his right arm. He is the best pure passer ever to play at East St. Louis. "I never have to tell him anything twice," Shannon says. "And I've never had a boy who could throw like he can."

Singleton has spent the summer throwing in the gym, but outdoors, in full eleven-man formations, his arm is even more impressive. He has the strength to throw the deep out pass, where a poorly thrown ball can hang long enough to be intercepted. He has the touch to feather a screen pass or a long fade pattern that has to be looped precisely. And though Singleton makes mistakes, he makes them only once. "Can't do it that way, quarterback," Shannon yells. And Singleton doesn't do it that way again.

Shannon's players never have to wonder what the coach is thinking. He announces his impressions loudly and immediately, sometimes with withering sarcasm. This day, Stick Eubanks, the senior who had thought the job was his, is lackluster in drills, and Shannon is all over him. A pass is thrown behind a receiver, and Shannon says sarcastically, "Nice throw—shows how hard you've been working."

Eubanks barely glances his way and says nothing. He's used to this by now. "He's got that look in his eye," Shannon mutters, watching Eubanks's half-hearted efforts. "I just hope he isn't the kind of guy who'll quit if he can't start. He can still make a contribution, and he might still be a Division II college prospect if he sticks around. But he's a senior, and he just sees it from his point of view, and he thinks the job should be his."

If Eubanks doesn't stick around and Singleton gets hurt, Shannon will be in deep trouble. The only other candidates are Jerry Creer, a senior fullback who has never taken a snap at quarterback, and the two sophomores, Kenvir Dixon and Ben

Williams. Dixon didn't help his chances by showing up today wearing an earring (he was shipped immediately to the defensive backfield). And Ben Williams shows up late for the afternoon practice, not exactly the leadership qualities Shannon is looking for. Williams tells him he didn't know what time practice started.

"Funny how everybody else knew it," Shannon tells Williams in front of his assembled teammates. "Let me tell you guys something. You get into the habit of missing practice, you'll be the best-conditioned athletes in the state of Illinois you'll be running so much."

Shannon is all over the practice field during drills, screaming and interrupting plays, getting into his players' faces and glaring at them. "You got to pay attention," he yells. "We don't have time to make mistakes. Our job is to teach you and then you have to do it. We're young, we're going to make mistakes, but we can't make many of them.

"You coaches, never assume anything. Never assume these guys know the first thing about the game of football. If you assume, and he doesn't know, then it's not him who has messed up, it's the coaches who have messed up. You've got to tell these guys everything, and then you guys have got to do it. If we tell you, and then you mess up, then it's your fault and I won't have that. Do it again."

A little after six o'clock, he sends the players through sprints and then sends them home, telling them to be back before 8:30 in the morning. The assistants sit around a while, enjoying the evening shade, and then they, too, drift away. Finally Rucker locks the equipment room, and he and Shannon head for their cars. "A little ragged, but it's the first day," Shannon says. "Got to get the rest of these kids out here. We're missing too many people. But over all, it wasn't bad. Not too bad."

Even on this first day of practice, Shannon already has a pretty firm idea of which players are going to start for him, which plays they're going to run, and where his weak spots are. Fifteen years of building football teams have given him an intuition about such matters and a system he follows rigidly. "Ain't no secret to it," he once told an admirer at a national coaches convention who asked how his teams won year in and year out. "It's just hard work."

From time to time, however, there have been suggestions that he cheats. It's not uncommon for high school football coaches to stack their decks. In Texas, for example, junior high school players have been known to repeat a grade at the suggestion of a high school coach so that when they're eligible for high school ball, they'll have another year's growth. High school coaches play recruiting games, moving players into their school districts to live with relatives, even "adopted" relatives or guardians. Across the river from East St. Louis, coaches in St. Louis suburbs have taken advantage of a court-ordered school desegregation plan to recruit top black athletes out of St. Louis's inner-city schools. Schools in predominantly white suburban districts wind up with football teams with black players at most of the so-called "skill" positions in the backfield and at wide receiver. The practice frustrates inner-city coaches, who can't compete with the athletic and academic facilities found in the wealthier suburban districts.

This option is not open to Bob Shannon. Few students go out of their way to attend high school in East St. Louis. His recruiting is limited to hanging around the three junior high schools in the East St. Louis school district, looking for young athletes who have the choice of going to either of the two high schools in the district. On occasion he'll arrange transportation so a boy who lives near Lincoln can get to and from Eastside.

From time to time, however, there have been charges that he stockpiles his team from more exotic climes. The charges are never proven, but the very fact they are made infuriates him.

"Eastside is always suspect because black inner-city coaches are always suspect," he says bitterly. "In 1983 we beat a team from Romeoville in the playoffs, and all I heard was that I had gotten my good players from Florida. Florida! Man, these kids are lucky to even know where Florida is, much less to have been there. But some guys will do anything to win except what it takes, and that's hard work.

"Winning has never been our emphasis. We feel if you get the right players and do things the right way, winning will take care of itself. We don't produce athletic bums. Yeah, because of where we are and the kind of kids who live here, we're going to have a few outstanding guys every year. Let's face it, a lot of young black guys are good young athletes. And life is pretty tough here. A kid doesn't get to be fifteen or sixteen years old in this town without learning a little bit about being tough. By the time they get to me, I know I've got a chance because they've already been through a lot, and they wouldn't be choosing to put up with me if they didn't have a reason. But we don't win just because we've got all these great players to choose from. Look at Lincoln. They get their players the same place we do, and they don't win like we do.

"You don't succeed every year with all outstanding guys, because you don't have all outstanding guys every year. You succeed with the average guys. You succeed with average guys who are smart and willing to work hard. It's like Bear Bryant said: 'People who are tough and not smart will get you beat.' I'm after smart kids who are the right kind of kids."

The search for the "right kind of kid" never ends. It is the cornerstone of Shannon's program. "When I first became head coach back in 1976, I had a vision," he said. "I didn't share this vision with anyone else, because they would've thought I was crazy. My vision was to have one of the best high school football teams in America. The way I look at it, if you're going to do anything, you should try to be the best you can possibly be. I didn't buy the idea that because I was coaching in East St. Louis I was going to have to settle for halfways."

Shannon had been an assistant coach at Eastside for four years when he got the head coaching job and the vision that went with it. He'd spent his first year in town as an assistant at Lincoln, but there was talk at the time that Lincoln would be phased out and the district would consolidate its high schools in the new building at Eastside. With an eye toward security, Shannon accepted an offer from Cornelius Perry, then the head coach at Eastside, to work for the Flyers instead. "That's one reason the Lincoln people don't like me today," he says. "I left there to come here. I think they resent the success I've had. People here are trapped in a time warp, man, always talking about when they were in high school. A lot of it has to do with there not being much else to do. You get together, have a drink or two, and talk about what happened twenty years ago. I hear about it from the fans, always talking about how they could've beat us way back when they were playing."

As a young assistant under Perry, Shannon coached the Flyers' sophomore team in its limited schedule of four games and worked with quarterbacks and wide receivers. They were good years—Eastside was a good team long before Bob Shannon—but they never won a state championship. The 1974 team, led by Kellen Winslow and Eugene Byrd, came close, losing 19-13 in the state championship game when they made the mistake of taking an opponent too lightly. "I learned a great lesson from that game," Shannon recalls. "You can have all the great talent in the world, but if you're not disciplined, it won't matter."

Certain key words—and "discipline" is one of them—trigger an almost automatic short lecture from Shannon. "Discipline" pushes a button and triggers "commitment" and "preparation" and "character" and "the right kind of kids" and "get it done." By the time a kid is a senior, he's heard this lecture nearly every day for three years. It doesn't mean the kid has absorbed it, though that's the hope. "You know what's bad?" Shannon asks. "It's when one of the players gets into trouble, with the law, say. It always says in the paper that he's an East St. Louis football player, or a former East St. Louis football player. It doesn't say what else he is or what else is happening in his life, but it says he's a football player. That's bad, because it reflects on every other kid on the team. But that's the way it is, and we can't have that. The way you stop that is to get the right kind of kids."

The "right kind of kids." He pauses, letting the key word cue up the rest of the lesson.

"Good people will do good things, and they'll stay with you. It's easier to get them into the mold to do the things they're supposed to do if they're the right kind of person. I assume that every kid who comes out for football is a pretty good person. But I don't stop with that assumption. I keep watching, looking for something that will prove to me who they are and what they believe in. I look at the people they hang with. Too many times the heroes in this town are the wrong kind of guys, the guys with the flashy clothes and the flashy cars. I know what they do, and so do the kids, and I want them to know that I know.

"You know, it used to be that being a part of our football team was a big thing around town. It still is, but it ain't as big as it used to be. Nowadays the big thing is to be working a hustle, to be selling drugs or having yourself a 'position.' The big thing for a lot of these guys in town is not having a job, because you got to work if you have a job. They all want a 'position' where they get paid without working. You got to play ball with the politicians to get yourself a position. I won't do that, and I won't let these kids do that. I've got this philosophy that anything that's worth having is worth working for. The things that come easily are not greatly appreciated in the long run. I make sure that being part of the football team does not come easily.

"These kids know they're being evaluated twelve months a year, not just from August to November. I don't bring them in and talk to them very often, but they know I'm around, watching. We evaluate them on the playing field and on the practice field, and we evaluate them when they're not practicing, when they're getting ready for practice. I want kids who are in a hurry to get out on the practice field."

Shannon is a watcher. When he's not coaching or teaching, he roams the halls of the school or sits on a chair in his corner of the gym, watching gym class. He says very little, but he doesn't miss much. He will get in his car and drive through the streets, watching the hangouts, cruising by the drug corners. He'll spot the new earring or the new friend, the expensive new coat or the new pair of Air Jordan basketball shoes. His eyes will narrow, stopping down to f/16, and click, the impression is stored.

"It starts the first time I see a kid. I like clean-cut guys. I won't even ask a guy with an earring in his ear to come out for football. Maybe someone will come to me and say, 'Coach, he's a pretty good guy,' and I'll give him a shot, because I like for the kids to stand up for each other. They know what I'm looking for, and it's good for them to be thinking along those lines. I'll see a boy I haven't seen before, a big kid, and I'll ask one of the older players about him, and they'll say, 'Coach, he's pretty fast and he's pretty strong.' Then I say, 'What kind of guy is he?' And if they just shrug or something, I won't even waste my time on him. He might have all the talent and ability I'm looking for, but no character. What's the use in that? He might be in jail in three weeks. I've got lots of confidence in my ability to coach them, but we have to have people who can stay eligible, who want to do it, and who are going to stay around.

"The big thing is the off-season. That's when you make this football team. We expect them to improve in the classroom then, because that's the time when they don't have to worry about practice and games. I want to see academic improvement and athletic improvement. I want to see some of that dedication and preparation and discipline. I'm down there in the gym and the weight room all the time. I'm a little looser in the off-season. I talk to the kids, try to motivate them. By the time we start out here in August, I know who's going to play for me. I take the individuals who come closest to having the qualities I'm looking for. Some coaches look for talent first. Not me. I look for good kids. Kids at this age are changing so fast, maturing so fast, that if you get one who wants to do it, and if he's got anything at all between his ears, I feel we can teach him."

Shannon spends most of his afternoons during the school year in the gymnasium, supervising his own players and monitoring physical education classes. Many of the students he sees there are bigger, stronger, and more agile than his football players. He checks them all carefully, like a shopper inspecting peaches in a supermarket, discarding one after another for various imperfections. Too lazy. Bad habits. Bad company. Poor grades. Not the right kind of guy. He is always looking, always checking, searching for the raw material from which he is utterly confident he can make a football player. He is a watcher, and he watches his players most carefully of all.

"The one thing I have to do in the off-season is find me some leaders," he says. "I read a book once by a guy named Robert Preston about personnel in complex organizations. He divided people into three basic groups. He said there were the upwardly mobile, the guys who share the goals of the organization and who exert a lot of effort on the job. Then there were the indifferent ones, the ones who say, 'I just work here.' They just go on and do the minimum they can get away with. And then there are the ambivalents, who can't ever get started. You need these upwardly mobile types to be your leaders, so they can communicate your goals to the others. I'm looking for people who take what I say and then repeat it in the locker room, or in the huddle. They can hear me talk about something all the time, but if they hear it from another kid, it sinks in. It's the way kids are. That's why Dana Howard was so important to us last year. He was a big guy and nobody wanted to mess with him. But he was such a good kid, and he made everybody around him want to be like him. I don't see anybody like that this year, not yet.

"The quarterback, maybe, if he keeps improving, but he's just a junior and you need your seniors to be your leader. Maybe Jerry Creer and Homer Bush, but they're both kind of easygoing. Clarence Green is the closest, but he's so quiet. I tell those seniors they've got to take charge, and they say, 'Yeah, coach,' but it's hard for them to do it if they're too worried about their friends and what they're gonna think. I got a couple of big guys on the line that have that leadership ability, but I don't know about their work habits. It'd be bad not to have anybody like Dana, but it might be worse to have the wrong kind of leaders. Chris Moore wants to be that leader, but that might be the worst thing of all. I don't know about Chris Moore."

Chris Moore is five feet, ten inches tall and weighs 185 pounds. He is only a junior, but already he gets a dozen letters a week from college recruiters. As a sophomore in 1989, he shattered Shannon's "sophomores don't play" rule by the sheer force of his talent. He gained 1,191 yards on 127 carries. He averaged more than 9 yards per carry. He gained another 671 yards on punt and kickoff returns, averaging 27 yards per return. He scored twenty touchdowns. He became a big star, and he began driving Bob Shannon crazy.

His off-season workout habits were sporadic. Shannon spotted him hanging out with people he disapproved of, kids he knew had disciplinary problems at school. Chris spent a lot of time goofing off, scrounging french fries in the cafeteria, showing off for girls, leading around a pack of admirers.

"It's like Chris always wants to be the center of attention," Shannon said shortly before fall practice began. "He's been mad since I didn't take him to the Mizzou camp in June. I only took eleven guys, the quarterbacks and the receivers and some of the seniors who'd been working hard. It's a big deal for them, two days out of town. I didn't take Chris. Too many teachers had come to me and said he wasn't coming to class on time and not working hard. Acting like somebody owed him something. He got suspended one day because he wouldn't take off his cap when a teacher told him to. What kind of thing is that to do? Why should I reward him for that? The thing is, he lost status in the eyes of his teammates when he didn't go to camp, so he's been talking about transferring to Lincoln.

"He's got all these Lincoln fans hanging around, telling him he'll never be a big star over here, and that he'll be the center of attention over there. I said fine, if that's where he wants to go. What Chris don't know is that I haven't even planned for him to be here. I've got to be planning the offense we're going to run, and I got to know who's going to be here. I can't count on Chris Moore being here, so he ain't in my plans. We're going to throw the ball, and if he does show up, he's not going to carry the ball as much as he did last year. Chris thinks he's as good as he needs to be. That's not my philosophy. He thinks he's going to come in here and carry the ball every down, he's in for a big surprise. You see a lot of guys like that. They realize in their senior year that they've got to get to work, and by then it's too late. Young people always think they've got time."

But lo and behold, Chris Moore did show up for fall practice, wearing a cap tilted sideways on his head and a chip on his shoulder. "Chris is still talking about going to Lincoln, coach," one player told Shannon during a water break. "Says a Lincoln man going to pick him this afternoon."

"That's fine," Shannon said. "Chris looks a little heavy to me. He won't help them that much."

The kid laughed and disappeared into the mass of players crowding around the orange water coolers. Shannon knew his message would be delivered.

Chris Moore grew up on Fifty-eighth Street in East St. Louis, not far from Eastside High. His father, Lawrence Moore, drives an oil truck. His mother, Sarah Moore, works as a secretary. His parents do not live together. For a while, Chris tried to split time between his mother and dad, an arrangement that would lead to all kinds of troubles for the Flyers. When you can run with a football the way Chris Moore can, where you live becomes a matter of grave importance to high school coaches.

Chris Moore started running with a football when he was eight years old, in a midget football league. "I always been a running back," he says. "Since the first time I played. I seen people pay more attention to running backs than anyone else."

He played running back at both Clark and King junior high schools in the East St. Louis district, setting three different rushing records in three years. He was a hot ticket, but there was never any question where he'd go to high school. His older brother, Lawrence Moore, Jr., had gone to Eastside and then signed a professional baseball contract. "For me," says Chris Moore, "football is a chance to make some money."

He is a medium-sized kid with a compact, muscular build. He walks through the halls of East St. Louis High as he runs on a football field, on the balls of his feet, almost springing along, his eyes darting back and forth. He wears his hair cut very close to his scalp and practices keeping a grim look on his round face. He speaks softly, in broken phrases, snatching one thought after another out of the air, mumbling his words. He is eager, he says, to get this amateur part of football behind him, to go somewhere where he can get rewarded for carrying the football. He doesn't want to wait in line, taking a year off as a freshman— "redshirting," the colleges call it—to get used to college. "Wherever I go," he says, "I want to break some records. I want to go to college, somewhere they got a running back who's about to graduate. I ain't gonna redshirt nowhere. I got to play."

He is impatient, too, with practices and school and everything else that fills up the time between Saturday afternoons in the fall. "Football ain't no fun except on Saturdays," he says. "I like the games. I like the ball. I like getting a lot of attention."

He is impatient, too, with Coach Shannon. "I knew about him when I came," he says. "I thought about Lincoln, people wanted me to go there. But I was used to being on a winning team, and I knew he had winning teams. They told me he was hard. They told me he wanted you to do right. They told me he was a good coach on the field, but off the field they say he ain't a good man, telling the scouts about all your problems."

And now, after putting up with Shannon for a while, what does he think about what he was told?

"He's a good coach. He wants you to do right. All the rest of the stuff, I got no problems. He be on me about my weight, how I got to show him I want the ball. It don't bother me. I'll show him. I got no problems."

One thing that worried Bob Shannon about the first week of practice was the weather. It was much too nice, unseasonably cool for the Midwest in mid-August. "Yeah we can get a lot of work in," he said. "But you know it's going to be hot in September when we have to play. We won't be ready for it. If you're going to play in the heat, you have to work in the heat."

He got a break at the end of the week. Hot, muggy weather

returned, and so did his pads and helmets, freshly repaired and cleaned and paid for. Now the work could begin in earnest.

"I've been tolerant this week," he tells his players as they line up in the parking lot to run their laps. "From now on, no tolerance. You don't miss practice. You don't come late. I'm getting tough from now on, and I suggest you all do the same."

To show them what he means, he takes out a stopwatch and announces that this morning's laps will be run against the clock. "I want you to challenge yourselves," he says. "The first group that runs is going to have to finish in a minute-twenty. Now who thinks he can run one in 1:20?"

A dozen or so kids crowd forward. "Come on now," the coach says to the group lagging in the back. "Get up here and join group one. These are the guys who are going to get it done. We can count on them. These are the money men. How do you feel about yourselves, fellas? Group two is going to be the one-thirty guys, they're going to be kind of shaky. Group three is going to be the one-forty guys, the guys who want to take the easy road. Come on now, tell me who can get it done here."

The first group takes off, and as it hits the end of the parking lot, the second group takes off, and then the third. At this point, Chris Moore, who is the last player out of the locker room, arrives. "Well, here's Chris Moore all by himself," Shannon says loudly to his assistants. "Chris likes that special treatment, so we'll give it to him. You wait until everyone else is finished and then you do me one, Chris."

Moore smiles, embarrassed, but almost happy to be singled out. The first group finishes strong, and the second, and the third group straggles in, big overweight linemen for the most part. The players are sucking for air in the morning heat and humidity. Shannon sends Chris Moore off with the hoots of his teammates in his ears. Moore turns once and glares at them. "Look how slow he is," Shannon tells the team. "I told Chris all summer he wasn't working hard, and now he shows up fat. He's gonna be surprised at the guys who catch him from behind this year."

The players watch Moore run his laps, and then they gaze upward to watch planes from nearby Scott Air Force Base doing low-level passes over East St. Louis. Shannon counts half a dozen planes and two dozen players. Among the no-shows is a young man with the kind of excuse you hear only in places like East St. Louis.

"His stepbrother got shot in a tavern last night," Shannon said. "A guy said don't come back in here, but he came back in anyways and got shot. They say they don't know if he's going to be all right. The kid said he'd come on in, but I told him to stay at home with his family."

Shannon learned later that the player's stepbrother had died of his wounds, and that he had been the second member of the boy's family to die in the violence that is a part of life in East St. Louis. The city's per capita homicide rate is the highest in the country. "We've never had a player murdered," he said, "but around here, you never know. This is a tough place for a kid to grow up."

Shannon is annoyed at the unexcused absences from practice but pretends not to be. "I can't be concerned with those that ain't here," he says, repeating his refrain. "I got to get it done with what I've got."

Rucker passes out practice equipment, a motley, mismatched collection of old jerseys and hand-me-down pants that he has scrounged from various sources. Rucker spends a lot of time on the phone, tracing used equipment and then telling Shannon what it will cost. One year's big bargain was a lot of old football shoes bought from Vashon High in St. Louis. Vashon is an inner-city public school, but it had managed to find money in its budget for new shoes, and Shannon was glad for the leftovers at a dollar a pair. "Kids got to practice in something," he says. "I remember last year we went over to Busch Stadium to practice for the state championship game. They've got artificial turf in there like they do at Illinois State where they play the finals, and the Cardinals always invite us over to practice there. They invited Hazelwood East, too, because they were going to play in the Missouri championships. Our guys were looking at Hazelwood East practicing, and they all had their names on the back of their jerseys. The kids say, 'Coach, why are they practicing in their game jerseys?' I said 'Guys, those are their *practice* jerseys.' They couldn't believe it. Man, our practice jerseys aren't even all the same color."

East St. Louis never seems to have money for equipment, so Rucker and Shannon have become adept at finding backdoor sources. Last year Rawlings Sporting Goods, headquartered in St. Louis, donated new game uniforms. The year before, a local university had changed coaches, and the new coach wanted a new style uniform. The university passed on its old practice uniforms, at least those that were still serviceable, to high school teams, the Flyers among them. Some businessmen in St. Louis had donated enough money to buy a washer and a dryer so the uniforms could be kept clean. Shannon and Rucker jury-rigged the plumbing so the machines would work. Previously Rucker had had to cart the uniforms off to a nearby laundromat, armed with a roll of quarters.

The big addition this year is a commercial ice machine donated by a benefactor in St. Louis. What with the ice used to treat sprains and bruises and the ice used in water coolers, football teams use hundreds of pounds a week. Before the gift of the machine, Shannon paid for all of the ice himself. "Now the only thing I've got to do is find a way to lock it up so somebody doesn't steal it," he says. "Around here, it don't matter what it is, you have to lock it up. Ice machine might weigh two thousand pounds and they'd steal it in a minute."

The ice is a blessing in the heat and humidity of this Saturday morning. Rucker and his student assistants have filled four twenty-gallon coolers with ice water and lugged them out to the shade of the gym wall. The only thing missing is cups. Coach Art Robinson volunteers to go pick some up. Shannon reaches into his wallet and pulls out a ten-dollar bill. "Where you going?" he asks Robinson, handing him the cash.

"Just going to run over to the Red Fox," says Robinson, referring to the convenience store up the street.

"You be careful over there," Shannon says. "They're liable to be real excited to see cash at the Red Fox, they see so many food stamps. Got them food stamp prices, too."

At that moment a sophomore player trots up, shirtless, to say that Rucker sent him out to talk to Shannon. "A guy stole my jersey," he explains. "Coach Ruck said I had to ask you for another one."

"Fellas," Shannon says to his team, scattered on the grass outside the locker room, trying on their new, old equipment. "This sophomore has lost his jersey. Someone want to tell him about the rental fee?"

"Three swats!" answers a chorus of seniors and juniors.

"That's the way it is, son. Three swats. You know how it is around here. You don't leave equipment around for even one second, not even to go to the bathroom. Go see Ruck and tell him you came to pay the rent. The rest of y'all, let's go to work."

With the players finally equipped, Shannon is in his element. He has a team, in pads, and the hitting begins immediately. Some coaches don't like heavy hitting and scrimmaging in early practices, preferring to work up to it and avoid injuries. Shannon sees it differently. "We hit every day, twice a day," he says. "It's when you don't hit every day you get injuries. We learn to hit right and how to take a hit. We teach them to deliver a blow. Look at Chris Moore."

When you see him with a football in his hands, it becomes apparent why Chris Moore feels a fuss should be made over him. He is a gifted back, with a loose and powerful gait that lets him react instantly. He has a sense about when he is about to be hit, and he reacts to counter the blow, driving his shoulders and pumping his legs. "The only time Chris gets serious is when he has the ball in his hands," Shannon says. "But then he gets real serious."

The scrimmage is long and repetitious, and strictly according to the play sheet Shannon holds in his hand. Each night he diagrams a dozen plays on a single sheet of paper and then carefully inserts it into a plastic sheet protector. Today's sheet is the basic Flyers' offense for 1990, half a dozen running plays and half a dozen passing plays. "We're so young, we have to keep it real simple," he says. "What we try to do is run the same basic plays out of four or five different formations. That gives us fifty or sixty plays, depending on the defense we see. We'll add a few more as the year goes on, depending on who we're going to play and how quickly these guys pick up what we're doing. The key to our offense is being able to do what we want to do, no matter what the other guy does. We do it right, execute, and we don't need a lot of plays."

In these early days that means endless "reps," or repetitions. Tailback dive right, tailback dive left. Fullback dive right, fullback dive left. Tailback draw right, tailback draw left. Shannon likes draw plays, designated "bandit" in his terminology, that allow Chris Moore to wait for the quarterback to bring the ball to him, giving him an extra second to read the holes in the line. Time and again Shannon makes the offense run the same basic play. "Pro-right red, 23 bandit," he says. "Run it again."

It is a draw play to the weak side, in this case the left side, the one away from the tight end and the flanker. It is designated 23 because the number 2 back, the tailback, runs off the number 3 hole, between the left guard and left tackle. The offense lines up in split backs, the tailback and the fullback side by side, two steps behind the quarterback. In "pro-right red," the "red" means the tailback is to the left of fullback. "Blue" is the code for the fullback to line up on the left.

Shannon thinks 23 bandit will be his single-most-effective play this year. "We have a great split end," he says, meaning Homer Bush. "Everybody knows it, and normally, that means they're going to drop somebody off the line to take away the quick pass to him. That means the defensive tackle has outside containment. He has to go in high, to watch the sweep, and we'll get a good angle to block him outside and run inside of him. Sometimes we'll run it with a trap block by the right guard, and sometimes with other blocking schemes. The line will communicate with each other depending on the defense they see. If they're in a 4-4, the center will pull and take that outside guy and the fullback will take the end."

Another key to the play's success is the Flyers' right guard, a stumpy senior named Clarence Green, Jr. "Junior" Green is Shannon's best offensive lineman, a team captain, the too-quiet, hardworking kid who more than any other player on the team has taken Shannon's lectures to heart. He wants desperately to go to college and figures football is his only chance. At five feet nine, he is at least four inches too short for most major college programs, and at 230 pounds, he is very slow. But he lifts weights religiously and practices intensely. Shannon has told him that if he is strong enough and smart enough, a smaller college might take a chance on him. Green plays every down as if his future depends on it. Sooner or later, he figures, a college recruiter will ask who's opening those holes for Chris Moore on 23 bandit.

"Junior's a smart guy," Shannon says. "The weak-side draw is one of the most fundamental running plays in football, but when you add the variations to make it work against all the defenses, it gets pretty complicated. That's why I want intelligent players. It's complicated, but they get all of it or else they're out of there.''

On this day, they're getting it right. Singleton takes the snap, turns to his left, takes two quick steps back and puts the ball into the tailback's—Chris Moore's—belly. Junior Green pulls from his right-guard slot, moves quickly across the center and kicks out the defensive end. The left guard and tackle are double-teaming the defensive tackle. Moore reads the blocking and takes off. Nobody touches him.

Between now and the first game of the season, he will practice it a hundred times or more, and its right-side counterpart, 24 bandit, another hundred times. The other plays on his sheet will get a similar number of reps, until the coach is satisfied it is second nature. After each rep of each play, Shannon will stride into the middle of the field, finding fault or giving praise.

"What'd you do wrong there, tackle?"

"Whose man was that, linebacker?"

"Who you supposed to block, fullback?"

"Do it again."

And then without telling the defense, he will call 1-23 bandit, split end post corner, a passing play based on a fake. The "1" is his terminology for a play-action pass. Singleton puts the ball into Moore's belly, and then pulls it out, stands up and throws a deep-corner pass to Bush, who is all alone. The cornerback assigned to cover him has seen 23 bandit so often he overreacts. "You've got to read your keys, cornerback!" Shannon screams. "You've got to be smarter than that."

It is a joyless, intense practice, all business. The assistant coaches are screaming, Shannon is glaring. The slightest error brings a coach, sometimes two, into the offending player's face. And yet when the player gets it right, a "not bad" is tossed his way, and sometimes a "better," and sometimes the highest praise of all, "Now you look like you might help this football team."

After the offense works, the defense gets its work. Tackling drills, brutal one-on-one encounters that stress hit-or-be-hit, head up, butt down, drive through the man. Young sophomores, who until today have only heard the horror stories about what it's like to tackle Jerry Creer or Chris Moore, find out the stories are all true. Quarterbacks don't have to hit, but they fill the time climbing into a one-man harness to drag a heavy sled back and forth across the field, building leg strength. Shannon calls frequent water breaks and lets the players stretch out briefly in the shade, then it's back to work. The practice goes late, well past 6:00 P.M., and ends with wind sprints. Any player who had ideas about staying up late and partying on Saturday night is having second thoughts.

Sunday will be a day of rest, and there will be no hitting on Monday, either, because Shannon and some of his assistants will be out of town. They have scheduled a half-day visit to the University of Illinois, 150 miles north in Champaign, where they will sit in on the defensive backfield sessions with Illini coach John Mackovic. "Some of us got to get our minds right about zone coverage," Shannon says. "I can't afford the time, but we can't afford not to do it either. Some guys don't like to change. Hey, I don't like to change, but sometimes you've got to do it."

"**Y**eah, he's changed over the years," says Terry Hill. "He's gotten a little softer. He got on you a little more back then, so you were afraid to mess up. He'd make a joke about you in front of everybody, make you feel bad. He don't do that anymore. I guess maybe he's a little easier on kids today."

Hill, who coaches the Flyers' running backs, was an all-state halfback in 1977. He gained 1,579 on 219 carries that year and earned a scholarship to the University of Missouri. He left Missouri in a feud with the coaching staff after his junior year, played a year of small-college ball in Oklahoma, and bummed around the edges of pro football before returning to East St. Louis in the early 1980s.

"My talent was just a God-given gift," Hill says. "I never had to work at anything until Coach Shannon came in. I remember when he put in his summer program, made us all come in all summer long to work out. We hated it, but then went to the playoffs. I had never had any plans to go to college, but he gave me confidence, and I went to Missouri. There's just so much going on out there in the streets, you have to mold yourself into the attitude of not giving up. He'll do that for you, but you have to listen to him. He talks all the time about using sports to help you in life, but I had to learn it the hard way."

Hanging out around the pros and then back on the streets, Terry Hill developed a drug habit. He'd gone to John Davis, the track coach at Eastside, and Davis helped him get treatment and then helped him get a job as an assistant track coach. "Coach Shannon, he was watching me, and then when he decided I was serious, he came to me and asked if I'd like to coach football, too," he says.

"Man, I wanted back in. I came back, and I had even more respect for him. A lot of people around town had changed; he hadn't, not in the important ways. Maybe he was more relaxed, but he was helping people more. I tell kids out there they don't realize how much he's helping them until they leave school. Some kids don't make it through the program, but when they do, they remember him. He intimidates a lot of them, but that's just the way he is. I tell them, if you can deal with that man, you can deal with college. I tell them they'd better hit the books, because he stresses those books, and that's part of the deal. I tell them he built this program, and you can be a part of it, but you have to do it his way."

As three-a-day practices hit their final week, any misconceptions among the players about who is in charge are long gone. So are a lot of the players. Only forty or so remain. "People are always impressed when I tell them I never cut anybody from the football team," Shannon says. "What I don't tell 'em is that I don't have to cut anybody. My program does it for me. People weed themselves out. We tell 'em what they have to do, tell 'em they have to invest something of themselves in it, and if they don't, they're gone. They make the decision, not me. We make it possible for them to come in the mornings all summer, or the evenings, and we tell them it's up to them to get it done. Anybody who wants to make the team so he can get a uniform and wave to his girlfriend, he's gone by now. The people who are here now are the guys who are going to be on the team. A kid who hasn't been around, been skipping practice, if he shows up next week to get a jersey, he's going to be in for a surprise. The other thing is, it seems like every year we have someone who shouldn't be here. He's too slow, too small, got no ability. But if he comes out, and stays through all of this and does his work, he's going to make the team. I tell the fellas they have to earn my respect, and their teammates' respect, by doing the best job they can. It's not about being an All-American, it's about getting the job done to the best of your ability. And that kid that's too small, he's going to earn respect just by being out there. And if I stick by him, it shows everybody else I mean what I say about trust and respect."

Occasional visitors drop by the field during this last week of three-a-days. Some, like Ronnie Cameron, the former Flyers quarterback who was a blue-chip recruit at Missouri in the mid-1980s, are welcome. Players like Cameron are held up as examples, each one passing on a lesson. "You know what I liked about Ronnie Cameron," Shannon says, loud enough for Deondre Singleton to hear him. "He couldn't throw the ball like Deondre, but he was fast and he could run and he was a winner. He was always the first guy on the practice field, weren't you, Ronnie? This young man here, we can't get him out of the locker room."

Singleton, who likes to take his time doing things, reddens, but says nothing. Cameron beams. The message has been delivered.

Other visitors to the practice field are not so welcome. Shannon's eyes sweep the parking lot constantly, looking for people he can't identify. The Illinois High School Association has strict rules governing how much a team is allowed to know about any team on its schedule, and opposition coaches aren't permitted to view practice. But you never know who is scouting for whom. With Sumner and Larry Walls up first on the schedule, Shannon wants to know who everyone around the field is. "I'm not usually paranoid, but I know how those guys are," he says.

If he is not paranoid, he is at least unusually cautious. He never gets so caught up with what is happening on the field that he stops watching. He watches the parking lot. He watches the sidelines. He watches his back. A week before the season starts, there are still rumors that Chris Moore is being courted by Lincoln High. So when Moore trots up to ask permission to leave a practice early because he has a ride waiting, Shannon says, "I was wondering who was in that car. Why don't you tell him to get out of the car and come say hi."

You can't ever be too sure, particularly where Lincoln is concerned. Shannon may not be paranoid about Sumner, but he is about Lincoln. "The thing is, all these politicians around town, all these people on the board, they're all Lincoln people," he says. "They went to school back when Lincoln was the black high school and we were the white high school. In some of their minds, we're still the white school. Seems like we're always getting the short end of things. It's like now that the blacks have the power in the city, some of them are still getting even for the things that were done to them when they were growing up."

In the fall of 1990, East St. Louis High School has an enrollment of 1,708 students. One is white. "Coach Shannon is right about that," says Sam Morgan, the principal at Eastside. "In some people's minds, this is still a white school, and for some of them, that makes a difference."

Ironically, Lincoln chose a white man as its head football coach, Jim Moncken. "I think that's because I'm black," Shannon says. "They're going to tell me they're color blind."

"Lincolnoia" is rampant at Eastside, where every budget shortfall is blamed on pro-Lincoln sentiment at the board of education. If there are broken windows at Eastside, someone will go check the windows at Lincoln. If there is no money for band uniforms at Eastside, someone will note the spiffy uniforms of Lincoln's state-champion marching band. If there is a player who can't cut it on Shannon's teams, either for grades or disciplinary problems, the coaches will smile and joke that they'll be seeing him soon wearing the black and orange of the Lincoln Tigers.

Lincoln's basketball and track teams beat Eastside's regularly, and Lincoln's marching band is world-class. And Lincoln may get top priority in equipment and facilities. But on the football field, the competition is mainly in Shannon's mind. The Flyers haven't lost to Lincoln since 1978; the average score of the last four Lincoln games has been 45-4. Still, Shannon is obsessed with Lincoln. He has made the Tigers the locus of his frustrations with life in East St. Louis.

He frets and lectures about the evils of Lincoln, particularly now when players can still transfer before classes start. Players will bring him gossip about one kid or another who is said to be thinking of transferring, and Shannon will make sure the kid hears a Lincoln lecture. "You know, son," he says to one sophomore player during a water break one afternoon in late August. "I had a guy's mama tell me just the other day that she almost made him go to Lincoln. Then she told me it would have been the worst mistake she ever made, because over there all you'd have to do is play ball. Here you have to worry about academics, too. Before you go deciding, you'd better check with your mama."

In the last week of practice, it has become clear that Homer Bush will be the focus of the team's offense. "He's going to be our 'go-to' guy," Shannon says. "Our whole offense is going to be geared toward getting the ball in his hands as often as we can. We got the quarterback who can get the ball to him, and we got the running game to take the pressure off him. He's a senior, and I like to get the ball to a senior when things get tough. They've been there before, and they don't make mistakes."

Bush is a splendid athlete, very fast and very agile, with a variety of darting moves and sure hands. More important to Shannon, he is always one of the first players on the field for practice, and he never shirks his work. He will get plenty of it. Shannon plans not only to throw the ball to him as often as possible, but also to use him to return kickoffs and punts, and to play free safety on defense.

"With his moves, any time he touches the ball he's like to get us six points," he says, watching passing drills one afternoon. Bush runs a deep out pattern, and Singleton drills the ball low to the sideline. Bush dives for it, catches it, and drags his feet inbounds for a completed pass. "That's the way, A. G.," the coach says. "That'll help you if you do that in a game and we get it on tape. Those college guys like to see that. And you know what? You make a catch like that, it'll help us, too."

Homer Bush's nickname is "A. G." It started out as "H. G.," for Homer G. Bush, but the "H" got slurred into "A." Everybody calls him A. G., which is a good thing, since he doesn't look like a garden-variety Homer. Tall and lean, he wears his hair in long Jheri curls, which reinforce his resemblance to a preplastic-surgery Michael Jackson. He is the most popular player on the team, quiet and friendly, hardworking and diligent, an excellent student.

As a little boy, Bush would hang around the Flyers' practice field shagging balls. He remembers going to games at Parsons Field and wondering if he could play for the Flyers when he grew up. "Eastside football isn't that big a deal for most kids, but it was for me," he says.

"I'm the type of guy, once I start something, I like to finish it. I came out last year, I was the split end, and I didn't do the job. I lost my position. Coach Shannon told me I could have the job back if I worked hard enough. I had to see if I could do it. I worked hard and got it back in the playoffs. I made seven catches in one playoff game, and I decided to see just how far I could take it.

"The quarterback and I, we'd come in here every day after school, and during the summer. It started right after the state-championship game last winter. Coach gave us a ball so we could work even if he wasn't here. We got the timing right. People would come up to me all the time and ask could I fill Kenny Dunn's [last year's all-state receiver] shoes. I had a lot of pride, pride in my family, and I thought I could do it. I knew I had the potential, I just wasn't using it."

Shannon tells him that, time and again.

"Coach really gets in your face," he says. "It's like talking to your father. If you're not doing wrong, it's no problem. But if you are, it's a big problem. He doesn't care who you are, either. He's always talking about grades, and I don't care who you are, if you don't get the grades, you don't play. He's always saying, 'It's not the kind of player you are, it's the kind of guy you are.'"

Bush had thought his athletic future lay in baseball. He is a shortstop, and a gifted one. The same reflexes that help him catch a football help him field ground balls and lash curveballs into the gaps. He batted well over .400 as a junior and in American Legion ball, and was approached by professional scouts. "I was shocked," he says. "But I really want to go to college. I think I'd like to go into law enforcement, maybe law school. I've been thinking about the FBI."

With the Sumner game two days away, Shannon has pushed up his intensity another notch. On the other side of the school, sirens are wailing. Someone has set fire to some bushes in front of the school, and the fire department has responded in force. Shannon ignores the confusion and orders everyone else to do the same. He is all over the seven-on-seven passing drills, critiquing, criticizing, coaching. Singleton is the only player who talks back to him, asking questions and nodding his head, and Shannon is on his case hard.

"Dumb, dumb, bad decision," he says as Singleton throws a ball high and late for an interception. "I hope Sumner has a guy like that, throwing the ball late. You can't do that. You've got to get outside quick, get your shoulders around, be ready to deliver the ball. Do it again.''

He is pushing Singleton hard to learn to throw the ball rolling to his left in a strong-side right offense, away from the strength of the opposing team's rush. The plan is for Homer Bush, at split end, to break open on the weak side of the secondary. But Singleton must be able to deliver the ball while moving away from his right, or natural, side. Singleton works hard on it and gradually learns the technique of swiveling his hips on the run, squaring up his shoulders, and throwing sharply. Shannon watches him do it two dozen times before he is satisfied. "Now we got to find out if he can do it in a game," he says. "That's the big unknown. You never know how a kid's going to do with people watching him and cheering, and with the pressure on. I think he's going to be all right, but I can't get a read on the rest of the team. Last year I had guys like Dana Howard and Kenny Dunn, and I didn't have to worry about their attitude or how they'd respond to pressure. Those guys would take care of it. This year, I don't know. We're going to be good, but I like to be machinelike. I have to keep asking them about leadership. These guys are all too laid-back."

Machinelike precision will have to wait. This Thursday, two days before the opener, he coaches his last heavy practice. The Friday session will be a light run-through. There is never enough time, and today time runs out. He coaches this practice as if trying to overcome all that laid-back attitude all by himself. He is in the middle of every play, screaming and yelling, and glaring if screaming and yelling don't work. Glaring almost always works.

"Down, double him, down."

"You're too high, get your butt down. Drive him."

"Slant now. All right. Quicker!"

"Good hit, there, now you're helping us."

"When you gonna get tough, linebacker? You ever going to get tough? You got to be able to knock somebody down and then laugh at him. Let him know you going to be there next time."

Singleton hits Bush on a long fly pattern, and Ben Williams, the sophomore quarterback, says, "I'll be doing that next year."

"Why the hell don't you do it this year instead of messing around?" Shannon says. He is very unhappy with Williams, who has a chemical burn on his forehead from a home hair treatment. The burn means he can't get a helmet on, and even though as a sophomore he probably wouldn't play anyway, Shannon is not pleased.

Late in the afternoon, he runs his goal-line offense for the first time all summer. There hasn't been enough time for the specialty teams, but he must give them a chance to stack up strong and punch the ball in from inside the five-yard line. Besides, he hasn't found a placekicker yet and hasn't had time to practice kicking points after touchdowns. There has been too much other work to do to worry about the kicking game, so the goal-line offense will also be his conversion offense. Two or three plays are put in, power dives and a quick out pass. Each one is run a dozen times, and finally, late in the afternoon, he calls a halt. If it's not done now, it'll have to wait.

The kids are excited. The worst is over, the big game is less than forty-eight hours away, and today is uniform day. Today they'll find out who wears what number. Today they'll get their game uniforms, the game jersey they can wear to school on Friday and impress the girls. Rucker, who has spent all week sorting and patching uniforms, carries a box of jerseys and a clipboard onto the field. Singleton gets number 11, Chris Moore 12, Homer Bush 16, Dennis Stallings 89. The kids on the fringe of the team watch anxiously—will they or won't they get a uniform? Shannon has told Rucker which players to suit up and which ones haven't been out often enough or worked hard enough. "We got guys here today who haven't been out here in two weeks," he says. "They're going to be mighty disappointed, but I don't give 'em no sympathy. I told 'em what the rules were, and they made the decision. They don't do what they're supposed to, they don't get to play."

Those who don't get shirts drift off, trying not to be seen. Those who do get them peel off their sweat-soaked practice jerseys and shoulder pads and try on the game jerseys, bright blue with white numerals, trimmed in orange.

"Fellas," Shannon tells them. "Listen up. We got some rules for these shirts. Don't take it home. Don't be wearing it down State Street and some guy with a gun come up and take it off you. Then you don't have it and we don't have it and maybe it's got a hole in it and maybe you got a hole in you. You give it back to Coach Rucker. You want to wear it to school tomorrow, that's OK Ruck'll be here early, you come in and get it. No, you can't take it home and show it to grandma. How do I know you ain't wearing it somewhere on the street? I might have to come by the crib and check it out, just you, me, and grandma.

"Now go on. Give 'em to Ruck and get on home. Be here tomorrow. We're going to work on kickoffs. I hope like heck we get to kick off some."

The kids hustle off, still talking. The coaches gather in the shade of the gym wall, shooting the breeze, drinking iced tea that a booster brings by. Shannon sits apart from the rest of them, forward a little, swigging from his water jug. They talk about the kids who showed up and the kids who didn't. They talk about Sumner a little bit, wondering if Bulldog coach Larry Walls has any tricks up his sleeve. One year he tried "quads," four wide receivers at once, hoping to confuse the Flyers' defensive backfield. Shannon doesn't think he'll try it again, but he's practiced against the four-wideout offense just in case.

As the coaches sip tea, Bruce Hill, the East St. Louis fire chief who moonlights as a football referee, strolls up. He's just inspected the remnants of the burning bushes in front of the school. "Old bushes wouldn't even burn," he says. "The trash under them did a pretty good job, though."

"What you got that gun on for, chief?" asks Shannon, noting that Hill is wearing a 9-mm. automatic on his belt.

"I'm an arson investigator now, coach," Hill says.

"Well, I guess you need that gun, then. Guys around here will set a fire just so they can shoot at you."

Hill rides the coaches for sitting in the shade drinking iced tea. The coaches ride him right back about the fire department's new physical training program. "I hear they got you guys swinging on ropes down there," Shannon says. "If you can't be a fireman, you can be Tarzan."

They talk over plans for Saturday's game, which Hill will be refereeing, and Hill says he'll drop by practice Friday to go over the rules with the players. Shannon likes his players to have the law laid down before game time. He will not tolerate any cheap-shot tactics and asks Hill to go over the antispearing rule for his players. Spearing, or diving into an opposing player helmet first, is a primary cause of neck and spinal column injuries. The tactic has been outlawed, both by the coaches and the rules, but Shannon wants it emphasized.

Hill, finishing his tea, promises to go over the rule. "Some of us got to work," he says, hitching his belt and turning to head back to his car.

"Tell that to the rest of the guys downtown," Shannon shoots back.

Hill grins and waves and drives off. One by one, the assistant coaches follow him. "Well, gentlemen," says Shannon, "not much time left now. Not much time at all."

CHAPTER

3

To Bob Shannon's amazement, Parsons Field has been lined—in chalk, not weed killer—for the opening game. Art May, the Eastside athletic director, visited the stadium the afternoon before and found the grass uncut and the field unlined. May, who sometimes can work small miracles, has gotten the school district's maintenance crew out in time to do the work. So when Shannon and his team get off the yellow school buses that have ferried them from the high school, the field looks as good as it ever looks, despite ninety-five-degree heat that would have wilted the grass if it hadn't already been brown.

Undaunted by the heat, a big crowd—fifteen hundred or so is a big crowd for Parsons Field—has come out for the matchup between the Flyers and those Sumner Bulldogs. Despite their reputation, the Flyers don't attract many fans in their hometown. Part of that is because the team is taken for granted and because a lot of folks in town root for Lincoln High instead. Part of it is because Parsons Field is located in a section of town that's dangerous even for East St. Louis. And much of it is simply because folks in town have bigger worries than wondering if a bunch of teenagers are going to win a football game.

Even so, Eastside has developed a hard-core following among sports groupies in the St. Louis area. White and black, they come out to see what Shannon has wrought. They seek the shade of the single covered grandstand, or bask in the sun in the bleachers. Curbside vendors set up barbecue grills and ice chests, peddling foot-long Polish sausages or barbecued pork snouts—snoots, they call them. Just looking at them can cause your arteries to clang shut.

Shannon doesn't eat on the day of a game until long after the final whistle. He is far too nervous for that, pacing back and forth in bright blue bell-bottom polyester coach's pants and one of his orange Fightin' Illini golf shirts. He wears a bright blue baseball cap with a cursive E on the crown, the hat pulled low over his head. On game days he worries less about what he wears than what he eats.

His team is dressed in orange pants and bright blue jerseys, uniforms that were donated the year before by businessmen who'd read that the team had played for the state championship in tattered uniforms. The team looks good, except for Chris Moore, who has customized his uniform to befit a star. He has oversized shoulder pads, a huge neck roll, and strips of towel tucked into his pants like a flag football player. When he runs, the towel strips stream out behind him, like pennants in a used-car lot. "Chris wants to make sure nobody misses him," Shannon explains.

Across the field, Larry Walls's Bulldogs are dressed in white uniforms with maroon helmets and numbers. Walls and Shannon do not speak; they never do. Even when they are in the same room, such as for the annual selection of the *Post-Dispatch*'s all-metro team, they sit with their backs to each other. Walls is among the coaches around town who find Shannon's aloofness bordering on arrogance. Shannon says he couldn't care less.

"Larry's one of those guys who think I'm not outspoken enough," Shannon says. "He likes to make football a platform. That's not what we're about. Plus last year we beat them 39–0 and then they went unbeaten the rest of the year, so that says something right there."

Opening ceremonies aren't much. The Eastside band plays a flat rendition of the national anthem, but public address announcer Irl Solomon is hampered by a PA system that functions only sporadically. It works just long enough for him to say, "Welcome to ancient but venerable Parsons Field, the stadium that will not die." Solomon, a twenty-year veteran of Flyers football and a history teacher at Eastside, is beside himself. "Nothing ever works around here," he complains. "We asked them to fix the windows one time and they told us we should just wear heavier coats."

Bruce Hill, the arson investigator, has taken off his gun and put on his striped referee's shirt. He tosses the coin to start the season. Sumner wins, takes the opening kickoff, and starts marching through the Flyers' defense. They march forty-two yards in four plays and are deep in Eastside territory. Pacing the sidelines, Shannon screams, "Watch the reverse!"

Sure enough, Sumner runs a reverse. Clarence Green bursts

through from his defensive-tackle position, sets up, and pops the Bulldog flanker as he comes back across the backfield. The ball flies loose and Green recovers the fumble.

Shannon grabs Singleton as the offense trots onto the field. "Pro-right red, 23 bandit," he says. Time to see if they can run the play for real. They can. Moore, pennants flying, gets eleven yards. Shannon, who calls all the plays, sends flanker backs shuttling in and out with one running play after another, most of them for Chris Moore. Now that it's too late for him to transfer to Lincoln, Shannon puts Moore to work. And he gains two yards, eight yards, twenty-five yards, plowing up the field. Shannon calls 1-23 bandit, split end curl, and Singleton hits his buddy Homer Bush for thirteen yards on the first pass completion of the year. Shannon goes back to Moore, and he takes it in from the nine-yard line. Four minutes, forty-two seconds into the season, Eastside has a 6-0 lead. Shannon's face relaxes for an instant, and then he calls a flanker over to send in a play for the extra point. There hasn't been time to work on the kicking game yet, so the Flyers will try two-point conversions all day. He calls a play action pass, a fake to Moore and a soft lob to fullback Jerry Creer. It works perfectly and the lead is 8-0.

The Flyers are off to the races. With their coach stalking along the sideline, speaking to no one except the quarterback and the shuttling flankers, his plastic-covered play sheet rolled up in his hand, the team starts coming together. The defense forces the Bulldogs to punt shortly before the end of the first quarter. Shannon calls 23 bandit again, and this time Moore goes fifty yards before being caught from behind at the one-yard line. He comes out of the game to catch his breath, walking very slowly to soak up the praise from the fans standing along the roped-off sidelines. His teammates pound him on the shoulder. The long gallop gives him 126 yards on ten carries in the first twelve minutes of the year. Moore stands at the water cooler, pouring water over his head. Shannon calls over his shoulder: "Wouldn't nobody caught you last year, Chris."

Singleton scores on a quarterback sneak. The two-point conversion falls short and the Flyers lead 14–0 early in the second quarter. Two possessions later, Green lays a devastating trap block on a Sumner tackle and Creer bursts through the hole for sixty-two yards and another touchdown. Singleton hits Bush with a conversion pass and the Flyers take a 22–0 lead into the locker room at halftime.

The players are gassed. The heat is taking a toll. They loll in the cavelike locker room under the grandstand, sucking water. Shannon tells them to drink up, but wonders why they're so tired. "Y'all aren't playing hard enough to be tired," he says.

He goes over mistakes, singling out the offender. He goes over what he likes, which is the blocking by the offensive line and the hitting by the defense. He sends them back onto the field.

Though the referees call frequent time outs for water breaks, the sun and the heat are crippling. Players are falling with muscle cramps, getting the cramps massaged out, and running back in. Neither team does much in the third quarter, but in the fourth quarter, Sumner starts making mistakes. Defensive end Robert Perkins blocks a Bulldog punt. Dennis Stallings picks up the rolling ball and returns it forty-nine yards for a touchdown.

Cornerback Marcus Bester steps in front of a Sumner pass, picks it off cleanly, and goes forty-seven yards for another score. With the game winding down, his first team exhausted, and a 36–0 lead, Shannon sends in the second team to run out the clock. Sophomore running back Richard Jenkins gets his first chance to carry the ball for the Flyers on the last play of the game. He sweeps right end, the horn sounds to end the game, and a Sumner player pulls the ball from Jenkins's grasp. Most of the Flyers are celebrating their shutout victory as Sumner's Tony Dotson is taking the stolen football into the end zone. The officials rule it a touchdown.

Shannon is livid. Not with the officials, but with the lapse in concentration. He had another shutout over Larry Walls and a sophomore mistake ruined it. He calms down quickly, shakes hands all around, and finally allows himself to smile. Yes, he lost a touchdown, but he won the game. The season has started. Life can begin again. "For a first game, it wasn't bad," he says. "I like us to be machinelike, but it takes a while. Yeah, it takes a pretty good while."

The Monday after the Sumner game is Labor Day, a school holiday and a light practice day for the Flyers. On that morning, Morris Hunt, an East St. Louis businessman who volunteers as an assistant coach, goes hunting for a lineman named Vaughn Johnson. Shannon and his coaches have been hunting for Johnson most of the summer. He didn't show up for off-season workouts and he wasn't around when practice started. Classes started the previous week, and Vaughn Johnson, who would be a senior, hasn't shown up for school either. Under normal circumstances Shannon would have written him off. "You can't save everybody," he often says. "Sooner or later, a guy's got to do something to save himself."

But these are special circumstances. The Sumner game showed a definite weakness in the middle of the Flyers' defensive line and along the offensive line, too. It happens that Vaughn Johnson had started a few games as a nose guard as a junior and also played a pretty good offensive tackle. And then he'd been a successful heavyweight wrestler after the season, getting bigger, stronger, and quicker in the process. Bob Shannon wants Vaughn Johnson badly.

He and his coaches started asking around. Kids said they'd seen Johnson, whose street name is Ubay, off and on during the summer. They said he'd been living with his sister, but the two hadn't gotten along, so now he was living with a girlfriend. Morris Hunt had tried the sister's house and had been trying to track down the girlfriend. On Labor Day morning, Coach Hunt came to the end of his search.

"I went by the house where he was supposed to be living every day for a week," Hunt said. "I finally found him Monday morning at 7:30. He was sound asleep. I told him to come on back, Coach Shannon wanted to see him. Shannon says he don't cut these guys no slack, but with Ubay, he kind of gritted his teeth."

Ubay came in. Shannon talked to him. He told him the team needed him, and more than that, he needed the team. Shannon told him he was letting the team down and letting himself down. He told him that for his sake, and for the team's sake, he was going to break one of his cardinal rules and give him another chance.

Ubay came back.

"Yeah, well, what am I going to do?" Shannon asked later. "He comes from a family situation that's bad even for East St. Louis. He had no one else to care for him. To see a guy like that overcome all that stuff and still succeed would be gratifying to all of us. Some guys, you know, aren't going to stick with it, other guys you just cross your fingers and hope. His mom didn't know where he was, and he and his sister didn't get along and she put him out. He got involved with some girls, evidently an older girl, and she wasn't exactly the kind of girl you'd like your own son to be involved with, but who was there to tell him the difference?"

Shannon second-guessed himself watching Ubay's return to practice, where his teammates welcomed him like the Prodigal Son. A huge, almost square kid, five feet, eleven inches tall, 245 pounds, he has a large, triangular head and a nose flattened like a nose guard's should be. The Flyers' line got 100 percent better the first time he lined up, but Shannon wondered if he'd merely rationalized the situation.

Ubay had violated most of Shannon's rules about off-season workouts and senior leadership. His grades the previous semester had been bad, and he hadn't even shown up for the fall semester until Morris Hunt tracked him down. Part of Shannon had wanted to toss Ubay to the wolves, but he'd needed a tackle. Maybe, Shannon reasoned, Ubay would grasp this last chance and make something of himself. Go on to junior college, get an education, get off the streets of East St. Louis.

"Yeah, I know it looks bad," Shannon said, "and yeah, maybe if I didn't need a tackle so bad I wouldn't do it. But knowing the whole situation—that here's a guy who if he doesn't have this team, he doesn't have anything. He's not a bad kid, and that was in his favor. He'd been in the program for two years, and was always pretty solid until this came along. I came up hard myself. You have to appreciate some of the things these guys go through."

Robert Lavern Shannon began life in a cabin in Port Gibson, Mississippi. His first memory is of standing in front of a fireplace in that cabin, trying to get warm. He does not, as he often says, like to look back. But when he does look back, and when he warms to the subject, the stories spill out of him.

"That must have been some time in winter of '46–'47 or thereabouts. I was born in July 1945, and they say you can't remember anything until you're almost two. We moved to Natchez in 1948 so my father could get work in a sawmill. I can't remember what my dad did before that; he never really did say. Most folks around there sharecropped, so maybe he did that. I kind of doubt it though. He liked to tell stories about hoboing around during the depression, about hobo camps in places like Cairo, Illinois. He liked to ride the rails. I always thought he was a wanderer."

From time to time David Shannon would ride the rails back to

Port Gibson. It was there in that small farming community in western Mississippi one Saturday morning that he met a country girl named Lucy Yarborough, the daughter of sharecroppers who came to town only on Saturdays. After Lucy Yarborough and David Shannon were married, they moved to town and David stopped riding the rails. David did whatever David did, and Lucy worked as a domestic. That wasn't enough for a family that was growing at the rate of one a year—first David, Jr., and then Robert, and then Fred, and then eight more until there were eleven in all, five boys and six girls.

In Natchez there was work stoking boilers at a sawmill along the Mississippi River, Leonard's Mill, on a hill called Leonard's Hill. Mill-owned housing was available in a shantytown below the hill in an area called Under Leonard's Hill, a place of shotgun houses with privies out back and water you pumped from a well. The houses stood on blocks against the water from the spring flood. "Had this old wood floor with cracks between the boards," Shannon recalled. "You could look down and see through the cracks and see chickens under the house."

David Shannon would rise in the middle of the night and climb Leonard's Hill to Leonard's Mill, where he would spend twelve hours a day, six days a week, shoving logs and scrap lumber into boilers that fired the steam engines that ran the screaming saws. At midday Lucy Shannon would fix her husband's dinner, and Robert would run up the hill with it and then linger, talking to his father and the other millworkers during dinner hour.

"I liked hanging out there," he said. "I liked watching the men work. I liked being around them. A guy named Rayfield

Wright would give me a sandwich. A millwright named Sonny
Crump would share with me. They were also so kind to me, just a
little guy, and I liked watching how things worked. I've always
been amazed by machines and machinery.''

After dinner he would return home with the dirty plates and
cups. Later, after he started school, he would see his friends at the
mill only in the summer, or on Saturdays. Still later, when he was
ten years old and his father, who had long suffered from asthma,
began having trouble breathing, he would rise in the middle of the
night with his dad and help him stoke the boilers. The trip up the
hill with his father wasn't bad, but the return home, at four in the
morning, meant he had to pass the Hanging Tree alone. The
legend was that a man had been lynched in the old oak tree on
Leonard's Hill, his body hoisted high so it could be a lesson to
everyone who passed by on the rolling river. Robert Shannon
feared the Hanging Tree, and he would close his eyes as he
passed it, sprinting hard for home.

School was far better, even though the kids from Under
Leonard's Hill had to walk to school since they lived just outside
the city limits and the bus only carried city kids. And lord help
you if you were late. The principal at Broomfield Elementary
School was a man named Robert Lewis, and he would stand in the
doorway with a belt, just waiting for latecomers. Robert Shannon
was always on time, and even today he is a chronically early
person.

"Mr. Lewis was one of the first people to really help me,''
Shannon said. "He was a man who had expectations for you, and
you'd do anything not to disappoint him. I remember one year, I

must have been eleven or twelve years old, and it was New Year's Day. I didn't have nothing to do and was just walking around the streets. He called me in off the streets, gave me some cake, and let me watch the Rose Bowl game on TV. We didn't have TV at home. I'd seen it before, but this was the first time I'd ever seen color TV. I can tell you what was on, Michigan versus Southern California, and all the colorful balloons and everything. I was so amazed.''

Years later Shannon, by then a veteran of a dozen years as a head coach, was visiting Natchez and dropped in to see Robert Lewis, old and arthritic, but his mind still vital. He was still living in the same house where Robert had gotten his first full-color glimpse of the world outside. Peter Hernon of the *St. Louis Post-Dispatch* made that trip with Shannon and later wrote of the meeting with Lewis in a series of articles that appeared in the paper in 1989:

> Unburdening himself, Shannon spoke of students who don't want to learn and teachers who don't want to teach; he lashed out at indifference and corruption and how he has less patience than he used to. How, as he likes to put it, "You can't save 'em all."
>
> Gently chiding him, Lewis said: "It's so hard to say, 'When do I stop trying?' What do you do with the troublemakers, the indifferent, the low achievers? The one thing I know is that you can't give up. Maybe you can get through to them. Coaches have such great influence. You mustn't give up. You'll never know when you'll reach a young man."

The Flyers' second game of the season will be played on the road, in the northeastern Oklahoma town of Muskogee. The game entails a nearly five-hundred-mile bus trip and a night in a Holiday Inn for the Flyers, but Shannon has to go to extraordinary lengths to find strong opponents for his team. In a nine-game regular season, the Flyers play the five other schools in the Southwestern Illinois Athletic Conference, and crosstown rival Lincoln High, and then must find three other nonconference opponents. Since none of the Southwestern Conference teams present much of a challenge to Eastside—the team has lost only one conference game since 1981—Shannon looks to his nonconference opponents to provide tough opposition. "For us, the playoffs are everything," he says. "If we get to the playoffs without having a tough game, then we're in trouble."

In recent years, of all the schools in metropolitan St. Louis, only Sumner and Soldan High—another St. Louis inner-city high school—and DeSmet Jesuit in suburban St. Louis, have had the nerve to schedule East St. Louis. Shannon and Art May must pick up opponents where they can find them and then try to talk the school district into paying for the travel costs. That means Muskogee this week and Robeson High in Chicago next week. "Scheduling is always a headache," Shannon says. "You've got to find someone with an open date the same day we've got one, and you want to find somebody that's pretty good. Then you've got to get the guys on the road, put 'em in a hotel, feed 'em, and get 'em back the same night because they dang sure ain't going to pay for us to be gone two nights. We had an assistant superintendent call up the other day and tell us they didn't have the money for this trip. Art told him, 'Well, we already signed the contract and we'd have to pay them off if we didn't go.' So they found the money somewhere.''

The school district's incessant shortage of money for his team is a constant irritant. Even though the crowds at Parsons Field usually aren't very big, each person through the gate pays a two-dollar admission fee, and there's money from concession stands. Even after paying for game officials and the required ambulance attendants and emergency medical technicians, he figures, there ought to be something left over for niceties like equipment and travel. "But they ain't ever got any money," he says, "and I ain't ever seen a budget sheet. I know someone's getting that money. I'd just like to know who."

But that's a worry for another day. Today's concern is why Muskogee scheduled him in the first place. He exchanged game tapes with the Muskogee coach and is singularly unimpressed with what he sees of the Muskogee High Roughers. "I can't figure out why he wants to play us," he says. "They're pretty good, but they ain't that good, and he sure didn't invite us down there to lay fifty on him."

So he prepares for the worst. "I believe in being overprepared," he says. "I prepare for every game like we're playing the Green Bay Packers."

Unfortunately, the bus drivers assigned are less prepared. The ten-hour trip is quiet and uneventful—Shannon has a strict rule that all stereos must be equipped with earphones: "I don't like that bump-bump stuff and they don't like my jazz and blues"—but the drivers aren't happy they have to turn around and drive

home after the Friday night game. They stand in the Muskogee
Holiday Inn parking lot, grumbling about union rules, threatening
to stop the buses for a nap when they've driven their allotted
hours. "Well, sir," Shannon tells the lead driver. "If you think
you can sleep, I guess that'll be all right."

The driver eyes the players loading equipment and baggage
onto the bus and thinks about trying to nap with a busload of high-
energy boys. "We'll see," he says.

"Just do what you have to do," Shannon says.

He walked off to run the team through a late-afternoon walk-
through practice in the motel parking lot. It's a session designed
more to calm nerves than practice football. The session draws a
small crowd of locals; the Flyers find themselves minor celebri-
ties in Muskogee, a football-crazy town in the Oklahoma oil
patch. The local paper has ballyhooed their visit, and reporters
from Tulsa and Oklahoma City are on hand for the game. "Guy
stopped me in the restaurant and said they'd been pointing to this
game all summer," Shannon said. "People in this town are crazy
about their team. It's a little different where we come from."

Indeed, despite a drizzling rain, by game time some six
thousand fans have crowded into the "Indian Bowl," a well-
tended old football stadium near downtown Muskogee. They buy
two-dollar copies of the Roughers' yearbook, thick with advertis-
ing, player photos, and gushing profiles of the Roughers' coaching staff. At Parsons Field, they sell photocopies of game rosters
for a quarter and have trouble paying for the copying costs.

Maybe the Flyers are intimidated by it all, because they play
terribly in the first half. Deondre Singleton throws an interception

that Muskogee cashes in on. He is sacked and fumbles and they cash that one in, too. The Roughers recover an on-sides kick—another thing Shannon hasn't had time to prepare for—and they cash that in, too. Late in the second quarter, the Flyers are trailing 26–8. It's apparent that Muskogee has studied films of the Sumner game, because they are keying on Chris Moore and shutting down the Flyers' running game.

So Shannon goes to the air. Singleton hits Bush three times on a sixty-yard march that ends with a twenty-two-yard touchdown pass to Bush with a little over four minutes left. Muskogee fumbles on its next possession, and with time running out in the half, Singleton demonstrates why Shannon has fallen in love with him. On a play called 81 switch, Singleton pump-fakes a pass to Bush and then calmly turns back to his right and picks out Chris Moore, who is streaking up the middle of the field. He lays the ball over Moore's shoulder for a forty-eight-yard touchdown pass. Eastside goes to the locker room down 28–20.

Shannon is furious. "We could easily be out of the ballgame now," he says in the steamy, dank room. "And we could just as easily be beating these guys. We gave them a touchdown, just gave it to them. But I want to tell you something. We can still beat 'em, but you're going to have to shut them down in the second half.

"I told you I was scared of them because they were so fired up. They're more fired up than you. They got good athletes and they're fired up and that's why they're winning. When both teams have good athletes, athletes cancel each other out. That's when it's up to us as a coaching staff to come up with something. But guys, this is where it's going to pay off. All that running, all that conditioning, all them practices. We're gonna have to win a ballgame in the second half, and to do that, you're going to have to believe you can win."

With that, Shannon goes to a blackboard. He tells his defense to split wider and slant toward the holes instead of driving straight ahead. He instructs John Davis, the defensive coordinator, to call more blitzes by the linebackers and safeties. "We're getting blown off the ball, and this is gonna stop that," Shannon says.

On offense, he diagrams several weakside draw and counter plays to offset Muskogee's unbalanced line. And it all works like a charm. Having seen what Homer Bush can do to them, Muskogee drops an end off in coverage and suddenly Moore bursts through for a touchdown on 23 bandit. When the defense keys back to Moore, Shannon calls trap plays to fullback Jerry Creer. Eastside grinds sixty-nine yards in thirteen plays to take the lead. In the fourth quarter, the Flyers then have a chance to ice the game, but Dennis Stallings drops a sure touchdown pass in the end zone. Undaunted, Shannon calls the same play, and this time Stallings catches it. The final score is 38–26. Shannon has wanted a game to test his team, and he got it.

He is jabbering with relief after the game. "We're definitely going back to the whip next week," he says. "This was my fault. I didn't have them ready. The good thing is we didn't panic when we were down. Good ball clubs don't panic. We don't get down enough to know how to handle it, and that's my fault for not telling them it could happen. Muskogee came out and played with emotion and we didn't. But it's tough to play four quarters on emotion. We're looking for players who can execute and stay calm. But this is a great one to win, because we can always point back to it and say, 'Remember what happened when we got down.' If you don't work hard, you find yourself in this situation. That's why I believe in working hard. You can get down, but if you know how to work hard, you can get back up."

"**I** always had a job when I was a kid, even as a little guy," Shannon recalled. "I remember I used to get up real early in pecan season. I'd look out the window and see if the wind was blowing, and if it was, I'd get out of bed and hustle down to the pecan groves. They had these pecan trees along the streets and in the parks, and the wind would blow those pecans out of the trees. But you had to get up early to beat this old guy, Mr. Gene Barnes. He thought those pecans belonged to him.

"I picked some cotton, too, but I discovered early that was a losing proposition. You'd get on that truck at 4:30 in the morning and try to pick 150 pounds, cutting your fingers and your fingernails on them ol' bolls. And they had this company store there, you know, where you get bread and pop and bologna to make you a sandwich, and they'd just give it to you and say they'd take it out of your pay. Well at the end of the day, you didn't have nothing left. I remember an old guy, they called him Uncle Jabbo, that old guy could pick 300 pounds of cotton a day. They said he done time behind the walls, in prison, and in Mississippi that's where you learned to pick cotton.

"I always had a job. I always wanted that money, to buy bats and balls and gloves. I always had my own glove, but I had to buy it. I remember my big disappointment as a kid was not getting to play Little League because the field was so far from home and there was no way to get there. We'd go up to the mill and get some old pieces of lumber and my father's friends would cut 'em down for us for bats. We'd buy balls with money we'd get from odd jobs, and go out in the pasture and play. We used cow patties for bases. I played with my brothers until they got a little older, and then all's they wanted to do was hang out down at the Dixie Inn, gambling and playing pool. I never could see the sense of that, gambling. I worked hard for my money. Why should I let another guy take it from me?

"I always bought my own clothes, too. As a kid I had two pair of blue jeans, and I'd wash 'em myself. My mother taught me to iron, and people who knew me then will tell you about the creases I kept in my jeans. And whenever I had any money, I made sure I bought me something to eat. I always got me a nice meal. Seems like I never had enough to eat. It was rough."

It got rougher in 1955 when David Shannon's asthma, compounded by emphysema and heart disease, forced him out of work for weeks at a time. The elder Shannon's weekly wage was thirty-two dollars, and when he didn't work, he didn't get paid. To save money, Robert and his younger brother Fred were sent to stay with their aunt Beatrice Carroll in Buffalo, New York. "Plus my mom wanted us to get away from my brother David for a while. He was shooting hookey a lot, and when he skipped school, we'd skip with him. I was also getting beat up a lot. There was this girl, Janice Mae Harden was her name, and she'd have her brothers beat me up. I left school many a day with those boys chasing me down that rock road. I don't know what she had against me, but I was glad to get away from there. I think my aunt Bea needed a couple of dependents, too, so things worked out for everybody.

"It was a different world there in Buffalo. We'd been going to this one-room school, and all of a sudden, we're in this big ol' school. I learned a lot there. I learned about gangs. Folks told me don't go into this certain neighborhood along Purdy Street there. I said I didn't believe there was anyone who had anything against me on Purdy Street, so I walked on through there and this gang of guys came up to me. I was lucky there was one guy there who knew me, and he told them I was OK, and they let me go. I couldn't believe there were people who would take action against someone they didn't know just because they didn't know him."

Buffalo opened his eyes in other ways. There were myriad sports and activities programs, and there were organized recreation centers, things that were still decades away for the rural South. "It was good for me," Shannon recalled. "I got some exposure to how other people live. My aunt was hard on me, but she was pretty much OK. She worked for a steel company there, and she had this big house where she'd rent out rooms."

Bob and Fred lived in Buffalo for only a year, until their father died in 1956. "He'd managed to save $250 in his whole life, and someone stole it from him down at the hospital or the funeral home," Shannon said. "He was making $32 a week when he died, and drinking up a lot of it, but he managed to put some of it away—only when he died, it was gone.

"He could've done a better job raising us, supporting us, but he was never allowed to. He drank a lot because that was what black men did back then. The white folks encouraged it, you know, 'Let them have a good time on the weekend and it'll keep them quiet during the week.' I could understand why they did it. There wasn't nothing else to do and they had to get some enjoyment out of life somehow. They were so depressed by the situation they were in that they tried to put on a front. They'd get dressed up on the weekends and drink and gamble.

"That was the system there, and my dad was subservient to the system. He was never really allowed to be a real man. That was the way it was done in those days, and it drove a lot of people to drink. It was the plantation mentality, you know. Keep 'em drunk and happy and never let 'em see there's a way out. I think that's one reason I stay apart from the system here. I want to control my own life. I don't let the little things get to me. I was only eleven years old, but I saw what it did to my dad.

"It was a situation where you had that poverty, and you got into this mind-set that you could only accomplish so much, that you could get a job driving that tractor on the white man's plantation and that was about it. It became a convenience, a crutch. It was easier to believe it than challenge it. If a white guy told you something, you couldn't argue with him, you couldn't challenge him and feel you'd live to tell about it or that there wouldn't be some other kind of reprisal."

Financially, Lucy Shannon and her eleven children were better off after David's death. Social Security brought in a hundred dollars a month to add to the twelve dollars a week Lucy made cleaning white folks' houses. "There wasn't nothing like food stamps back then," Shannon said. "There were surplus commodities that they gave away sometimes, rice or flour, but my mom was too proud to pull that wagon all the way home. We had to work for our own stuff. My mom wasn't any good with money. She was always letting con men talk her into buying cheap stuff we couldn't afford, and then it would break before it was paid for. We were always in hock to the furniture store. They'd either repossess it or we'd break it. It taught me something. It taught me to have things of value, to take your time and get something that would last."

The house rules were simple: Lucy would do the best she could, but everyone had to fend for himself. But still someone always needed shoes, and there was never enough to eat.

"Let me tell you something about eating. I'm thirteen, fourteen years old, and I'm an athlete, right? So I'm always off somewhere playing ball or practicing. I learned I'd better get home on time. Someone would always save something for me, but lots of times someone else would go in and find what had been saved for me and eat it. I went to bed hungry a lot. We'd eat neck bones and a pot of beans. Meat was very rare. I had this thing about butter. I always wanted to be able to afford butter. I find that funny because now I can afford it, and I can't eat it because I'm watching my cholesterol.

"I was in college before I had a whole steak to myself. I'd seen one, and maybe had a piece of one, but a whole one? Now I can afford steak, but I don't eat red meat anymore. I eat fish, and maybe that's because we ate a lot of fish back then. People would fish the river, right down below where we lived. You'd go down there and they'd pull one out of the trap for you, knock it in the head, and give it to you. Catfish, gar, buffalo, drum. Nobody ever wanted drum, because it had all those bones, so they'd give it to us on credit. Days there wasn't no fish, there wouldn't be anything. We'd have to go to the neighbors or somewhere and ask for a bag of beans.

"I remember one day when I was about fourteen, it was the hungriest I've ever been in my life. There was this woman, a four-hundred-pound black woman they called Big Mama or Big Baby, and she ran this house of ill repute. She kind of specialized in black girls for white guys. I knew about her—everyone did—but I'd never been in there. But I was so hungry that day I went in there and asked if there was anything I could do to earn a meal. I never asked anyone to give me anything free, but I always asked if I could work for it.

"She said, 'Come on in.' She had a bunch of dogs there; the whole place smelled like dogs. She said she'd fix me a meal and then she wanted me to clean up her yard. She fixed me bacon and eggs and bread, toast, you know? It was a fine meal, and then I went out and cleaned up her yard. I heard later, five or six years later, that they'd found her dead, lying in her bathtub with her skull fractured. They said somebody must have killed her and put her in there, because it wasn't big enough for her to fall down in."

The skinny kid in the well-creased blue jeans became known around town as someone you could depend on to do a job right. "I always made sure I asked if they were satisfied with the job I'd done, and if they had anything else I could do, or knew of anyone else who needed something done. There was only three things I wouldn't do. I wouldn't pick up garbage or ride that garbage truck. I wouldn't shine shoes. And I wouldn't sell papers on the street. Those were desperation jobs, and I didn't want to be desperate."

Work hard enough, he figured, you didn't have to be desperate. Shannon got a job delivering liquor from the Four-Point Tavern, pumping the bicycle he'd bought from his jobs all over town, delivering liquor from three in the afternoon to nine at night for ten bucks a week plus tips. "I had to quit that job one day, though," he said. "One of those drunks had gone into the bathroom and instead of using the stool to crap in, he'd used the urinal. The boss told me to clean it out. I said, no, I didn't believe I wanted to do that and I'd just be moving on down the road."

He got a job one summer painting dormitories at Natchez College. "We finished that and then the boss, old Bob Lee Williams, said we were going over to paint the college president's house," he said. "I said, 'Wait a minute, Bob Lee. That wasn't in the deal. I want my money now.' He got all mad at me, said I thought he was trying to cheat me, which I guess I did. He paid me half of what he owed me and fired me.

"I had a lot of jobs because my mom was a domestic, and the people she worked for would ask her if she knew anyone who'd cut their yards, paint their porches, or whatever. And she always said, 'My boy Robert will do it.' And I'd go there and try to do the best job I could because I always wanted to go back. Any job I had, they hated to see me go. My mom expected me to be better than the rest of them, and so did my dad.

"The best job I ever got, the one that did the most for me, was delivering furniture for this store in town. It was the furniture store where the rich white people shopped, and when we delivered the stuff, I got to go into some of their houses, the big old mansions there in Natchez. I couldn't believe that people lived like that, fine furniture, carpets on the floor. I kept looking down at the carpet, feeling it under my feet, and thinking about our house where you could see through the floorboards to the chickens. I saw that and I remember thinking, 'I'm going to get me some of this. This is all right.' That was when I decided I was going to go to college no matter what it took."

School became his focus, school and athletics. "I knew athletics was going to be my vehicle," he said. "Education wasn't really pumped into our heads. My folks gave us choices. My brothers didn't really want to go to school. They were like my dad; they liked to wander. They'd take off, be gone for two or three years, we wouldn't hear from them. One day my brother Fred said he was going to Buffalo. He walked out of the house with ten bucks in his pocket. We heard from him two weeks later; he said he'd made it. We didn't have any money but we had choices, and we had independence."

When Robert Shannon let it be known that he was thinking about going to college, he found any number of people who said they'd help him. "People had high expectations for me," he said. "My high school coaches, Eugene Marshall and George Smith, they were always telling me I could do it. They convinced me I could do it, get out and be successful. You have to hear that message—you can if you want to. Don't be afraid to try. Just go out and work hard and do the best you can.

"I wanted something better than we had. They showed me how to look around and see the situation for what it really was. And there wasn't anything. That was no way for people to live. And I figured if I could get some of those things, those nice houses and furniture and carpets, by going to college, you're doggone right I wanted to go."

In the locker room next to his office, the Flyers were preparing noisily for another practice, yelling, banging lockers, chasing one another through the hallways. Shannon got up from his desk, opened the door, and told them to keep the noise down. At once it was as quiet as a cathedral.

"That's why I'm so hard on these guys," Shannon said, peeling off his shirt to change into his practice clothes. "They have to hear what I heard. You have to treat people with respect, you have to try to be a good person, you have to try to do what's right. I was always taught to treat older people and women with dignity. When I hear these guys, some of them, talk to young women the way they do, I get after them. And I get after the girls, too. I tell them, 'Don't let them talk to you like that. If you don't respect yourselves, how can you expect them to respect you?' I believe in respect."

He changed into shorts and a faded blue shirt, folding his teaching clothes neatly and laying them over a chair. He put on a blue baseball cap and grabbed his plastic-covered play sheet. It was time to go to work.

"Like I said, athletics is just a vehicle," Shannon continued, "but you need something like that to help you accomplish what you need to accomplish. No way I could have done what I did without athletics and the people who were associated with athletics, people who'd been in a situation like mine and who could influence me. Guys like Eugene Marshall, who told me how poor he'd been. It put a realism on it, made it seem possible, made it look like it could happen for me. The key is you have to be willing to try. Growing up in the South, a black kid hears so many times that he shouldn't even try. After a while, you hear something often enough, you begin to believe it. My brothers did. They hung with the wrong people, and they never heard the kind of talk I did. You need that positive influence.

"Bad as it is here, a lot of these kids don't want to leave. They're comfortable here, they know they can get along somehow. They're afraid, some of them, to try it somewhere else. They don't know if they can make it somewhere else. My job is to teach them to succeed."

In the week after the Muskogee trip, two days before the Flyers will play Robeson High School in Chicago, Shannon gets a piece of bad news. Chris Moore's eligibility is being challenged by Fred Curtis, the principal at Belleville East High School. East, as it's known around the Southwestern Conference, is one of the Flyers' rivals.

"I haven't talked to Chris yet," Shannon says. "What I hear is that he's actually been living in Fairview Heights, with his mom, but he's been down here keeping tabs on his father. If he's living in Fairview Heights, it means he's in East's attendance area. I'm thinking they took a look at Chris, said, 'Well, he's a pretty good back, maybe we ought to try it this way.' It's always something around here.''

As if to punctuate that, James Rucker sticks his head in Shannon's door to report that someone has walked off with the detergent he uses to wash the football uniforms. "You didn't lock it up?" Shannon asks.

"Yeah," Ruck says, "but I ain't the only coach around here who's got a key to that room.''

"If it ain't one thing it's another," Shannon complains, pulling a twenty-dollar bill out of his wallet and handing it to Rucker. "Maybe you better lock it up with our stuff.''

Rucker takes off on a detergent run, and Shannon begins rummaging through some of the boxes of football shoes stacked in his office. The game against Robeson will be played at Gately Stadium in south Chicago, and Gately stadium has artificial turf. He has to find some low-cleated turf shoes for his players in his pile of hand-me-downs from the Phoenix Cardinals. "Those guys play on grass now," he says. "There must be some turf shoes in here someplace.''

He throws the shoes around angrily. The missing laundry soap, on top of the challenge to Chris Moore, has him a lot more upset than he wants to let on. "You get these guys who can't beat you on the football field and they figure it can't be their fault so you must be cheating," he says. "It bothers me that they would think I had to cheat to beat them. We don't cheat. We don't have to cheat.''

Early in his career, Shannon had to forfeit some games for using ineligible players. Once he used a player who was too old, thinking that because the player had been eligible as a junior he would be eligible as a senior. It turned out the kid had turned nineteen before the season began, making him ineligible under Illinois High School Association rules. Another time he forfeited games because a player didn't live in the East St. Louis school district. The kid had moved and hadn't bothered to inform Shannon, which is apparently the situation with Chris Moore. "I was just starting out then," he says. "I didn't keep up too well with the administrative side of things."

Administration is still not his long suit. He would not knowingly play an ineligible player, but neither would he spend much time checking and rechecking records either. Nor would he delegate such responsibilities to anyone else. He does not delegate much of anything, because he doesn't trust many people. Twenty years in East St. Louis have convinced him to trust only himself. He is suspicious and hostile toward people or rules he doesn't control. The adage that sometimes you have to go along to get along is lost on him.

"They don't pay me to be an administrator," he says. "I ask the kids, and they all tell me they're eligible. I don't have time to check on all of them. That ain't my job. That's somebody else's job, and if he didn't do it, I can't worry about it."

But he is worried about it. Moore may have a dual residency: with his mother in Fairview Heights, a bedroom community near Scott Air Force Base, and with his father in East St. Louis. It will be up to the IHSA to consider what his primary residence is and whether there was any intent to deceive. In East St. Louis, where broken families and unwed mothers are common, residency is not a simple matter. "How am I going to keep up with that?" Shannon asks. "It's not like I brought Chris in from somewhere else. He grew up in East St. Louis schools. You can bet if he'd gone to Lincoln nobody would be saying anything about this. This whole thing ain't about Chris Moore. It's about politics.

"Besides, if we lose him, we lose him. We don't look at him as just a kid we need to win. We're trying to get him involved in some things that will do him some good outside of football. It's not that way everywhere else. If he goes to East, he's going to have to work his way up. It'll take the right kind of attitude, and I don't know if he has it. We've been trying to get him to work. I could just let him alone and hope he plays good on Saturdays, but that's not the way I work. At this age, it's hard to get a young man to look very far down the road. I've been telling him that, and now look what's happened."

Things got worse for Chris Moore in the game at Chicago. He pulled a groin muscle and spent most of the afternoon on the bench. The Flyers didn't miss him. Shannon plugged fullback Jerry Creer into Moore's tailback slot, and Creer had a big day. So did Deondre Singleton, scoring one touchdown himself and throwing touchdown passes to Bush and Stallings for two other scores. The Flyers won 33–8.

"Going to Chicago is like being on Broadway for us," Shannon said after the game. "Seems like every coach we might see in the playoffs is there to watch us play. We didn't play very good, but the quarterback had a big day and Jerry Creer played well.

That's got Chris Moore bothered more than his injury or this residency thing. I've been telling him he's not the player he was a year ago, and he's beginning to see I'm right. That's the thing about football he doesn't understand. There's a whole lot more to it than Saturday afternoons.''

Bob Shannon was in the eighth grade when he first began learning about football. His teacher was Mae Marshall, whose husband, Eugene, was the football coach at Sadie V. Thompson High School in Natchez. Mae Marshall was an unpaid scout for her husband. "She asked me did I want to come out for football,'' Shannon said. "I said, well, I didn't know. So she told Coach Marshall about me, and he asked me to come out. I didn't know if I really wanted to play, but I went on out. I wanted to play wide receiver, but he made a quarterback out of me. I was really a baseball player, a third baseman, but I thought maybe football could get me to college.''

With men like Eugene Marshall and his assistant, George Smith, drumming college into his head, and with the work ethic he'd already developed, Shannon became one of the most dedicated athletes Sadie V. Thompson High School had ever known. And it paid off with a scholarship offer from Jackson State University, the separate-but-equal public university into which the state siphoned black students. Bob Shannon really wanted to go to Jackson State. It had a good football team. It was just up the road from Natchez. It was a great source of pride for blacks in his hometown. And last but not least, his high school sweetheart was already going to school in Jackson.

"I was going with a young lady named Frances Floyd," he said. "I felt very strongly about her. She was going to school at Millsaps College in Jackson, studying to be a nurse, and I figured if I played at Jackson State and she'd be at Millsaps, that'd be just the thing.

"But there was this guy by the name of Bob Zuk, who was a scout for the Pittsburgh Pirates. He'd seen me playing sandlot baseball and the Pirates had drafted me in the seventh round. He'd asked me before they drafted me if I would sign with them. I'd told him yeah, but after they drafted me they only wanted to give me eight thousand to sign instead of the sixteen thousand he'd mentioned. He wouldn't go higher than eight, and I wouldn't take less than sixteen, which is what I figured it would cost to go to college. I figured college was less of a gamble than professional baseball, so I told him I was going to play football."

Zuk, who later gained fame as the man who signed baseball Hall of Famer Willie Stargell, was a determined man. He followed Shannon to Jackson, where he'd enrolled in summer school to get a jump on his courses and to be near Frances Floyd. "He'd pick us up in his car and try to talk her into talking me into playing baseball. She just said I'd be making my own decision, so then this strange thing happened. He got together with this other guy, a coach at Alcorn State, and they got this guy at Jackson State to give me this old TV set. It was just an old ragtag TV that wouldn't hardly work, but then the guy at Alcorn State turned me in. It supposedly was an illegal inducement, you know, giving a TV set to a player. They got me ruled ineligible for two years in that conference. I guess he figured if I couldn't play football I'd go ahead and play baseball.

"The guy who'd recruited me at Jackson State, a guy named Rodney Page, told me, 'Well, Alcorn got you ruled ineligible. You can either sit it out here, or I can call this guy I know at Tennessee State. They ain't in our conference and you can play there.' That's where I met up with Big John Merritt."

John A. Merritt was the football coach at Tennessee State in Nashville. He rolled into Jackson in a big brown Cadillac and picked up Bob Shannon to take him for a look at the campus. "He was a great talker," Shannon said. "We rode along, talking about Tennessee State and everything I would do there. He took me to the campus and pointed his hand out and told me I'd get everything I wanted there. He said I'd meet my wife there. I said no, I was going to marry my sweetheart back in Jackson. He said, 'No, you'll meet her right out there.' And he was right."

Shannon enrolled at Tennessee State, promising Frances Floyd he'd be back to see her often. "I remember I wrote her a letter [later that year], one of those letters, you know, that says you're really busy and getting into other things, all that stuff. I mailed it and then I thought better of it. But before I could get back to her and apologize, she went and got married to this other guy. My intentions were always to get back to her, but by the time I got around to it, it was too late. I can't even say today why I did that. I was very fond of her.

"She married a white guy, which in Mississippi in 1966 was just something you didn't do. I remember one time when we were in high school, she went in all by herself to this drugstore and sat down at the counter and asked to be served. This was at the time, you know, just a few years after the sit-ins. Nobody knew why she did it, and her friends got her out of there before they had her arrested, and nothing ever came of it. But that's the way she was. She just did what she thought was right.''

In week four of the season, the Flyers play their first conference game, against the Belleville West Maroons. Belleville is a mostly blue-collar town on the bluffs above the floodplain where East St. Louis lies, the place where a lot of the white folks who left East St. Louis in the 1950s and 1960s wound up. Tennis star Jimmy Connors, for example, learned the game on East St. Louis's rutted courts, but polished it at Belleville's country clubs. The seat of St. Clair County, Belleville is the focus of much of the political resentment in East St. Louis. "The politicians in Belleville" and "the folks on the bluffs" get blamed whenever things don't work out in East St. Louis, which is most of the time. Belleville has two high schools in the Flyers' conference: East, which filed the challenge to Chris Moore; and West, which was next on the schedule. The games against Belleville are big games for the politically minded, who see the Flyers as an instrument of social policy.

"We can't score enough for some people in this town when we play those schools," Shannon says. "To me, that's silly. I'm not bringing social issues to my job. At the same time, some of those whites over there think we're running up the score on them sometimes. That's a real problem. I don't want to embarrass anybody, but we're getting ready for the playoffs, and sometimes I've got to leave my starters in long enough for them to get some work."

Things work out just right against West. Homer Bush puts on a show, catching ten passes for 168 yards. The Flyers build a 32–6 lead by halftime, with Singleton hitting Bush, Stallings, and flanker Cory Dent with touchdown passes and reserve fullback Rolando Cameron scoring on two short runs. The Flyers even manage to kick a couple of extra points, Shannon having designated a defensive back named Roderick Fisher as his placekicker. Singleton and Bush hook up for another touchdown pass to start the second half, and Shannon calls off the dogs. The Flyers sit on their lead for the rest of the game and win 39–13. "We're not there yet," Shannon says. "But we're getting there."

"The thing I remember about leaving Mississippi and going to college was that I knew I could never go back," Shannon said. "That road was a one-way street. There was a lot of pride in having the opportunity, because so many people didn't have it. The way out for them was working on that plantation, driving that tractor, and that tractor don't get out. People felt that once you had the opportunity to succeed, you'd better take it. They expected you to do well. A lot of people in that town were expecting me to do well."

People in Natchez, people like Robert Lewis and Eugene Marshall, made sure that Robert Shannon had what he needed for a decent start. When he needed a new suit for his senior prom, they scraped money together to help him buy it—and a pair of dress shoes, too. They'd invite him in for meals, make sure his family had a decent Christmas dinner. "It all goes back to if you try to help yourself, people will see it and try to help you," he said. "I was raised never to ask for charity, but to try to help yourself. They wanted me to succeed."

Determined not to let them down, he hit the ground in Nashville running. He registered for classes, bought his books, and went to work. "I remember one of the first nights after football practice, one of the coaches came through the dorm, checking on us," Shannon said. "I was lying in my bed, reading a biography of Winston Churchill. I had this history course, you know, and I wanted to get ahead. That coach couldn't believe it. He thought I was pulling something on him.

"The first test I took, I made a 92. The professor took it to the football coach. Football players didn't normally make a 92. They just tried to get by. I told the coach I didn't do it that way, and I still don't. What's wrong with being the best? What's wrong with spending a little extra time, going a little deeper, being a little bit better prepared, so you can do a better job?"

Nashville was a different world. There were three square meals a day, serious people who wanted to talk about books and making it in the world, a regimented schedule that fit his need for orderly boundaries. And there was college football, a far cry from the low-rent glories at Sadie V. Thompson High.

"Before practice started, everyone was telling me about this guy named Eldridge Dickey," he said. "I was a quarterback, you know, and I thought I was pretty good. They said, 'Man, you ain't seen Eldridge Dickey.' He'd gone off to Texas for a year and then he'd come back, and the whole campus was buzzing. 'Dickey's back, Dickey's back.' They called him 'The Lord's Prayer.'

"I said, man, can't nobody be that good. The first time I saw him, I was in my room, studying, and there were a bunch of guys out on the lawn throwing a football around. Suddenly everyone started clapping and cheering. The Lord's Prayer had just walked up. He took the ball and threw it over a guy's head. He threw another one into the ground. I said, huh, that ain't so good. Then he threw one, must've gone fifty yards and hit this guy right on the numbers. I said, whoa, this guy may be as good as they said he was."

Bob Shannon went back to studying. He'd seen the Lord's Prayer and he knew he'd be spending his football career on the bench. "I was a pretty good quarterback, but I was never as good as I could have been, and I only got to start one year. I was between Eldridge Dickey and Jefferson Street Joe Gilliam, and I wasn't as good as either of them. Both those guys went on to play pro ball. I made sure I prepared myself for other things."

Between his college scholarship and summer jobs, Shannon was living better than he'd ever lived before. He never had enough money to spend vacations at home, as if going back to Under Leonard's Hill was anyone's idea of a vacation. He always worked, one summer in an ice house, moving huge blocks of ice—"that was a great summer job, man; you'd work like hell all day long, but at least it was cool"—and other summers building grain silos. "I was the motor man, worked that motor hauling those blocks up."

After summers in the silos, football was a relief. Still there were lessons to be learned on the football field. Big John Merritt had a terrific coaching staff, including Alvin "Cat" Coleman,

J. C. Coffey, Howdy Green, and Joe Gilliam's father, Joe, Sr. "They were an outstanding group of men, great role models," Shannon recalled. "The only fault was that John wouldn't tell you the truth all the time. He kind of told you what he thought you wanted to hear. He kind of pampered his stars, and I learned a lesson from that. They didn't turn out to be as good as they could've been if John had demanded more of them.

"The guy who made the biggest impression on me was Cat Coleman, who was our offensive coordinator. He was always telling us, 'Y'all are either going to sacrifice now and enjoy life later on, or you'll enjoy it now and sacrifice later on.' I never forgot that, and I tell our guys that every day. But people nowadays don't want to learn from other people. They want to do things for themselves, learn the hard way. I've always tried to learn from other people, and fortunately, I've run into some pretty good people coming down the road."

Shannon made a big impression on his coaches, too, in part because he was always around. "This virtually became his home for five years," Joe Gilliam recalled from his office at Tennessee State, where he became head football coach in 1983. "He spent most all of his time on this campus. He visited home, but he never went back to Natchez. We could never figure him out, but we enjoyed having him around. He was such a serious young man, such an outstanding student, a dean's list student. Considering his background, that was very unusual.

"We knew about his background, of course, because he was always working, sending money back home, and we knew he was troubled by it. But he never let on. He was a great entertainer, an actor. Back then we traveled by bus to our road games, long trips, fourteen hours sometimes. And Bob would entertain us, singing and acting out things. I always thought he could have been a Hollywood actor, because he could change roles so astutely. He had that acting role in his personal life, too, because he never let on about all the troubles he had back home. He'd talk about it, but he never would complain or ask for help. The only thing we did was make sure he always had work in the off-season and the summertime."

Because Eldridge Dickey was in the class ahead of his, Shannon was the starting quarterback in only one year, his senior season, when Tennessee State had a record of seven wins, one loss, and a tie. "He had this consuming interest in football, whether he was starting or not," Gilliam said. "He had a mind like a sponge, and he always had a great ability to call plays. I called a lot of the plays then, but Bob got to the point where we let him call his own plays. He was just determined that nothing was going to stop him, determined he was going to succeed. He worked very hard to maintain his demeanor of being relaxed. He just would not let anything bother him, or at least he wouldn't let it show."

In the summer of 1970, after his senior year, Shannon took a postgraduate course in football under the great Vincent T. Lombardi. Lombardi, who had built his legend coaching the Green Bay Packers in the 1960s, had moved on to the Washington Redskins. The Redskins spent a twelfth-round draft choice on the Tennessee State quarterback, thinking maybe his athletic ability and work habits would make up for his lack of foot speed. It didn't, but Shannon spent eight weeks with Lombardi before he was cut.

"I was going to try to learn whatever I could, and if you're thinking about being a football coach, that's a pretty good guy to learn from," he said. "Hey, that man was in charge. He was in total control of the whole thing. He ran a tight ship, and he was very demanding. He didn't accept anything but your very best, on every play and every drill, and he was a winner."

When the Redskins cut him, the Atlanta Falcons offered him a free agent's contract. But Shannon knew enough about football and the NFL by that time to know that his own abilities didn't match up. He thought he might be able to coach the game, but he couldn't play it anymore. He went back to Tennessee State to do his student teaching, the only requirement left before he could get his education degree. Somewhere, he figured, there was a school that needed a coach.

"I got into it because I wanted to stay close to the game," he said. "I like football. I like the discipline of it, I like the point and counterpoint. You do one thing, and the other guy does something to counter it, and you have to figure out how to counter him.

"But I also got into it because the way I was helped was through the people I dealt with in football. I thought if you could show kids to play the game the right way, with dedication and sportsmanship, you could teach some lessons about commitment, which might be a lifetime value for them, the same as it was for me.

"Also I liked the game. I was never as good a player as I wanted to be, and that propelled me. I'm going to create an environment for them to improve their skills, to be as good as they can possibly be. And I'm going to give them an opportunity to improve their skills. But in the end, it's all going to fall on them."

CHAPTER

4

The Flyers will mark the midway point in their nine-game 1990 regular season schedule with a game at Granite City, another mostly white blue-collar town just north of East St. Louis. Granite City is not Shannon's favorite place to play; in 1986 the Granite City Warriors upset the Flyers 17–14, ending Eastside's forty-four-game winning streak. Shannon hasn't lost a regular season game since, but that 1986 game is still very much on his mind. Obsessed with football all year long, at this point in the season, he's become oblivious to anything else. Looking for something to worry about, Shannon's convinced himself that history is about to repeat itself.

"They've got a pretty good team this year," he says. "Their defense has been playing real good, and I don't know yet how good we are. This team is slow coming along. It has to do with experience and leadership. You need that leadership to set the tempo, keep down the bickering. Right now we don't have that vocal-type guy who'll make sure the others understand why we do what we do. You get that bickering at the end of practice, when we do our running. We make them sprint down to the fire plug and sprint back, must be eighty to a hundred yards. Last year we had a Dana Howard to make them do it, set the tone. This year they all want to complain. We should be in better shape than we are. They don't want to get themselves into shape, and then they want to gripe at us when we make them do it.

"But I guess we're coming along. The passing game is coming along, the running game is OK. The offensive line is coming together, but it hasn't gotten there yet because we've got some new guys in there. The defense is all right, but we haven't been tested much, except down at Muskogee. I don't know about that defense yet. Hopefully, this game against Granite City can be the one where we come together for the stretch run."

Shannon isn't the only one who smells an upset. A huge crowd turns out at Granite City's stadium, buoyed by the Warriors' 4-0 start and boisterous because their town's depressed economy has gotten a big boost today. Granite City Steel Company, the town's biggest employer, has added a whole new shift, putting two hundred people back to work. The mood in the stadium seems to say that tides are turning.

East St. Louis has its own omen to worry about. Yesterday, a state court judge ordered the city of East St. Louis to turn over title to its city hall to a man named Walter DeBow. In 1985 Walter DeBow, arrested on a traffic violation, was beaten senseless by another prisoner in the East St. Louis city jail. Courts found the city police negligent and awarded $3.4 million in damages to DeBow, now institutionalized with permanent brain damage. The city concocted a strange utility bond issue to pay the judgment, but DeBow's attorneys were unhappy with the plan and went back to court to force a settlement. The judge decided to give Walter DeBow two plots of land, a vacant industrial site and the city's four-year-old, $6.5-million City Hall.

"The kids are all talking about it," says Shannon as the Flyers warm up at Granite City stadium. "But it's one of those things you can't do anything about. It won't affect us."

Indeed, the new shift at the steel mill will be the only good news for Granite City today. Chris Moore takes the big crowd out of the game by going 71 yards for a touchdown on the fourth play of the game. Granite City then fumbles the ball right back, and Moore goes 19 yards for another score. In all, Eastside scores four touchdowns in the first quarter, two more in the second, and goes on to crush the Warriors 49–0. Moore, who's been cleared to play while the investigation into his residency status is under way, gains 164 yards on only five carries, including touchdown runs of 71, 19, and 27 yards. Deondre Singleton completes six of eleven passes for 164 yards. Homer Bush catches three of those passes, two of them for touchdowns, and scores a third touchdown on a 72-yard punt return.

The team plays so well even Shannon is satisfied. "That's the best we've played. I just hope we can keep it up. When you've got a good team down like that, you've got to keep it up. You've got to finish them off."

Shannon is so happy he even allows himself to think a nonfootball thought. When a friend jokes that at least one good thing has happened for East St. Louis today, he laughs and shakes his head. "It's crazy," he says. "They say you can't fight city hall, but in East St. Louis, you can own it."

Bob Shannon long ago decided the best way to deal with city hall in East St. Louis was neither by fighting it or cooperating with it, but by ignoring it. He sees the city and its problems as a diseased environment and has built a bubble to isolate his team from it. He is fiercely protective of his autonomy and snipes at anyone who attempts to interfere with it. He sees nothing in the political values of East St. Louis that he wants passed on to the boys he coaches.

But at the same time, he is fascinated by the town and the things that go on there. "I've been known to watch a western or two on TV," he said once. "I like those old westerns, and 'Lonesome Dove,' that was the best I've seen. And you know how in the westerns, there's always a sanctuary where the bad guys hide out? Sometimes that's what I think about East St. Louis. It's a sanctuary."

East St. Louis has been called an inner city without an outer city, a self-governing ghetto. Its history is unrelentingly bleak. No one there recalls the "good old days," because there have never been any. The very election that established the city was fraudulent. The man who was the city's first mayor later was assassinated. Things never got much better.

East St. Louis exists only because it lies adjacent to the confluence of the Mississippi and Missouri rivers. At first there were the Cahokia and Tamaroa people who lived on the shores of the Father of Waters and built their strange, inexplicable mounds on the flatlands of its floodplain. Then down the river from the Great Lakes and Quebec came French missionaries, and then late in the eighteenth century came a rough man named James Piggott to establish a village he called Illinoistown.

Piggott was enough of a visionary to see that people eventually would want to cross the Mississippi to get at whatever was on the other side and bring it back to civilization. He built a ferry landing and ran boats across to the village of St. Louis on the western shore. Another man, Richard McCarty, came along in the early 1800s and built a mill and a trading post not far from a sandbar called "Bloody Island," a favorite place for gun duels.

Thus was the character of the place decided—it would serve the city on the other side of the river, linking it to the industries in the East, and it would be a tough and violent place. In 1857 the Ohio and Mississippi Railroad cinched that role for Illinoistown, establishing its terminus there. In 1874 the great engineer James B. Eads spanned the river with his monumental bridge. The railroads from the East would terminate in Illinoistown, and the Eads Bridge would be the rail link to new markets in the West.

The land was well suited for the railroads, flat floodplain along the banks of the great river. What didn't come east by rail over the bridge could come down the Missouri to the Mississippi just above St. Louis and be loaded onto eastbound cars waiting in Illinoistown. The railroads came and were followed by mills and factories and stockyards to serve the railroads and the markets the railroads served. Thousands of railroad and factory workers moved to Illinoistown, finding shanty housing on the floodplain in towns the companies created. National City for the stockyard workers, Alorton for the Aluminum Ore workers, and nearly a dozen more. In 1861 Illinoistown badly needed an identity for itself, not to mention a tax base, and a referendum was put forth to incorporate under the name East St. Louis. The railroad workers were paid five dollars each to vote for the new name. A century later precinct workers were still getting five bucks a vote.

In 1861 there was no shortage of places to spend the money. The town was full of saloons and whorehouses, honky-tonks, and gambling dens for people who didn't feel like playing high-stakes games across the river. Sin became a major industry, much of it concentrated in an area near downtown called "The Valley." Prostitution and gambling flourished under the benevolence of police and politicians, who were well paid for their myopia. Competition for public office and its fruits was fierce; in 1885 a man named John Bowman, who'd been the city's first mayor, was shot dead for advocating reform a bit too strenuously.

The politicians were dependent on the sin industry in large part because other industries found a way around paying taxes. By incorporating company towns, and building their own shanty-towns for workers, big industry avoided paying municipal taxes. East St. Louis, which had a high service demand and low property tax payments, found itself perpetually broke. Politicians tended to skim interest payments and bond fees, and pay off judges and prosecutors to keep the system alive. So even though the city was booming, there never was enough money to pay its debts.

The nature of the people who moved to town only made things

worse. They were largely unskilled and uneducated, ethnic whites and the children of former slaves fleeing the South for opportunity in the North. Black and white alike were paid low wages and housed in shanties. They depended on the political system for everything from jobs and health care to transportation and entertainment. They were the serfs of the industrial revolution and never created the kind of middle class that advocates reform. Those few who did work their way into the middle class, as merchants or administrators, moved their families quickly out of the dank and teeming flatlands into the rolling hills of the city across the river.

Bad as they were, these days—from the turn of the century through the Second World War—were the best the city ever knew. Sure, the people were dependent and the politicians corrupt, but at least there were jobs and affordable housing that with a little effort could be made almost decent. There was opportunity.

No one was thrilled about working in the abattoirs of the National City Stockyards, or the Hunter, Swift, and Armour packing plants, but at least there *was* work there. There was work at American Steel and Alcoa, at the Obear-Nester Glass plant, at Hill Brick, and Moss Tie, Walworth Valve, Socony-Mobil, Phillips Pipeline, Continental Can, C. K. Williams, and a dozen other big smokestack industries. The factories sprawled across the landscape, inside and just outside the city limits. Neighborhoods grew up next to the plants, chockablock around them. It was an urban planner's nightmare, but no one cared.

At its high point in the early 1950s, East St. Louis had a population of just over eighty-one thousand but afforded nearly forty thousand industrial jobs. Workers from neighboring towns shopped there, too, in a thriving little downtown and in the shops along Collinsville and St. Clair avenues. The city had its own crusading daily newspaper, the *East St. Louis Journal*. The *Journal* never lacked for subjects to crusade about.

The city was dominated by an iron triangle—machine politicians on one side, business leadership on another, and the sin merchants on the third. Unlike other cities, where business leaders and their managers mobilized into a reform movement, East St. Louis's executive class didn't live in town. They were absentee owners and commuters who cared very little about living conditions in the city. Their companies benefited from snug relationships with the politicians who kept their tax assessments low. The city's merchants kept down their own taxes by loading assessments onto tavern owners who ran gambling and prostitution operations in back rooms. License fees were enormous, but so were the wages of sin.

The joints in the Valley were famous around the world; indeed, the Valley became a tourist attraction. More respectable merchants caught the overflow business, so they were content. During Prohibition, the Valley housed hundreds of speakeasies and night spots, some featuring great blues and jazz musicians in the front rooms and hookers and gamblers in the back. The bridges from St. Louis were busy all night.

The Second World War brought an end to the fun and games in the Valley. Many of the usual patrons were off to war, and the Army Air Forces threatened to post the city off limits to personnel at nearby Scott Field. City fathers—shocked, absolutely shocked to discover vice in the Valley—closed down the area. It was later bulldozed to make way for an interstate highway interchange.

But the high rollers just moved a few blocks over. Organized crime, in the person of one Frank "Buster" Wortman, who'd been a deputy in Al Capone's old Chicago mob, moved into the area in full force. The Wortman mob quickly gained complete control of gambling and prostitution in East St. Louis, and Buster's Paddock Restaurant became a noted tourist stop. He ran an efficient operation: plush casinos with expensive entertainment, wire rooms in the back and slot machines in the front, bullets for anyone who objected. Even the crummiest beer joint had slots, and the poshest nightclubs were precursors to what would soon be built in Las Vegas.

Federal prosecutors eventually put Wortman out of business, and large-scale sin became small scale by the end of the 1950s. Yet organized sin remains a part of East St. Louis's heritage, kept alive still by nightclubs and girlie joints downtown, and by strip joints and late-night clubs on the outskirts of town. Fun seekers in Missouri find that taverns there by law must close at 2:00 A.M., so many of them cross into Illinois to keep their parties going until dawn. "Going to the East Side," it's called.

Bob Shannon, who doesn't drink, smoke, gamble, chase wild women, or hang out with those who do, was nonetheless introduced to the East St. Louis vice scene very early in his career as an assistant football coach. "When I first came to East St. Louis," he said, "I lived with Dupree Davis, a politician. His wife was the mother of the principal at Hughes-Quinn, the junior high school I was assigned to. The principal's name was Wendell Mitchell. He asked his mother to take me in, because I was living in this house of ill repute, a little hotel on Missouri Avenue.

"I didn't have any money, and neither did this other new guy. I forget his real name. They called him Bo' Hog, because he was a big guy, a linebacker from Ohio. He and I were the new teachers at Hughes-Quinn, and Mr. Mitchell knew we needed a place to stay, so he'd called whoever it was owned the hotel and told them to let us stay for free until we got paid. The girls were a-comin' and a-goin', and we were living on the top floor, wondering what we'd gotten ourselves into. Old Bo' Hog figured it out pretty quick. He left town after one year. Said he'd seen enough. Maybe I'm more stubborn than he was, or maybe he was smarter than I was."

In the week after the big win at Granite City, college recruiters start showing up at the Flyers' practices. Their interest is focused mainly on the seniors, particularly Homer Bush and Jerry Creer. But they all ask about Chris Moore, and Deondre Singleton begins getting some attention, too. Shannon is frank when recruiters come by. "I never lie for a kid," he says. "What I tell the kids is I want the recruiters to come back and trust my judgment on the next group of kids. If a guy asks me about a kid's work habits or his grades, and they ain't so good, I tell him. I try to focus on their strengths, but I won't ignore their weaknesses either."

Grades can be a big problem. Under National Collegiate

Athletic Association (NCAA) rules, an incoming freshman must "predict" academic success by scoring at least 18 out of 36 possible points on the American College Test, the standard used in Illinois. Sam Morgan, the principal at Eastside, says the average ACT score at the school is 17. "That's not good," he says, "but we're up from 1988, when the average was 15.1. The football team is better than the rest of the school population in grades, because they have to stay eligible and because Shannon stays on them so much. So many of these kids, the only reason they stay in school is so they can play sports. They think sports can be the vehicle out of here, and maybe it can. You hear people saying it's pie in the sky for a kid to think he can play in the NBA or the NFL. I say, maybe it is pie in the sky, but I say good for pie in the sky. Anything to keep a kid in school."

When one of his seniors has a chance for a college scholarship but may be shaky on his grades, Shannon arranges tutoring for the ACT. His wife, Jeanette, a mathematics teacher, helps out, as do a few other teachers in the district. If the kid's parents can't afford the tutoring fee, Shannon comes up with the money himself. One way or the other, Flyer seniors usually predict.

But kids can't sign college letters of intent until February. This is still October, and Shannon is otherwise obsessed. He is spending twelve hours a day at the school these days, then going home to a late supper and a couple more hours poring over his play sheets. "Got to stay on top of things," he says.

He is unhappy that his team doesn't share his enthusiasm. The leadership he is looking for has not materialized. In fact, unexcused absences from practice are on the rise. "I'm going to put the burden on them," he says. "From now on, they're going to run an extra sprint for every player who's not here."

His team is 5-0 and coming off a 49-0 victory, but he is discouraged. "These guys are so different from the bunch we had last year. It seems like there's so much else on their minds. It's discouraging. We've put a lot of time into this, and it's meant a lot to me over the years. It's like the Roman Empire, destructing from within.

"I think back to when I first came to East St. Louis, down at Hughes-Quinn. My vision was that I could make a great difference. I overrated what I could do. It dawned on me over the years that some of these people don't want to improve their lot in life. I thought, back then, that everybody wanted to be successful, to move up and prepare themselves for a good life after high school, a job or college. I found out that was the farthest thing from a lot of people's minds, and it wasn't as bad then as it is now. What I think now is that some of them you'll reach, some of them you'll never reach, and some of them you won't know until they come back ten years later and tell you."

He stands up and stretches and begins changing into his practice clothes, to see how many unenthused no-shows he will have to deal with today. "The only thing you can do is do the best you can, be the type of person you're telling them to be. I'm just trying to get them to figure out they don't have to settle for what's out there on the streets. I always tell them, look around on those street corners. See those guys in the fancy clothes and the fancy cars and look at their faces. The cars and the clothes stay the same, but the faces change. They go to jail, they get shot, but there's always somebody else to take a dead man's place."

It turns out he was overly discouraged. Two days later, the Flyers destroy Belleville West 54–8 to go 6–0. "We may be all right after all," Shannon says.

When Bob Shannon moved to East St. Louis in 1971, he was following a trail cut by thousands of other black Mississippians. In the three decades of industrial boom that followed the completion of James Eads's railroad bridge in 1874, the city's population grew to nearly sixty thousand, of whom some ten thousand were black. The city was the traditional first stop for Mississippi blacks following the river north toward hope. Many moved on to St. Louis, or farther north to Chicago and Detroit, but many others found work in East St. Louis and stayed.

Industry was glad to have a brand new—and highly exploitable—source of cheap labor. A second generation of white workers, backed by union organizers, was beginning to agitate for higher wages in the packing plants and other industries. The companies responded by threatening to replace union workers with blacks. On the hot summer night of July 2, 1917, the tension exploded. A bloody riot took the lives of forty-six persons, thirty-seven of them black.

Shortly after that, whites began leaving East St. Louis. Black immigration increased. By 1940 blacks made up 22 percent of the population. By 1950 the figure was 34 percent, and by 1960, blacks accounted for 45 percent of the city's peak population of 81,712. In the 1960s white flight soared. Between 1960 and

1970, 26,000 whites left East St. Louis. The city's population plummeted to 69,996; 70 percent were black. By 1980 the population was down to 55,200; 94 percent were black.

Another way to look at what happened in the sixties and seventies is this: In 1959 East St. Louis's business community managed to get the city designated an "All American City" by the National Chamber of Commerce. By 1979, according to the Census Bureau's "liveability quotient" statistics for cities with a population of fifty thousand or more, only Mayaguez, Puerto Rico, ranked lower than East St. Louis.

Things didn't get any more liveable in the 1980s. By 1990 only 40,994 people lived in East St. Louis, of whom 98 percent were black. In thirty years, the population had been cut in half. The white population had almost disappeared.

So had most of the jobs. The 1960s saw the devastation of East St. Louis's industrial base. The meat-packing industry moved operations to the west, closer to the source of cattle. Heavy industries like Alcoa and American Zinc found cheaper places to do business. The railroads lost business to the interstate highway system and the airlines. Month by month, year by year, thousands of jobs were lost as big industries closed and hundreds more were lost as the support industries closed in their wake. By the mid-1980s, only about five hundred manufacturing jobs remained in the entire city.

Retailers followed the population out of town. East St. Louis had been the commercial center of St. Clair County, but when the customers left and property taxes kept being boosted for those who remained, the retailers fled on the new interstate highway to

Fairview Heights. By 1991 East St. Louis had a property tax rate of $21.16 for every $100 of assessed valuation, nearly four times the rate of surrounding cities. Even if someone did want to build a home or business there, the taxes would be prohibitive.

By 1990 the official unemployment rate in East St. Louis was nearly 24 percent, though of course that only measures those who are actively seeking work. Many East St. Louisans long ago quit looking. About 70 percent of the city's residents are on some form of public assistance, which means they're either unemployed or underemployed.

By the early 1990s, the biggest employer in the city was city government and the rest of the public sector, including School District No. 189. To get a job, or to keep a job, in East St. Louis, allegiance to City Hall or the Democratic Township Committee must be absolute. It is a city of connections—political, financial, or family connections, or usually a combination of at least two of these.

To the extent that it has been governed at all, East St. Louis has been governed by a Democratic political machine. In the early days, the machine was fueled by a coalition of white politicians, industry owners, and racketeers, all of whom exploited a population that had good reason to be convinced that its very existence depended on the machine. Blacks were easy prey. The machine controlled the jobs. Opposition was fruitless; people figured they might as well go along with the machine. They might as well take the five bucks on election day.

The white machine cultivated a black sub-machine. Black leaders got jobs and favors, often in the form of a share of slot-machine revenue, in return for getting out the vote. As late as 1967, when blacks made up two-thirds of the electorate, white machine leader Alvin Fields won reelection to his fifth term as mayor by a three-to-one majority over his black opponent.

Fields, first elected in 1951, had presided over the dissolution of his city. Not that it mattered to voters. The most lasting legacy of the Fields administration was the institution of "judgment fund borrowing." In East St. Louis, city suppliers, be they major (like utility companies) or minor suppliers (of such conveniences as gasoline for police cars) must in effect sue the city to get paid. A court then rules in their favor and the city issues bonds backed by property or utility tax receipts. Year by year the judgment bond obligations mounted until East St. Louis's property tax rate became one of the highest in the country.

By 1990 most American cities were reserving bond issues for major capital improvements. East St. Louis was using them to buy tires for fire trucks and stationery for City Hall. Even when someone managed to land one of the coveted City Hall jobs, he soon learned to bring his own toilet paper to work. Cash was reserved strictly to meet the city payroll, and even that was a dicey thing. One creditor or another usually was trying to attach the payroll, meaning the biweekly checks were almost always late. In 1990, when the state of Illinois decided to help bail out the city, East St. Louis was an estimated $40 million in the hole. The idea of declaring municipal bankruptcy was never considered seriously. Bankruptcy would have meant turning City Hall over to court-appointed receivers and thus a loss of political control.

In 1963 Mayor Fields came under pressure from business

people and community leaders to do something—anything—to stop the city's decline. In response, he hired a professional urban planner named George Washnis to be his administrative assistant. Washnis, a clever administrator and frustrated reformer, had great success luring federal antipoverty funds to East St. Louis. A lot of public housing was built there, and every well-intentioned Great Society program developed in Washington was tried. Fields stymied Washnis's efforts to professionalize city government, but when it came to outside help, nothing was too off-the-wall for Alvin G. Fields. When the architect Buckminster Fuller proposed raising a geodesic dome over the city, Fields was all for it. Cynics called Fuller's proposal "peasants under glass." Not surprisingly, nothing ever came of it.

Fields and the machine loved the antipoverty and housing money because it meant more dollars for them to handle. The one program that slipped out of their control was a federal Model Cities grant. To their delight, Washington chose East St. Louis as a laboratory for various programs under the aegis of Model Cities and designated millions of dollars to back it. Unfortunately for Fields, Model Cities was designed to be run by neighborhood organizers. In East St. Louis those organizers were young, black, and ambitious, and Model Cities became the wedge that broke the white machine. Though it hardly rejuvenated East St. Louis, Model Cities did create a black power structure separate from the machine. And it demonstrated to blacks within the machine that they could have it all.

Fields decided not to run for reelection in 1971. Black politicians who'd been biding their time in the back rooms of the

Democratic machine immediately grabbed for control of the party apparatus. Two black machine politicians filed for the nomination, splitting the machine vote. To their shock, the third black candidate in the race—a legal aid lawyer and reformer named James Williams—was elected. It was a stunning defeat for the machine. Not only had a black man been elected mayor, but a reformer to boot.

The loss of machine control was only temporary. By 1975 Williams had been frustrated repeatedly in his efforts at reform. He wouldn't play politics, so he didn't get anything done. The machine had changed colors, but not tactics. In 1975 a politician named William Mason promised enough people enough different things to get himself elected mayor. Mason had his own set of problems, not the least of which was that he'd promised the same things to too many different people. Taxes were still going up, people and jobs were still leaving town, federal funding sources were drying up, and Mason became another one-term mayor.

Primed and ready to take his place in 1979 was a bright, well-spoken young man named Carl Officer. He was the son of Marion Officer, the city's best-known funeral home operator and one of the most popular men in town. When he won the 1979 mayoralty election, Carl Officer was only twenty-seven years old. Handsome and charismatic, he vowed that his election meant the dawn of a new day.

Carl Officer was utterly confident, given to calling press conferences to announce new development schemes on the slimmest of pretexts. One Monday he called the press in to announce that East St. Louis would be the home of a new prison that would be run by private enterprise. Quizzed about who would run the prison, Officer replied, "I don't know. I just dreamed this up yesterday, but I should have a group together by Wednesday."

The new mayor was an elegant and stylish bachelor who dropped broad public hints about his sexual conquests. He liked to prowl nightclubs in the company of four police officers who were his bodyguards. One of the bodyguards was nicknamed "Pit Bull." Another always carried an Uzi submachine gun. One night, when the mayor was in the men's room of a nightclub, the bodyguards beat up a patron whose only crime was that Mother Nature had called him at the same time she had called the mayor.

Carl Officer became mayor the same year Bob Shannon won his first state championship. In two reelection campaigns in the eighties, Officer steamrolled his opponents pretty much the same way Shannon steamrolled his. As the 1980s began, they were two of the most popular men in town. As the decade ended, they were two of the least popular. Officer spent the eighties consolidating political power but driving the city deeper into despair. Shannon spent the decade winning football games and antagonizing people with his attitude.

For sure they didn't like each other. Carl Officer thought Bob Shannon was a carpetbagger, typical of all the "outsiders" who criticized the city but didn't live there. For his part, Bob Shannon thought Carl Officer embodied all that was wrong about East St. Louis.

The weather got cold and rainy in mid-October, turning Shannon's practice field to mud but raising his spirits. "Chicago weather," he says, pulling on a yellow rain suit one afternoon before practice. "We'll catch this kind of weather up there during the playoffs. This is a chance to get used to it. We got to do the things we do no matter what kind of weather we get. You get some coaches, when it rains, they won't throw the ball. Not me. You got to get the job done anyhows."

A knock at the door interrupts him. One of his players has come to ask for toilet paper.

"You didn't bring any?" Shannon asks. "I told you guys, you have to bring your own. You know they ain't going to leave any for you. What happens if I give you mine and you leave it in your locker and it's gone? What happens if I need it?"

The kid, a huge, soft-looking sophomore in whom Shannon saw the makings of a useful offensive guard if only he could be toughened up, shifts from one foot to the other out of embarrassment or maybe something more urgent. Shannon glares at him and then tosses him half a roll of paper. "You bring that back to me, you hear?" he says. The kid takes it and runs.

"Gotta teach that boy his mama ain't here to take care of him," Shannon says. "You find that over here a lot of time. Some of their mamas don't care about them at all, and some of them are so protective they do everything for them."

Still, a roll of toilet paper doesn't seem like so much to ask.

"Shoot," Shannon laughs, topping off his rain gear with a battered blue stocking cap. "That ought to be easy for them to remember. I bet he'll remember the next time."

He walks out onto the muddy field, across the yard to where Singleton and the other quarterbacks are trying to throw wet footballs with a strong wind at their backs. Shannon uses rubber footballs on days like this, the better to preserve the leather Rawlings R-5s he prefers. He buys some of the footballs with his own money and he doesn't want them ruined. Besides, he reasons, if you can teach a kid to throw a wet rubber ball, he should have no trouble with a wet leather ball. "Watch your grip and take your time," he tells Singleton and the others. "Try to fade it with the wind."

A half hour of throwing with the wind is followed by a half hour of throwing against it. Shannon concentrates on his favorite short passing play, designated 95 on his play sheet. It is a basic outside hitch pass to the split end, Homer Bush. Thrown with the proper timing, with the ball in the air before the receiver makes his cut, there is no way to prevent it from being completed for a six-yard gain. And if the back is giving Bush too much cushion, trying to prevent him from running past him, Bush has the moves to turn six yards into sixty for six points. Time and again this season, Bush has run a 95 route, caught the ball, planted his feet, spun and run right past the would-be tackler. On a wet field, with cornerbacks giving more ground because of uncertain footing, the play should be even more effective. Shannon loves 95 because Singleton throws the out pattern crisply and with impeccable timing, making it a low-risk pass. The two friends have practiced it a thousand times, over the summer in the gym and throughout the fall. Today they are making it work in the rain.

But Shannon calls a halt after forty-five minutes. This is a big day. The Flyers are expecting a celebrity guest, and over his shoulder, the coach sees that the guest has arrived. A forty-foot-long luxury motor coach is pulling regally into the parking lot. The coach contains Walter Payton, the National Football League's all-time rushing leader, and a crew from the ESPN cable network. Payton, the former Chicago Bears running back, is a principal in a group trying to attract an NFL expansion franchise to St. Louis. The ESPN crew, headed by sportscaster Tom Jackson (a former all-pro linebacker with the Denver Broncos), is doing a piece on Payton's life after football. The plan is for Payton to speak to the Flyers, which will inspire them; ESPN will get a tape of it, which will help their piece—and the St. Louis NFL Partnership will get valuable national publicity. Payton, after all, is a black man—another poor kid who used football to get out of Mississippi—and the NFL has no black owners.

The trouble is that it's raining and muddy, and Payton has on an expensive suit and dress loafers. It's warm and dry inside the motor coach, which belongs to one of Payton's would-be NFL partners, a beer wholesaler in St. Louis named Jerry Clinton. The motor coach has a fully stocked liquor cabinet, draft beer, and a supply of canned nuts and pretzels. Inside the coach, Payton is munching honey-roasted peanuts and looking out the windows. He is like a visitor from another planet, safe inside his hermetically sealed capsule, looking out at a strange and hostile environment.

He gets a briefing on Shannon and the Flyers and nods his head. "Got it," he says. "I been there." He puts down his peanuts and steps outside the door. He shakes hands with Shannon—one man in an eight-hundred-dollar suit, the other in a yellow rain suit and a blue stocking cap—and they talk like old buddies about Jackson State, where Payton went to college.

"I want y'all to meet a man who was a pretty good football player for a guy from Mississippi," Shannon says to his awestruck team. "I want y'all to pay attention, because this is a man who knows what it takes. This is a man who used football to get a pretty good thing going."

And Payton says all the right things, about paying the price, about being tough, about staying in school. "Y'all are 6–0," he says. "But it's going to get tougher now. You gotta stay tough."

The players are nodding their heads and ripping strips off a roll of adhesive tape. They put the tape on one another's helmets and then bow their heads to Payton, who autographs the helmets. Tom Jackson and his ESPN capture it all on tape. Shannon watches this with amusement for about five minutes and then announces, "All right, fellas, it's time to go back to work."

Payton signs a few more autographs for the crowd of students who have gathered around, and then he follows the football players out onto the practice field, his loafers squishing in the mud. He has a few private words with Chris Moore, who someone has told him might need a few reminders about not squandering his talent. And then for a few moments, Walter Payton, arguably the greatest back in the history of football, stands by himself watching the ragged and muddy East St. Louis Flyers work out. Tom Jackson walks up to him. "I remember this," Jackson says.

"So do I," says Walter Payton. Then he turns away, and he and Jackson climb back into the luxury coach and head back to civilization.

Three days later, the Flyers, with Walter Payton's autograph on their heads, trounce the Alton High Redbirds 55-7. They are 7-0, with the hated Lincoln Tigers next on the schedule.

Carl Officer did not attend Lincoln High School; he went to a private school in St. Louis. Despite that, Shannon says he's a "Lincoln guy."

"All them politicians are Lincoln guys," he claims. "They all grew up when Eastside was the white high school, and now that they're in charge, they're getting even. They tell me, 'Oh, coach, you wasn't around then. You don't know how it was. It was bad. You have no idea.' I just say, 'Yeah, right. I was in Mississippi then, and it was burning.'"

Racial politics dominated East St. Louis during the 1980s, the decade when most of the boys on this football team began attending school and learning about the world around them. The city got ever deeper into debt. The federal government cut back aid to cities. East St. Louis lost another 27 percent of its population and a few more of its remaining industries. The city's accumulated debt passed the $40 million mark with barely a wave.

Heavy floods in the fall of 1986 caused the city's sewer system to break down and a third of the city was underwater, water in which raw sewage was floating. The city's police cars and fire trucks broke down repeatedly. Often there was only one police cruiser available for the entire city, and sometimes the police radios didn't work either.

The crisis was made more acute by the advent of crack, the

cheap rock cocaine that devastated America's inner cities in the eighties. East St. Louis became the crack capital of southern Illinois. At one point, the state police estimated that 40 percent of the crack in Illinois had its origins in St. Clair County, a remarkable figure given that Chicago and its suburbs are fifty times bigger than East St. Louis and its suburbs. If there was a good side to the crack epidemic, it was that it gave some focus to gang warfare in East St. Louis. Previously, street gangs like the Warlords had been given to random violence and theft. With crack in the picture, the violence became organized and business-like.

The city, never a garden spot, began to look like a battle-ground: "the Beirut of the Corn Belt," according to one newspaper editorial; "an American Soweto," according to another. Public housing projects became no-man's-land with crack peddled at drive-by pit stops to blacks from East St. Louis and whites from St. Louis who followed the old vice trail across the bridges from the west. Abandoned buildings were eviscerated by junkies looking for stuff to sell. The worst of the buildings were demolished with federal urban renewal funds, but nothing was ever built in their place. The sprawling abandoned factory sites sat and rusted, waiting for new industry that never came. The city was a place of wide open spaces, overgrown with weeds and dotted by enclaves of people hanging on and hoping for better days. The city's churches, led by a courageous coalition of ministers, encouraged the good people of East St. Louis to hang on and pray.

But even the churches were touched by the epidemic. Mayor Officer's good friend and supporter, the Rev. Joe Davis, pastor of the Fifteenth Street Baptist Church, was the man the mayor pointed to as a leader of the good folks who were trying to do something about the drug epidemic. The Rev. Mr. Davis, who styled himself as "the street preacher," was on the radio regularly talking about the problems of drugs and gangs until the federal government indicted him as a major crack dealer, charging that he'd used his church to launder drug money. Davis was convicted in 1989 and sentenced to thirty years in prison.

In 1986 Illinois Governor Jim Thompson sent the state police in to help patrol the city. Another state police unit was assigned to patrol the city's public housing projects. Drugs were the big problem, followed closely by assault, burglary, theft, and arson. By some accounts, the city's murder rate of forty to forty-five a year made East St. Louis the deadliest place in the country.

The city's own police force developed severe morale problems. Not only were East St. Louis cops burdened with patrol cars and police radios that couldn't be depended on, they often went three or four weeks at a stretch without being paid. Their health insurance was canceled because the city didn't pay the premiums. The city asked cops who weren't being paid to climb into patrol cars that might not start to patrol some of the most dangerous streets in the country, armed with the knowledge that if they got into trouble, they couldn't use the radios to call for help—and if they got shot, they'd have to pay their own medical bills.

Even so, police protection was more dependable than trash collection. The city stopped collecting trash in 1987 because it could no longer afford it. Residents either paid private haulers or hauled their own. Dead-end streets became impromptu landfills.

City residents dumped trash there, as did haulers from throughout the St. Louis area who wanted to avoid landfill fees.

The mayor, despite being reelected twice in the decade, provided a sometimes curious role model for law and order advocates. In 1989 he wound up in the St. Clair County Jail when he ignored a subpoena to show up in court to explain why the city hadn't repaired sewers in one housing project. The mayor and his attorney, who was paid $100,000 to defend and prosecute the myriad lawsuits the city was involved in, said the judge's order was political. The judge had them arrested. Officer's response was to release a letter he said he'd written in jail. "Some of the best political writing in history has been done from jail," he said, comparing his epistle to Dr. Martin Luther King, Jr.'s immortal "Letter from a Birmingham Jail."

Despite the chaos and embarrassment, Officer thrived in the eighties. His dominance of City Hall and its patronage system was absolute. He blamed the city's troubles on racism: racism by the federal government, racism by the county politicians in Belleville, racism by white reporters whom he said were interested only in portraying the failures of blacks. He said whites were determined to undermine the efforts of blacks to control their own destinies. He spoke of a broad conspiracy to drive the blacks out of East St. Louis so whites could buy up the city, prime real estate on the banks of the great river in the heart of the country. His remarks found an audience. Officer was reelected with huge majorities in 1983 and 1987, each time saying that prosperity was just around the corner, and that it was a *black* prosperity.

Officer was a master of forming ad-hoc coalitions, doling out just enough in the way of jobs and city contracts to control whatever it was he needed to control. He worked with, but stayed apart from, the city's Democratic machine. He demonstrated just how powerful he was in 1987 when he won reelection against the machine's boss, Clyde Jordan. Jordan, in addition to being president of the school board and supervisor of the East St. Louis Township Democratic Committee, was also a member of the East Side Health Board and publisher of the *East St. Louis Monitor*, the city's major black weekly paper. Had he been elected mayor, he would have controlled nearly every public job in town.

Clyde Jordan had never lost a political race in his life, but he lost to Carl Officer. His heart wasn't in the race. Already gravely ill with cancer, he died just three weeks after the election. Ironically, Officer missed him more than anyone. Jordan, a very practical politician, had tempered the wildest of the mayor's schemes. With him gone, the mayor had no anchor at all.

He staked the city's hopes on complicated development schemes. One called for building the world's largest auto-racing track. Another called for the huge rail yards along the riverfront to be relocated so the land could be used for parks and upscale housing and brand-new industry. This plan had the acronym MARGE, for Metro Area Rail Gateway Enterprise, and Officer loved it. "I'll fool around with anyone," the mayor said, "but MARGE is my steady girl."

But MARGE was just fooling around herself. The project never went anywhere. The federal government offered to develop part of the riverfront as an expansion of the Jefferson National

Memorial and Gateway Arch grounds directly across the river. Officer was not enthusiastic, claiming it would use land that blacks were going to develop into profit centers. He came up instead with an exotic scheme to issue $456 million in redevelopment bonds to build condominium projects, a trash recycling center, and a transportation center along the riverfront. With the help of a New York bonding firm, Matthews & Wright, Officer got the bonds approved by voters, and Matthews & Wright began selling them. The mayor spent many happy hours traveling to and from New York, dining in fine restaurants, talking to architects and consultants and bond wizards, and holding press conferences to boast about the black prosperity that was just around the corner. He was like a lamb being led to slaughter.

The FBI had begun nosing around in Matthews & Wright's business practices. The feds discovered that the firm had arranged $2.5 billion in bond issues in impoverished communities around the country, reaping millions in fees from each issue. Very few of the projects were ever built. In East St. Louis alone, Matthews & Wright raked in almost $20 million in fees. Officer and his administration spent another $1 million on various consultant's studies. Not a single shovelful of dirt was ever moved. Eventually the bonds went into default. Matthews & Wright entered into a plea agreement, admitting its actions amounted to criminal fraud. One of its officers went to jail. Investors were repaid with interest. The city was left holding the bag on a huge civil liability problem from investors who found they owed taxes on investments they'd thought were tax exempt.

Officer was undaunted. He quickly switched gears, deciding

that the city's future lay with legalized gambling on Mississippi River excursion boats. The state government had authorized issuing five gambling licenses to communities along the river. Officer was convinced that hordes of high-rolling tourists would flock to his depressed city, creating a demand for hotels and restaurants. He began taking applications from would-be casino boat operators and setting forth conditions. One condition was that city officials, including himself, would be entitled to free food and drink aboard the riverboats. Someone had to make sure the boats were operating on the up and up, he explained.

In authorizing riverboat gambling, the Illinois legislature had set aside one license for East St. Louis. The thinking was that the state's cut would help pay for bailing East St. Louis out of its financial troubles. The $34 million bailout proposal had slogged its way through the legislature in the mid-1980s. It had been favored by Governor Thompson, a Republican, as perhaps the only way possible to restore economic promise to southwestern Illinois. But Thompson had vowed that not one cent of state money would go to East St. Louis as long as Officer was in charge of spending it.

Officer said this proved what he'd been talking about, that white politicians in Springfield didn't think blacks could manage their own affairs. He scoffed at estimates of the city's debt, which ranged between $47 million and $54 million, saying it was all just paper debt and that the city really owed no more than $4 million to $5 million. He balked at accepting the bailout because it would be supervised by a state-supervised oversight committee and not by a locally elected official, namely himself.

Officer seemed to feel he was bulletproof, that he could get away with anything, no matter how outrageous. He topped himself in mid-1989, when he was invited to join a delegation of black mayors on a junket to the African nation of Zaire. "I'm going to take my own blood supply in case something happens," the mayor quipped. "I don't want any of that monkey blood they got over there." He was promptly disinvited on the junket.

This was East St. Louis at the end of the decade—lawsuits piling up right and left, a staggering debt that was being denied, preachers going to jail, garbage stacked up in the streets, sewers overflowing, crack being sold openly on street corners, buildings being torched. This was the East St. Louis that was discovered by "60 Minutes." A producer and a camera crew from the CBS news show spent parts of six weeks in the city in the summer and fall of 1989, and correspondent Ed Bradley came in to finish the piece in early October.

The cameras caught the devastation, and Bradley recited the litany of the city's woes. But Officer was eloquent in the city's defense, saying that all the city needed was a break, but that "outsiders"—meaning white politicians, white investors, and white news media—had somehow conspired to thwart him. He portrayed himself as an activist mayor, inviting the CBS crew to ride along with him as he patrolled the city in his role as an ex-officio police officer. He even went so far as to leap out of his car and help police make a drug bust. The cameras rolled, but the footage of the crime-busting mayor was left on the cutting room floor.

What did air was a relentlessly depressing segment on a

foundering city, balanced only by a few hopeful shots of the East St. Louis Flyers football team, which was storming toward the 1989 state championship just as the CBS crew was in town. Ed Bradley sought out Bob Shannon and asked him what grade he'd give the mayor.

"I'd have to give him an 'F,' " Shannon said.

"You know, it was strange," Shannon said one afternoon before the Lincoln game. "That '60 Minutes' show appeared on a Sunday evening. The next day I had this lady visit me, one of the administrators for the school district. And she says to me, 'You should know there's a group of people out there trying to get up a petition to take your football job away from you because of what you said about the mayor.' "

As a twenty-year veteran in District 189, Shannon's teaching job is protected by union tenure rules. But his coaching job, all $2,500 a year of it, is renewable yearly. It's protected by his won-loss record.

"I said to her, 'Now, you're a Ph.D. You understand about individual rights and the freedom of speech. Why didn't you tell the folks in that group that I had the right to say what I said? Why didn't you defend my right to say it? You're a learned individual. I imagine some of the people in that group weren't so learned. Why didn't you help them understand?'

"Well, she didn't say anything. She just said, 'They didn't like what you said.' I said, 'It doesn't matter whether they liked it or not; the question is whether I had the right to say it.'

"I was a little disappointed in her. When a person gets a Ph.D., you'd think they'd have a little common sense. But that's the way it's been around here. People resent that football has given me a platform, and that I don't use it to spout the party line. I call it the way I see it. For years some of them have been sitting back, waiting for us to fail, so that what I say won't be important anymore. But we've been successful, and I've said a lot of things that people in the community don't like. They don't say it's wrong. They don't say it's a lie. They just say 'Why would he say that?' Because I have a right to say it, that's why, and I say what I believe."

Most of Shannon's political troubles have stemmed from school-district officials, not from city officials—not that the distinction is all that clear. The Democratic political machine controls school elections, too, which means that every job in the district, from superintendent to janitor, is a patronage job. "Every job in this district is for sale," Shannon said. "It's a fact. People don't even think much about it anymore."

For years Shannon has been at sword's point with a powerful politician named Elmo Bush. Bush briefly was school superintendent and, before that, administrative assistant to the school superintendent. Before that he was a school principal; a city councilman; commissioner of fire, health, and education; a candidate for mayor in his own right; and later, Carl Officer's campaign manager in Officer's race against Clyde Jordan. In a city of cagey politicians, Elmo Bush is among the cagiest. He even threw his political support to a Republican gubernatorial candidate in 1990. The Republican won.

"Any time there's some power to be had, Elmo's around," Shannon said. "He doesn't like me, but that don't cut too deeply with me. I don't go to too many union meetings, but I did when Elmo became superintendent. One of the first things he did was ask the teachers to give up two weeks' pay so we could settle all the bills in the district. Well, that sounded all right to me, it would work and we could sell it to the teachers. I would have gone along with that. But then someone asked Elmo if he was going to give up his twenty-thousand-dollar raise he got from going from principal to school superintendent. He said no, because it would be demeaning to the office of superintendent. That's where Elmo lost me.

"We just don't get along. It stems back to 1979 when he had a son playing for me. His son was a fullback, a pretty good player, but he wasn't as good as the other guy I had, a kid named Darryl Dixon. Dixon was a great player, a fullback and a linebacker. He went on to play at Michigan State. Well, one day I came out after practice to get in my car and there was Elmo, parked over there under a tree. He comes screeching up to me, slaps on his brakes and gets out screaming, 'What are you trying to do to my boy? Ruin his career? He should be playing.'

"I guess I was supposed to do him a favor by playing his son instead of Dixon, but that ain't the way it works with me. The kids from the projects get the same treatment as the politicians' sons. I preach fairness to the kids, and I try to be fair with them. I figure if you do your job and try to do it the right way, you're going to be OK, no matter what happens. But that ain't the way most people in this town work."

And that's why the Flyers' annual game with Lincoln is so important to Bob Shannon. For him it is less a football game than a morality play, his way against the politicians' way. He has not lost to Lincoln since 1978, and when he talks about the memorable games in Flyer history, the Lincoln games are at the top of the list. He can remember every score, every detail.

"We beat them 7–6 in my first year, back in 1976," he recalled. "We had to forfeit that game later because we had an ineligible guy I didn't know about, but we beat them on the field. They were really good back then, too, and our games were wars, man. Everybody in town would be out there rooting against us. We beat them good in '77, shut them out 26–0. They got us 7–6 in '78, but we shut them out again in '79 when we won the state championship. We beat them by one point again in 1980, but the game I really remember was 1981.

"They had this quarterback named Deandre Williams. They had a really good team that year, and the coach just ran him off because he didn't want him around. He came over here. He wasn't as good as the guy we had, and the guy we had wasn't all that good. We were only 5–3 in 1981 because we couldn't score to save our lives. But if a guy comes out and stays, we let him play, so we made Williams a kicker.

"Well, the guy we had playing quarterback didn't want any part of playing in that Lincoln game. He just dogged it. So Williams went out there. He wasn't too good, because we couldn't move the ball at all. But neither could they. It was 0–0 in the fourth quarter when they finally score a safety on us. They go up 2–0 and they get the ball back.

"They got greedy then and tried a pass deep in their own territory. We intercepted it. I figured, hey, we can't move the ball, we might as well try to kick a field goal. In trots Deandre and everbody's laughing at us. They figured we were going to fake it, so nobody rushed. He kept his head down and kicked it through there straight as an arrow, man. We got a sack in their end zone with a few seconds left and won 5-2. Our guys carried Deandre off on their shoulders after that game, and they don't do that much around here.

"That one game really helped us around town, because everybody knew Lincoln was better than we were, and we still beat them. And we've been beating them ever since. They hung in there with us for a few years, but lately we've been pounding them pretty good."

That's because Shannon likes to use the Lincoln game, with its big-game atmosphere, as a prelude to the playoffs. He hypes the game to his players, telling them about bragging rights around town, building the Tigers into a symbol of all the things he's been teaching them to fight against. The practices in the days before the Lincoln game are fierce, with Shannon warning the Flyers that they will never live down the ignominy of losing to Lincoln, that the Tigers have devoted their entire season to this one game.

Whether the players believe it or not is arguable, but Shannon believes it. He has come to believe that Lincoln boosters were behind the great Chris Moore residency challenge. "The way I hear it now," he says, "is that after they tried to get Chris to transfer over there, and he came back here instead, one of them Lincoln guys went over to Fred Curtis at East and told him Chris was living up in Fairview Heights. That's what got all this mess started."

The mess is coming to a boil. The Illinois High School Athletic Association has held several meetings on the subject, interviewing the various parties involved, and a decision is expected any day now. Depending on what the association decides about where Moore lived, and when, and why, sanctions could range from a slap on the wrist to forfeiture of every game Moore has played in.

"You'd hear a joyful noise around this state if that happened," Shannon says. "There'd be a lot of joy in a lot of Mudvilles, that's for sure. That means they would've found a way to beat us, because they sure as hell can't do it on the football field."

Despite everything he tells his players, Shannon knows that Lincoln is no match for the Flyers. He's seen tapes of their games, and his assistant coaches have scouted them. They draw their players from the same pool that the Flyers do, but they don't have the Flyers' discipline. They are prone to breakdowns and poor execution. To make things more confusing, their head coach, Jim Moncken, has suffered a slight stroke. Assistants are coaching the team, and the assistants are elbowing one another to be in position to succeed Moncken if he's unable to return.

Lincoln does have a highly touted quarterback, a tall, handsome kid named Lester (Duby) Anderson. "He's a good quarterback," Shannon admits. "He should have come here, but his daddy is Lester Anderson, the chief of detectives, and the politicians don't want their boys playing for me. His daddy's been telling everyone that Duby is the best quarterback in the state, but he ain't even the best quarterback in East St. Louis. You lay a big hit on Duby early, and he's gonna get gun-shy."

Sure enough. The Flyers get to Anderson early and often, sacking him twice early in the first period, knocking him woozy enough that he has to leave the game briefly. When he returns, he is tentative, and so are his receivers. They drop several balls, and the Tigers' offense bogs down.

In the meantime, the Flyers are rolling. Jerry Creer blasts twenty-one yards for a touchdown on a quick trap. Homer Bush makes a brilliant diving catch in the corner of the end zone for a second score. The Flyers are leading 14–0 late in the first half when Shannon sends in what he calls a "Fort Worth" formation, four receivers split wide. Deondre Singleton picks out the open man, Dennis Stallings, who scores on a forty-yard fly pattern as the half ends.

There is no calling off the dogs in the second half, not against Lincoln. Shannon keeps the throttle wide open. Singleton and Stallings team up for another score. Duby Anderson is sacked for a safety, and Chris Moore runs the ensuing free kick back sixty yards for another touchdown, finishing off the last defender with a vicious straight arm. Stallings, on defense this time, reads a screen pass and drops off the line into pass coverage. He intercepts and returns the ball sixty yards for a score. And finally, Homer Bush squares off a 95 route, spins around his defender and goes forty-five yards. The final score is 48–6.

Singleton finishes with thirteen completions in eighteen attempts for 220 yards and four touchdowns. Duby Anderson is six for twenty-five for 81 yards with three interceptions. And yet after the game, the two quarterbacks walk off the field with their arms around each other's shoulders. Around the field, players from both teams are mingling, laughing, and shaking hands.

They are, after all, friends and neighbors, summer-league baseball teammates. With their helmets and shoulder pads off, they
look like little kids who've just finished playing war. It's Arma-
geddon only to the grown-ups.

CHAPTER

5

Early one morning in the week after the Lincoln game, Bob Shannon makes his usual stop to pick up the newspapers at a convenience store just up State Street from the high school. The place is really less a convenience store than it is a package store with iron bars on the windows and a Smith & Wesson under the counter. It is typical of what's left of retail commerce in East St. Louis.

Shannon buys his papers and a can of Coke. Leaving the store, he looks up and sees a man weaving his way across State Street, waving his arms and shouting, "Coach Shannon! Coach Shannon!"

Shannon grimaces. He knows the man well. His name is Brian Lester. When the coach talks about the successes of his football program, about the young men he's helped go on to college, he's always careful to add, "We lose a few, too." Brian Lester is one he lost.

Thirteen years earlier, in the fall of 1977, Brian Lester, whose street name is "Hodap," had come off the bench to quarterback the Flyers to six straight victories. He'd thrown a touchdown pass on his first play from scrimmage. Hodap wasn't a great quarterback, but he was capable of handing the ball off to great backs like Terry Hill. Shannon had liked Hodap. "He was so dedicated when he was in school," he said. "He did everything I ever asked."

Shannon lost track of Hodap after he graduated. "I don't know what happened to him, what went wrong. But I didn't see him for ten years."

Hodap walked back into Shannon's life one day in August 1988, staggering onto the practice field one afternoon. He was broke and looking for money. Shannon violated one of his cardinal rules and reached for his wallet, handing Hodap a twenty-dollar bill. Hodap came back a few days later, looking for more. Shannon told him no. He said if Hodap wanted help, he'd try to get him into a drug-and-alcohol treatment center. But there'd be no more money. Hodap staggered off.

But now, two years later, Hodap has reappeared. "Two dollars, coach! Two dollars, that's all I need," he pleads.

Shannon sighs and reaches for his wallet again. "I gave him another twenty," he said later. "You should have seen his eyes. Then he disappeared into that liquor store. I know I said I'd never do it again, but Hodap's not all bad. I remember the discipline and hard work he put in. He was a good kid. But he got out there on those streets and got into something bad. He ain't even all there anymore. He's just trying to make it."

Very few of the kids Shannon loses to "those streets" venture back into the bubble he's created around his football program. "They don't want to see me, and I sure as hell don't want to see them," he said. "If they come and ask for help, I'll try to get them help, refer them on to someone who can get them some treatment. But most of them don't want that. They get out there on those streets, and they forget anything we might have taught them. It's up to a guy to take care of himself."

From time to time, one of his "failures" comes to call with malice on his mind. One such visitor was a young man named Reavis Barr, who was a sophomore quarterback on Shannon's 1986 team. Reavis competed with another sophomore, Vernon Powell, for the back-up quarterback's job that year. The next year Powell beat out Reavis Barr for the starting quarterback job. Vernon Powell was a gem, a small, quiet kid who was a deadly sprint-out passer and runner. He started for two seasons and then won a scholarship to the University of Nebraska, a football powerhouse.

Reavis was a different story. "His mom wanted to send him to live with his daddy because she couldn't control him anymore," Shannon said. "Reavis knew that, and he wouldn't stay with his daddy. He ran away from his dad, came in and out of school. One day he wrought havoc in the parking lot, smashed my car's windows and jumped into a guy's car while the guy was just standing there talking to another guy. He drove all around the parking lot with the guy hanging onto the door, screaming.

"I kept up with him after that by reading about him in the *Belleville News-Democrat*. He's doing a seven-year stretch for robbery now. I feel bad about it, because I watched him go wrong. He came in here as a sophomore and wasn't really a bad kid, but you could already see he was going in the wrong direction. I tried, but there wasn't anything I could do about it. His mother wanted him to do well. She talked to me and I talked to him and we *both* talked to him, but Reavis was a guy who wanted to do it his own way, and around here you do it my way. Some of them you can save and some of them you can't. The swamp is going to get some of them."

The final game of the regular season is played on a beautiful late October day, a Friday afternoon so that all the students who want to see their unbeaten Flyers in action can get over to Parsons Field right after school. Not counting the band, about a dozen students show up.

"I think the students are proud of the team, but they just don't go to the games," principal Sam Morgan says. "Some of them have jobs, some of them just won't go to Parsons Field, even in the afternoon. You notice we never have any night games. Nobody has been mugged there lately, but people are afraid of it. Maybe the new stadium will help attendance, but I don't know. I had a dollar-day this year for homecoming. Sold student tickets for a dollar. You know how many tickets I sold? Forty-two."

It isn't only the students who don't show up for the season finale. The home side of Parsons Field is almost deserted. The visiting Collinsville Kahoks bring a hundred or so fans with them, moms and dads for the most part, loyal to a team that is the perennial doormat of the Southwestern Conference. Collinsville is a soccer and basketball stronghold; the football is an after-thought. When Eastside coaches want to insult a player, they tell him, "You couldn't even play for Collinsville." So woeful are the Kahoks that not even Bob Shannon is worried about them. "I just hope we don't get anybody hurt," he says.

Eastside scores early and often. In the first quarter Deondre Singleton hits Dennis Stallings with a twenty-yard touchdown pass, and Chris Moore scores on a one-yard slant. That's just the warm up. In the second quarter, Singleton and Homer Bush team up for two twenty-yard scores, Moore returns a punt fifty-two yards for another score and then catches a forty-three-yard pass from Singleton. At halftime it is 40–0, and Shannon sends the reserves in for the second half. The playoffs start next Wednesday and he isn't taking any chances with injuries. Jerry Creer gets a touchdown in the second half, and Stick Eubanks, finally getting a chance to play, hits young Frank Spraggins with a seventeen-yard touchdown pass. Down 53–0, the Kahoks salvage some pride with a last-minute field goal.

"I was glad for Stick," Shannon says, "but I was kind of disappointed. I was hoping we'd stall out down there so we could try a field goal. We haven't kicked one all year and you never know when you'll need to try it."

The day's major disappointment takes place off the field. The Illinois High School Association finally hands down its ruling in the Chris Moore case. It's Solomonic in its wisdom, cutting the baby in half. The Flyers are stripped of three victories in September of the year before, during a period when the IHSA found that Moore had been living in Fairview Heights. Sam Morgan had reported that Moore's parents moved there in July 1989, but separated the following September. Chris and his father had moved back to East St. Louis on September 20, Morgan told the IHSA. In the first three games of that year—victories over Sumner, Chicago Robeson, and St. Louis DeSmet—Moore had been ineligible. Those victories are forfeited. However, no conference victories are forfeited, so the Flyers retain their state title.

"I guess it's as good as we can expect, considering it's all political anyway," Shannon said a few days later. "They had to do something, and nobody's going to remember that we forfeited those games. We've still got the state championship. What bothers me is the politics of it all. It'd be one thing if they cared about every kid who wasn't in school that was supposed to be. What if Chris Moore was a girl, say, and he wasn't living in the district? Do you think anybody'd care where he lived? Shoot, no, all they'd care about was that he was enrolled so they could get the state aid for him. They wouldn't even care if he went to class as long as they got the money. The IHSA says they're just protecting the kids, but they've got rules that work against the kids. Look at those jackets."

He stands up and walks to the rear of his office, where forty brand-new letter jackets are hanging from the water pipes. They're fine-quality jackets, blue wool with orange leather sleeves, orange lettering on the back reading EAST ST. LOUIS, STATE CHAMPS, 1989. They were purchased and donated to the team by the local Coca-Cola distributor, but under IHSA rules, Shannon can't give them to the players who earned them.

"We can't give them anything of 'tangible value' for playing football," he said. "Now, we could let them buy them, which is what they do at other schools. But what do you think those jackets are worth? Sixty, seventy bucks? How many kids in this school can afford that? You walk around here, there's a lot of guys who could use a nice jacket, and I've got forty of them in here I can't let them have. You tell me they've got the interests of the kids in mind."

Shannon usually manages to control his bitterness, but not today. In addition to being angered by the jackets hanging from the pipes on a cold day and the Chris Moore decision, he's irritated because he's just found out he has to play his first playoff game on the road. It's a critical scheduling decision, because with thirty-two teams making the Class 6-A playoffs and only four Saturdays in November, the first round of the playoffs must be played on a Wednesday if the championship game is to be played on the last Saturday of the month. It's bad enough preparing for a game with only three days of practice, but a team that must spend a day traveling gets only two days to work out. With an unbeaten team that is defending state champion, Shannon thought for sure he'd get to play at home. Instead the Flyers will open 180 miles across the state, very close to Terre Haute, Indiana, against the Danville Vikings. To save the cost of lunch on the road, the school district will require the Flyers to leave Tuesday afternoon, meaning Shannon will lose a day's practice.

"We can't practice at night, because we got to feed them when we get over there," he said. "We try to hit these all-you-can-eat smorgasbord places, and they close early. Feeding these guys can get expensive."

Practice time is precious. Daylight saving time has ended; it gets dark on the practice field by 5:30 P.M., and there's only a single floodlight for illumination, plus the uncertainties of sending players home in the darkness. Beyond that, Shannon's senior players have to take an English test before they leave town, and the teachers aren't cutting them any slack.

"I got to let them off practice, which is OK," he said, "but I wonder if they do things this way down in Georgia or Texas? This political stuff gets to me. The IHSA says they're going to make it up to us by letting us play at home the second week. But you know who we're going to catch in the second game? Either Lincoln or Granite City. Both of them made the playoffs and they're playing each other. We wouldn't have to stay overnight to play either one of them, and if Lincoln wins, we get a home game against Lincoln and it's their home field, too. It's all politics, and somehow Lincoln always comes out ahead."

His bitterness is evident in an interview he scheduled for today with a freelance reporter on assignment from the Voice of America. "I really don't have time to do this now," he says, walking out to meet her. "But this is the only time she can do it. I try to cooperate with press because I want people to know what we're doing here, but this is a bad time."

The "60 Minutes" segment has resulted in a lot of national attention for Shannon. *People* magazine sent a reporter and photographer to town for a week to do a profile that ran to five hundred words and four photographs. *Reader's Digest* has a story in the works. There were even three guys from Hollywood in town for a couple of days to talk about made-for-TV movies. And today there's the Voice of America, which will spread the word of Flyers to Eastern Europe. They can't draw a crowd to Parsons Field, they can't get a break at the IHSA headquarters in Bloomington, but the Flyers will be news in Budapest.

In his interview with the radio reporter, Shannon only occasionally lets his bitterness come through. "The biggest thing wrong with East St. Louis is we've got a lot of the wrong politicians in the wrong places," he said. "The great majority of the people in town hate it, but they don't do anything about it. A young man came in to see me a couple of weeks ago, a player from my 1979 team who came back for homecoming, and he said, 'My goodness, coach. What's going on here? It was bad when I played, but it's so much worse now.'

"The sad thing is that all the urban ills you see on the streets can be found in the school. We should be doing more for the kids who are in school to get an education and not just for the kids who are in school because they have to be here. We need someone to let the word go out that if they're here for the wrong reason, they aren't welcome. But right now there's nothing for the kids here who aren't in sports or band. Nothing but go out on the streets and hang out with the guys."

Shannon has other reasons for his bad mood as the playoffs begin. This is his favorite time of the year, the one month that makes the other eleven months worth putting up with, the one month that tests everything and everyone he teaches. The playoffs usually energize him. But as the 1990 playoffs begin, Shannon finds himself profoundly discouraged. The streets are getting to him.

"You know I was up 'til midnight last night, looking at tape and studying play sheets," he said one afternoon. "And I was over here opening up the gym at 7:30 this morning. And then I had a guy come up to me—one of the other teachers, a nice guy, didn't mean anything by it—and he said, 'Why are you working so hard?'

"It made me mad. I said, 'Because the damn job is getting harder.' The more it slips around here, the harder we have to work. The more I have to put into it. The adjustments I have to make are more difficult. I've never questioned why I've put so much into this thing before, but I'm beginning to now. I'm getting tired of fighting it. I could keep it up, but there's something else now, too, and that's what's happening out there on those streets. It's going to come to a point where there's a cloud of suspicion over the team because there might be kids on the team who are using or selling drugs. And that's where I'm going to draw the line. I'm going to leave then. I'm going to be out of it. That's the one thing I couldn't deal with."

No matter where you go in East St. Louis, drugs are never far away. Sam Morgan says he assumes there are drugs in the lockers in the hallways of his school. If you go around back of the school in the early afternoon, before Shannon unlocks the back door of the gym, you often can find two or three kids sitting on the steps of the fire escape smoking marijuana. Shannon knows of several teachers who are cocaine addicts. On paydays, these teachers sometimes disappear at lunchtime; one teacher borrows another's car to "run to the bank," and the first teacher doesn't return for several days. The car is recovered later outside a crack house. The kids can all tell you, but most of them won't, the names of students and teachers and people they know who are heavy drug users. But until this year, Shannon has never worried that his team has been infected.

"I'm beginning to have my doubts now," he said. "I could always say before, without a doubt, that the team was clean. I could always say the team didn't use steroids. I think we might have had a few marijuana users in the past, but we never had any kids who were using or dealing hard drugs. But right now, today, I can't say that with certainty. And that bothers me.

"It's just a feeling I've got. You deal with people. You hear little things here and there, and you know the type of kids you've got. I would say today we've got more kids who are capable of it than we used to. What's happening out there on the streets is finding its way in here, as hard as we fight to keep it out. And that bothers me. A lot of work has gone into this program. We try to do it the right way. We try to deal with the right type of people. But there's less of them out there now. A lot of kids start doing drugs in junior high, and they're already hooked when they get here. That stuff bothers me more than any opponent we've ever played.

"It's a tough world out there. How long can we maintain our standards? How long can we keep the right kind of people in here? Every year it gets harder and harder to find forty kids who are the right kind of kids. When we run out of the good people, the kind of people who make this worth doing, what are we going to do then?"

The values on the streets are 180 degrees removed from the values that Shannon teaches. The value of hard work is lost in a city where there is no work to be had. The value of teamwork is lost in a city where it's every man for himself. Cat Coleman's maxim at Tennessee State—"Sacrifice now so you can enjoy life later"—has no credence in a town where a kid can make fifty dollars just standing lookout for drug dealers, in a town where life is too risky to count on "later" ever coming.

"It's the environmental pressures that get to them," Shannon said. "They like those Nike shoes. They like to wear those. They're $125 a pair, and they got to have two or three pair. There's a lot of work in that. It's those Polo pants and shirts. They like to wear those. Those are status symbols in this community. It used to be a status thing to make this football team, but it's less so now because a lot of people take it for granted. These young people don't know what went into making this what it is. They want to fit in out there on the streets, and they want to fit in by being an East St. Louis football player and still dress well and fit in on the streets. You can't do both, man, but they're trying. In the past, they were just worried about fitting in here with me.

"That's what has me concerned, the effect it's going to have on this program when one of them gets busted. It's going to be big news: 'Eastside Player Busted for Drugs.' Might be ten guys arrested, but the football player is going to be the news. I understand that. But it's going to reflect on me, and it's going to reflect on what we've built."

Shannon preaches constantly, ceaselessly, and not only to the football team. He teaches two health-and-physical education classes every day, volleyball and archery laced with a heavy dose of hygiene and family relations. He cares less about whether his students can shoot an arrow than that they know about AIDS and family planning and the dangers of drugs. Always the danger of drugs.

"You're always working against the current, though," he said. "It gets back to the kids' values. You'd like to teach them good values, but they normally take on the family values and you can't do anything about that. It's very difficult to change those values once they've been established. Around here, so many people have the value that you've got to get it today, not tomorrow. You don't work hard to get into position so you have good things later on. You've got to have them now. These kids want things at age eighteen that I've worked my whole life to get."

Shannon's lectures in his health classes come straight from the textbook, though he stops frequently to ask questions to see if anyone is listening. Usually the girls in the front of the room answer the questions and take notes. The kids in the back of the room try hard to be ignored, and Shannon usually obliges them. Teaching is something he does now only so he can keep coaching.

"I used to enjoy teaching," he said. "I used to enjoy coming here. But the way these kids act now, the way their values have deteriorated, the way they're unconcerned about the future, the way they disrespect each other and disrespect authority, it's not any fun anymore. I remember when it wasn't like that, but to them, it's just the way they are. They don't know any other way.

"Some of them listen. Some of them come from good homes, maybe their daddy's not there, but he's around a lot, and their mom tries to do the right thing. But fewer and fewer are listening. The message on the streets is easier. The streets have immediate rewards. I tell them about money, about planning and saving and working hard, but hey, out there a guy is telling them about easy money he can have today. They can listen to me, sit there and try to visualize having it some day, but out there, it's happening now. A guy says, 'Here's the money, right now.' And here's me saying, 'Sacrifice now, get it later on.' Now who's a kid going to listen to?"

Shannon's said he first noticed the fallout from the drug culture two or three years earlier when the number of kids coming out for football began to dwindle. More and more kids were begging off football and other sports to get jobs. "Supposedly they were legal jobs, flipping burgers or something, but I'm sure there were a few of them doing other things," he said. "The whole thing was to get money so they could have those shoes and those clothes, buy themselves some kind of car."

Before that, his chief competition for players used to come from street gangs like the Vice Lords and the Disciples, who spent most of their time on pointless violence. "There wasn't a lot of money to be made burning houses or robbing some guy who didn't have any money to begin with," he said. "Besides, it was rather dangerous. I could bring a guy in here and tell him to stand back and examine the situation, and show him that it didn't make much sense. The gangs didn't have near the draw that the drugs have.

"In the past, I didn't feel like it would be a big problem, because we had some leadership on the team. But we haven't got those leaders this year. There's fewer and fewer guys I can trust, guys who know how much we've put into this program and appreciate what's been done."

Shannon's plan of action is to approach a few of the seniors and tell them of his concern. "When I can, I like to get the kids to deliver the message for me," he said. "A guy will listen to another guy more than he will a teacher. But I'm going to talk to a few of those people myself and try to get the message across that this program has been good for the young people in East St. Louis. I'm going to tell them that rather than derail what we're doing, I'd rather see them walk away from it. I have to challenge some guys to be leaders, but I have to be on solid ground when I do it.

"It's discouraging though. We've put a lot of time into this, and it's meant a lot to me over the years. And now we're getting like the Roman Empire, destructing from within."

The short view is much more encouraging. On Halloween afternoon, the Flyers get off their bus and annihilate the Danville Vikings 61–0. They run five plays from scrimmage in the first quarter and score three touchdowns. Singleton is seven for nine for 247 yards. Bush catches four passes for 185 yards. Moore carries for 146 yards. The defense throttles the Vikings at every turn. "Ah, man," says Danville coach Nate Cunningham. "What an awesome football team."

Bush goes over a thousand yards for the year in this game. He has ten more receptions than any other receiver in the state.

Singleton is ranked as the number two quarterback in Illinois. Chris Moore, having worked himself halfway out of Shannon's doghouse, is getting to carry the ball more and is piling up yardage. "The one good thing about that IHSA ruling was that Chris finally figured out he'd let the other guys down," Shannon said. "He's been a lot more cooperative lately. Plus he's been jealous of all the attention Hickey Thompson has been getting."

Hickey Thompson is the tailback for Althoff High School, a Catholic school in Belleville, who will earn a scholarship to Michigan State. He regularly is ripping off 250 yards a game and threatening the state's all-time rushing record. He has worked his way back from a leg injury a year ago, and Shannon wastes few opportunities to remind Chris Moore of how hard work is paying off for Thompson. "Chris wants that ball twenty-five times a game like Hickey gets it," Shannon said. "He's trying to show me now."

Privately, though, Shannon has less regard for Thompson's achievements. "He's a good back, don't get me wrong, but you can always design a way to stop one good back," he said. "I'd rather do it this way. You might be able to take Chris away from us, but then the quarterback's going to get you. You take Deondre and Homer away, the tight end will get you, and Chris Moore and Jerry Creer will run over you. I like that balance."

What pleases him even more than his balanced offense is that his defense has shut out Danville. Shannon has not been at all pleased with his defensive team, even though it's given up but seventy-seven points in ten games. "You might say we're only giving up an average of one touchdown a game, but averages don't mean that much. You've got to look at who we've played. Muskogee is the only real good team we've played and they got twenty-six points in a hurry. Danville is the only big school in their area and they hadn't seen much competition 'til they saw us. We ain't seen much competition either, but sooner or later we will, and I'm worried about what's going to happen then.''

Shannon didn't use to worry about his defense. He would merely turn it over to his defensive coordinator, an intense, wiry young man named Marion Stallings. Stallings was a brilliant, vocal coach who knew defense frontward and backward. He had a way of instilling his own controlled hostility into his players. "We built this thing together," Shannon said of Marion Stallings. "We started out together, and we learned what it took to beat good teams."

Together in 1985, Stallings's defense gave up fifty-three points in fourteen games. In the state-championship game that year against Brother Rice of Chicago, Shannon's offense scored forty-six points. Stallings's defense gave up zero.

Marion Stallings was the perfect complement to Shannon. Shannon was controlled and calm, Stallings all fire and energy. But in 1986 Shannon made what he later said was the hardest decision he ever had to make. He told Marion Stallings he didn't have a job for him anymore. Stallings was forced to resign. The swamp had gotten him.

Marion Stallings was twenty-one years old, fresh out of Washington University in St. Louis, when Shannon hired him as an assistant football coach. It was 1976, and Shannon had just become Eastside's head coach. Stallings had zero coaching experience, but he'd been a terrific player for the Flyers in the early seventies. At five feet eight, 140 pounds, he was all muscle and heart. He had been a defensive back who reveled in coming up to meet the run, popping much bigger players, knocking them down, picking them up, patting them on their butts and saying, "Get on back to the huddle, and hurry back so I can hit you again."

Stallings had been a good enough student to win an academic scholarship to Washington University, one of the top universities in the Midwest. Washington U. plays small-college football in the NCAA's Division III, and Stallings earned All-American honors playing defensive back for the Battling Bears. He earned a degree in education and turned down a teaching and coaching job in suburban St. Louis to apply for a job back home in East St. Louis. He wanted to coach at his alma mater. Shannon hired him on the spot, recognizing a kindred spirit. Stallings was just as obsessed with football as he was.

"They'd just started the playoff system in Illinois," Stallings said. "Before we'd always had good teams, but we always got cheated when they voted for the top teams in the state. The Chicago-area coaches would vote for themselves, and we'd never be ranked number one. I was from East St. Louis, and I was proud of it. I knew we were better than they were, and I wanted to prove it."

In the late seventies, Shannon and Stallings traveled around the country, talking to college coaches, attending clinics, studying football. "He knew I was a die-hard Eastside guy," Stallings said. "Some of those other coaches had come out of Lincoln and he never trusted them. He knew I like to win, whatever it takes, and he knew I'd work as hard as he does. We went all around together, went up to Notre Dame, we learned football together.

"In '78, we went to the quarter i finals and got beat. Coach said we were going to get beat, the other guys were better than we were, and he was right. The next year, we went all the way. We had a couple of down years, and then it seems like everything came together. We got some players in here who took pride in winning. We had the worst equipment you ever saw, no uniforms, no shoes, homemade blocking chutes. We didn't have anything, but those guys we had weren't caught up in appearances. Everything else was falling apart in the city, but our team became a source of pride. The players took pride in that, being the one positive thing. Tough guys, man."

They were the glory years, the years of the forty-four-game winning streak and three consecutive state championships. It seemed that the tougher things got, the better the team got. Stallings was on top of the world, teaching physical education and biology, coaching football. Things were tough in East St. Louis, but as far as Marion Stallings was concerned, that only made the winning sweeter. Cocaine made it sweet, too.

"I was fresh out of college, single, making what for me was a nice bit of money," he said. "I didn't start out in the fast lane, but once I accumulated some things, it didn't take me long to move into the fast lane. I started hanging with some guys, I wouldn't call them the bad crowd, because they were other teachers for the most part, but they were into the drug scene.

"I'd had some exposure to drugs in college. Washington University, we had the best of everything. We were football players and that counted for something. We'd get invited to parties at frat houses and stuff, and drugs were big at the time. It was the thing to do. I came out of college, I kind of slowed down. I'd drink a little bit, maybe smoke a joint, but when I got to Eastside, I met some guys who were into heavier stuff. I figured, hey, I was a tough guy. I could handle it. I didn't handle it. It handled me."

At first there were Friday and Saturday night parties, hanging out in clubs. Cocaine was part of the good life. Later there was crack, a bigger hit at a fraction of the price. Getting high became part of the daily routine.

"I started, and then it got worse. And then it got worse and worse. It affected me, changed my personality. I wasn't the same person. Before, football was everything. After a while, I'd be late for practice, or I'd miss a game I was supposed to be scouting because I was out getting high. I got into trouble with a girl, a student. On drugs, you know how they say you're out of control? I was out of control. My appearance changed, my habits, everything. The whole nine yards. Probably I should be dead."

Shortly before the 1986 football season, Shannon told him he didn't have a coaching job for him anymore. "He was up front about it," Stallings said. "The man is fair. I knew he was right. I decided to resign. That was the best thing to do, but it was rough. I spent two years, just searching. I looked for another job, but I had trouble doing that. I did odds-and-ends jobs, tried moving to Chicago. Nothing worked."

The worst part about those two years was missing football. Stallings never came around the practice field, but he lived and died with the Flyers. He wouldn't allow himself to buy a ticket for the games. Instead he'd stand outside the fence at Parsons Field, where crowds of men would gather to drink beer and second-guess the coaches. "I'd just stand there and watch," he said. "God, I missed it. I'd go home afterwards and just be by myself. It would bring tears to my eyes. When they lost in '87 and '88, I hated myself. I wondered if I could have made the difference."

In 1988 Stallings checked himself into the drug rehabilitation program at St. Elizabeth's Hospital in Belleville. He came out clean, but he couldn't find another job he liked as much as the one he'd left. He spent most of his time killing time. The closest he got to sports was playing a peculiar St. Louis variation of baseball called corkball. Corkball involves a broomstick, a small, cork-filled baseball, and lots of beer. "The guys in my neighborhood, they don't do nothing but hang around, barbecue, drink beer, and play corkball," he said. "So that's what I did."

Stallings spent a lot of time with his sister's 15-year-old son, Dennis, a top junior-high-school athlete who was trying to decide between Lincoln and Eastside. The guys in the park told him he could get even with Shannon by sending Dennis to Lincoln. "I said, 'Man, you must be crazy. What happened between Shannon and me was because of what I did. This boy's going to Eastside.'"

In the summer of 1989, he heard Shannon was looking for a defensive coach. James Rucker kept bringing up Stallings's name, telling Shannon that Stallings didn't have anything else to do, that he was clean again. Shannon invited him back, and for a while, everything was wonderful again. Stallings got a job teaching in St. Louis, but he was able to get over and help with the defense after school. The 1989 team won the national championship, and Stallings celebrated by dabbling with cocaine again. Shannon heard the rumors. Before he could fire him again, Stallings got sick and almost died.

As the Flyers were slogging through the early part of the 1990 season, Marion Stallings was flat on his back at St. Elizabeth's Hospital. He had severe abdominal pains, nerve damage, and a fever that spiked as high as 110 degrees. He lost forty pounds. The original diagnosis was Hepatitis-B, but doctors at Barnes Hospital in St. Louis later decided he'd been infected with a rare strain of bacteria. The infection was treated with powerful antibiotics, and Stallings slowly recovered. He lost much of the feeling in his hands and feet, and was so weak he could barely stand. What he wanted more than anything was to be well enough to see the Flyers in the playoffs.

"Coach Shannon came to visit me a lot in the hospital," he said. "We talked about the team and the problems he was having on defense. It made me realize how much I missed it. I kept wondering, you know, how much drugs were to blame for me getting sick. That stuff is poison. The more we talked, the more I thought about football. Football was what I cared about, and drugs had taken it away from me."

As Shannon predicted, the Flyers' second-round playoff opponent—the one for which they get the coveted home-field advantage—is none other than the Lincoln Tigers, their neighbors at ancient but venerable Parsons Field. "The only good thing about it is we don't have to worry about scouting them or exchanging tapes," Shannon said. "It's not like we don't know what kind of team they've got."

"Scouting" for East St. Louis generally means that Art Robinson or another assistant coach gets in a car and drives to wherever the next opponent is playing. At playoff time, when a three-hundred-mile trip to Chicago usually is involved, Shannon will rent a car so Coach Rob won't pile up mileage on his own vehicle. As for videotapes of opponents' games, the IHSA permits teams to exchange tape of only two games, to prohibit wealthier schools from stockpiling tapes of their opponents. With the advent of home video equipment, however, a thriving underground tape market has been created. Coaches with friends in other districts usually can lay their hands on as much tape as they want. In Chicago, a local cable outlet even televises a high school game of the week, which permits coaches there to tape games in the comfort of their living rooms.

There is no need for such skulduggery against Lincoln. The scouting report is simple: Get to Duby Anderson early, and try to make the Flyers forget they beat the Tigers by forty-two points two weeks ago. "Those Tigers are ready for you now," Shannon says during his Thursday practice. "They'll be gunning for you. This is a championship game for them, to knock us out of the playoffs. This is the biggest game in the history of the franchise."

When Dennis Stallings runs by, Shannon grabs him by the arm. "How're your grades, Dennis?" he asks the big tight end, whose happy-go-lucky attitude extends to the classroom.

"Two B's and three C's," Stallings says.

"That ain't good enough. I know you can play. I don't know if you realize how important the other stuff is."

"I'm not worried, coach," Stallings assures him.

"*I* am," says Shannon, "because you ought to be."

The players don't seem to be too worried about Lincoln either. They're slow getting onto the field for practice, lingering in the gym where the St. Louis University basketball team is scrimmaging. "I'm glad they thought enough about us to bring their team over here," says Shannon, "but all I need is another distraction.

"I wouldn't say I'm nervous, but I'm uncomfortable. We don't have any depth. We can't afford any injuries. I wonder how good we really are? Can we play against the best defenses out there? A team like Lincoln, are we taking them too lightly? Moncken had a stroke, but he's out of the hospital, and he's going to be on the sidelines. Maybe that will inspire them. They've got size and speed. Their problem has always been getting those guys to commit to working hard and dealing with adversity. They might be able to get up for playing us, and I don't know if these guys realize that."

So he preaches against overconfidence for two days. But as game time for Lincoln II approaches, and Parsons Field fills up for what will surely be its last Eastside-Lincoln game ever—the new stadium will finally be completed in 1991—he is still worried.

"Our players don't think these guys can beat them," he says. "They saw them the last game, same as I did. The thing I'm most worried about is this Lincoln guy told me they were going to try to get our quarterback and knock him out of the game. I don't mean with a clean hit, either. I told Deondre about it, and he said, 'I ain't worried about it.' I said, 'I am.' I don't like that kind of play. You won't see us play dirty and you won't see us cheat either. You won't see any of that woofing at other players either. A guy does that, talk trash to the other team, and he's out of there. You have to win with class and lose with class."

In the first quarter, the Flyers pick up where they left off two weeks before. Dennis Stallings intercepts a Duby Anderson pass on the first play from scrimmage and returns it deep into Tigers territory. When Lincoln shows an overshifted zone to Homer Bush's side, Shannon sends in a play for his young flanker, Frank Spraggins. Singleton drills him for the touchdown and a quick lead. Anderson tries to get it back in a hurry, but cornerback Cory Dent intercepts and returns it fifty-six yards for a touchdown and a 13–0 lead. Eastside quickly gets the ball back and Singleton lets Bush outrun the coverage and then lays the ball in his hands for a twenty-seven-yard touchdown. One quarter, 20 points. If the Flyers weren't overconfident before, they are now.

So Lincoln storms back. The Tiger defense stifles the Flyers in the second quarter. Singleton takes a couple of hard shots and begins playing tentatively. His timing is thrown off and receivers are dropping the ball. Duby Anderson gets his arm cranked up, throwing two touchdown passes to his six-foot, seven-inch split end, Derrick Bogay. The Lincoln fans who jammed Parsons Field are rocking.

Shannon storms into the locker room, his face set in a grim mask. "All right," he says, calming himself down, "we're going to take the blame, us coaches, for what happened in the first half. We probably threw too many passes and they were laying back on us. We're going to change that. But if you thought this was going to be a laugher, you know better now. We missed opportunities because you didn't make the plays. The question now is if we're good enough defensively to hold them. I want to see what you're made of. We haven't been in a situation like this in a while, so let's be patient. I blame myself. You guys are too young to know something like this could happen. You seniors ought to know better, but I've been saying all along you haven't showed leadership. Now you know what I meant. Now this is what happens. You thought it was going to be easy."

Ears burning, the Flyers erupt in the third quarter, which turns out to be the most explosive twelve minutes Eastside has played all year. They score on four straight possessions, Singleton to Bush for thirty-six, Singleton to Stallings for twenty-four, Jerry Creer off tackle for fourteen, and Chris Moore up the middle for five, and throw in a safety to boot. Moore adds another touchdown in the fourth quarter to cap a 56–14 victory. Shannon lets the reserves play most of the final quarter; as much as he likes to roll up the score on Lincoln, he doesn't want anybody hurt. There will be another game next week, and the cream puffs are all gone from the playoffs. "Gonna get tough now," he says.

At 3:00 P.M. on a raw November afternoon a few days later, Shannon is standing on a pile of dirt on his practice field. The dirt was dumped there long ago to fill in a hole. The hole never got filled. The dirt remained, and Shannon uses it as a two-foot-high observation platform. He is watching Singleton and Eubanks throw passes to Homer Bush and three young receivers. The rest of the players are slowly trickling onto the practice field, bundling themselves up against the cold. They have on extra sweatshirts under their ragged practice jerseys. Some wear hooded sweatshirts, the hoods pulled up over the heads, and their helmets either jammed down over the hoods or the hoods stretched over the helmets. They've pasted strips of adhesive tape across the ear holes in the helmets to keep out the wind. A few have fashioned windscreens of tape across the face masks of the helmets. The linemen wear gloves, the backs and receivers tuck their hands inside the waistbands of their pants. The East St. Louis Flyers, defending state champs, readying themselves for a quarter-final playoff game, look like Kurdish refugees.

Shannon himself wears a stocking cap, three sweatshirts, two pair of sweatpants, and a heavy blue parka. His face is colder than the weather. "Don't say anything to anybody about this yet," he tells a visitor. "But I think I've about decided to give this one more year and then look for something else."

He stands silently on his little mound, staring at his players. He has never spoken of quitting before, although it's the question he's asked most. Coaches with records like his don't usually spend very many years in places like East St. Louis. Why has he not moved on to coach college football? Why hasn't he moved on to some other high school program, in Texas or Georgia or some place where his accomplishments would make him a hero? There are a lot of places with warm climates, fine facilities, and lousy records that would love to hire a coach who wins twelve or thirteen games a year. Why, after all these years and all these victories, and after all these hassles, is he still in East St. Louis? they ask. At long last, Shannon has begun to think about finding himself a soft spot to land.

"I'll have my twenty years in next year and be at the limit on my pension," he says. "I'd like to play one year in that stadium and then maybe move on. We'll have a good team. It'll be one to go out on. I'm tired of fighting it."

It has been a discouraging year. The team leadership hasn't materialized. The streets are closing in. His inquiries about drug use by players have led nowhere. He still has his suspicions but can't confirm them. The day-in, day-out struggle to keep the team moving ahead is getting harder. The school board is dragging its feet on a promised drug-rehab program for the district's teachers. He doesn't see things getting any better any time soon. Maybe, he says, it's time to move on, before he gets too old, while there is still time to start over somewhere, maybe down South, to take Jeanette back where they started. Find a nice house in a place where people are nice, a place where he doesn't have to bang his head against a wall every day of his life.

Shannon came close to leaving only once, after the 1984 season. His senior quarterback, Ronnie Cameron, who led the Flyers to two straight championships, was then one of the most hotly recruited athletes in the Midwest. The University of Missouri had just fired its head football coach, and the new coach, Woody Widenhofer, wanted Cameron as a symbol of how aggressive the new regime was going to be. The day he was hired, Widenhofer flew to St. Louis and drove straight to Ronnie Cameron's house. He recruited Cameron hard, and he recruited Bob Shannon hard, too. He offered Shannon a job as quarterback coach at Missouri.

Move to beautiful Columbia, Missouri, Widenhofer said. Help us put in an offense. See big-time, Big Eight college football. If you're concerned about being on the road all the time, don't worry. The only recruiting you'd have to do is in the St. Louis area.

Cameron signed with Missouri. Shannon didn't. Cameron had a miserable college career. So did Widenhofer. Shannon won two more state championships. Widenhofer got fired. In Shannon's mind, it proved he'd been right all along.

"In fifteen years, I've seen a lot of guys come through here recruiting," he said. "A great majority of them always say, 'You know, I had to try this college thing, but I left a great job back in high school.' You go to a college job the first time because it's a job you really want. But then the guy that hires you gets fired, and you're out of a job, too, so the second, third, and fourth time you get hired, you're going somewhere you don't necessarily want to go. You just need that job.

"All these young guys who start as graduate assistants, they all want to wind up at Nebraska or Miami or Oklahoma, some place like that. They've got good coaches who want those jobs, because it means a chance to win every year. You can count on that bonus money from a bowl game every year. A guy just getting into it might never get a chance to coach some place like that.

"You might get hooked up with some real good guy and be with him a long time, or you might get hooked up with three bad guys in a row and have to get out of it to save your mental health. Like ol' Woody, man. Look what happened to him. He was a good guy and a good coach, but he got into a situation he couldn't control, got fired after four years. He hooked on with Detroit, but what about the guys who worked for him? He couldn't help them that much."

Shannon has nothing but sympathy for college assistant coaches. He likes them, understands their importance, but doesn't understand how anybody could want that kind of job. "It's a double-edged sword," he said. "A guy has to have some goals he wants to achieve. Probably he wants to be a head coach himself and so he's just putting in time, putting up with all the stuff an assistant has to do. There are some good guys out there who make good assistants to good guys and enjoy what they do, but I don't think I could do that. Hey, I'm a head coach here. It may not look like much, but I run my own program and we've had a little success. I think for a coach that's the most important thing. Whether you win the state championship in Illinois, the National Championship at Miami or Notre Dame, or win the Super Bowl, winning is winning. You want a chance to be successful."

He stands on his hill, his arms crossed against the cold, watching the passing drills. His visitor finds them endless, tedious, and repetitive. Shannon has been watching them for twenty years. He finds them, especially at this time of the year with a quarterback who can throw the way Singleton throws, immensely satisfying.

"Here I get to define success the way I want," he says. "In college, it's all business. You don't win, you won't be there long. A lot of guys cheat now, good guys, but they cheat because that's the only way they can get good players. Here, I take whoever comes through the door. They're good athletes for the most part, and they keep coming. I don't have to chase them. I don't think I could put up with the attitude of the modern athlete, the real cocky guys you have to woo and con. You're wooing and conning him, and he's wooing and conning you, playing you off another guy, lying to you. That's a part of it I couldn't do.

"Besides, I like to be close to home. I don't want to be on that road all the time. You're on an airplane half your life and cars the other half. Back when I had the energy level to do it, I missed the boat. A college assistant who gets to be my age, they take him off the road. Woody told me I'd only have to recruit St. Louis and East St. Louis, but I knew there'd be a quarterback somewhere out there he'd need me to go see. My wife wanted me to do it. She likes that college atmosphere. But I saw it for what it is, a job. You wind up unemployed, looking for a job.

"It's like I tell these kids—everybody thinks he's going to be the exception. Bad things won't happen to him. It's the same with coaches. Whether it's stealing cars down the street or becoming addicted to some kind of chemical, or coaching in college, it'll happen to him. Everybody in college thinks, 'I'm going to be a great one. I'm going to be like Bill Walsh or George Seifert.' But there's lots of guys on that ladder out there. It doesn't matter if you're a good guy or even if you're a good coach. It's the final results they're looking for."

Standing there on his little hill in the cold wind, Shannon recounts his latest crisis. He has to take his team to suburban Chicago to play Larkin High School in Elgin, and there is still no guarantee that the money for the trip will be forthcoming. Two buses, one night in a Holiday Inn, three meals. Nobody ever budgeted for these things, even though Eastside is in the playoffs every year. Every trip is a crisis. One year, just to get to the state-championship game in Normal, he had to leave the morning of the game to save the money on a hotel so he could afford to take along all forty players on the team.

"I've got a thing I always tell the guys when things get tough. I say, 'We'll just have to roll our sleeves up a little higher and get it done.' Well, after a while the sleeves won't roll up any higher. You get tired of putting up with it. I've been rolling them up for a lot of years now, and we're about out of sleeves. This is one place where no matter what you do, they want you to duplicate it with even less. I'm tired of it, disenchanted with it. The way they keep the locker rooms, the way you can't even get a plumber.

"But you know, it's a fight. And to leave it would be like giving up the fight. I'd like to straighten out this mess before I go, but I don't know. I've always said I'll know when it's time to go. You work anywhere, you know when it's time to go. Right now, there's still a little more I want to do. I enjoy working with these guys, and the system hasn't become so bad that I can't function in it. But it's getting that way, man. You're fighting too many things environmentally. You just have to hope the kids won't get contaminated by it."

In the semifinals of the 1979 playoffs, East St. Louis beat Elgin Larkin and went on to win its first state championship the next week. The Flyers missed the playoffs the next two years, but have been back every year since then, winning four more state titles. Larkin hasn't been past the first round.

And so this quarter-final rematch eleven years later is front-page news in Elgin, a prosperous bedroom community in the far-northwestern suburbs of Chicago. The *Elgin Courier News* profiled the mighty Flyers in depth. The sports columnist chipped in a column about Shannon's achievements. The newspaper looked up players and coaches who survived the 1979 trip to Parsons Field. "It was one of the most memorable experiences I ever had as a coach," said Ray Haley, the former head coach of the Larkin Royals. "The kids viewed it the same way. It was cultural shock to a lot of kids. The area was like Vietnam, a bombed-out center. Buildings were burned out all around there."

Shannon laughs when he sees the story. "Hey, they should see it now," he says.

But this game will be played on Larkin's turf. The Flyers have scraped up enough school-board money and private donations to take two buses up on Friday morning. The players check into the Holiday Inn and change into their practice uniforms. George Walsh, the trainer-cum-highway-department-employee, has located a helicopter landing area on highway department land not far from the hotel. He got on the phone and got permission to use it as a practice field. Shannon is delighted, though he loses his good humor when the bus drivers get lost taking the team to the all-you-can-eat buffet restaurant for dinner.

He gets the team bedded down late, strict curfews imposed and enforced by the ever-present cricket bat. "We don't ever have any trouble in hotels," he says. "I tell the guys people are looking for them to make trouble, and it's their chance to change some attitudes."

Shannon's own attitude is, as usual, worried. He will have to play this game without Jerry Creer, his fullback, strong safety, and the closest thing the Flyers have to a leader. The injury bug, absent most of the year, has begun to bite. Two of his seniors are unavailable when he needs them most. Defensive end Robert Perkins has a badly sprained ankle and Creer has come down with pneumonia. Shannon has been impressed by what he's seen of Larkin's game tapes. They are well coached and disciplined and have a tough, quick defensive line, anchored by an all-state tackle named Mark Hornok. "They're the best team we've seen all year," Shannon says. "But you have to expect that in the playoffs."

The next morning the kids are up early, swarming over the video games in the hotel's indoor pool area. Shannon lets them have their fun for a while and then orders them into game uniforms for a walk-through practice in the hotel parking lot. It's a clear but cold day, and a bitter wind has the players with their hands stuffed into their pants. Shannon isn't concerned, but Walsh, the trainer, is. He dashes off to a discount store and buys $150 worth of gloves—fuzzy Orlon gloves for the linemen, cheap golf gloves for the backs and receivers. "Maybe we'll get the money back but probably we won't," Walsh says with a shrug. "But you can't come this far and lose the game because your hands are cold."

Larkin's fans come better prepared, dressed out of the L.L. Bean winter catalogue, carrying blue-and-white streamers, ready for the upset of the century. They fill their big, immaculate stadium, huddling together to keep warm. One busload of Flyer fans shows up and a few more come in private cars. One of the cars carries Jerry Creer, who's talked his father into taking him to the game even though Shannon has told him to stay home and rest. The Flyers are delighted to see Creer, and so is Shannon, though he won't admit it. "Maybe he can do something for us just by being here," he says.

It looks that way. The Flyers come out playing inspired football. With the wind blowing a gale, Shannon keeps the ball on the ground in the first quarter. With Creer on the sidelines, that means Chris Moore's moment has come. And he makes the most of it, ripping off yardage time and again, scoring two touchdowns in the first quarter.

Shannon is planning to put the ball in the air in the second quarter, when Singleton will have the wind at his back. But on the last play of the quarter, Singleton is tackled hard as he moves up the line on an option play. He limps to the sidelines, unable to put pressure on his left knee. Walsh and the state-appointed medical technician on hand for the game frantically probe the joint as Singleton gasps in pain. "A guy twisted it after I went down," Singleton groans. "I was down, the whistle had blown."

Shannon sends Stick Eubanks into the game. He never looks back at the bench where Singleton is being worked on. He tells his players they can't complain. They must get the job done with what they have. Now he has to do it, too.

Today Chris Moore will pay him back for all the aggravation he's caused. Untried and untested, Stick Eubanks is still capable of handing the ball to Moore. Thirty times Chris Moore carries the ball, and he gains 338 yards and scores seven touchdowns. He bobs, he weaves, he slashes, he lowers his shoulder and plows. He's waited all year for this game, and he is magnificent. He has scoring runs of 20, 6, 3, 48, 14, 7, and 61 yards. The Flyers need every bit of it. He's their only weapon. Eubanks can't get the ball to Bush or Stallings. Walsh tells Shannon that Singleton seems to have ligament damage. "We might be able to strap him up," Walsh says. "I don't think it's torn and he wants to play."

"No," Shannon says. "Maybe next week. Maybe next year."

The way Eastside's defense is playing, it doesn't look like the Flyers will be playing the next week. All of Shannon's doubts about his defensive team are proving correct. With Creer and Perkins out, and Chris Moore too exhausted from running the ball to play defensive back, the defense is helpless. Larkin moves the ball at will in the second half, rolling up 34 points in the half and 42 overall. The Flyers' defense gives up 532 yards, including 310 passing yards. Larkin quarterback Mike Rolando chews up the Flyers' cornerbacks, and when the defense backs off, the Royals run the ball through the holes that Perkins normally would fill, breaking tackles that Creer normally would make.

In the end, only Chris Moore and the clock save the Flyers. His last touchdown run, the sixty-one-yarder, gives Eastside a 49–29 lead midway through the fourth quarter. Larkin scores twice more, and with 1:30 remaining, tries an onsides kick. Eastside recovers, and Eubanks falls on the ball three times to end the game.

Bob Shannon doesn't know whether to be angry or relieved, so he is a little of both. Only once before in his career have the Flyers given up as many as forty-two points, and that was in his third season, when he was still tinkering with things. The injuries are a big part of this, but Shannon doesn't accept that excuse. "If you're going to say injuries are a part of football, you've got to accept them and not use them as an excuse," he says. "You've got to get the job done anyway, and we didn't do it. I've been suspect of these guys, and now I know I was right."

Youth, inexperience, and lack of depth have all played a part. Worst of all in his mind, the players lost their composure. Forty-two points in one game is about half of what he is used to giving up in an entire season.

Still, the Flyers have won. And Chris Moore has come through. There will be a game next week. Two of the people who come across the field to shake his hand are assistant coaches from Downers Grove North High School, which upset Conant High today and will play the Flyers in the semifinals in seven days. They want to know two things: can they have copies of game tapes, and just how bad is his quarterback's knee injury?

Shannon gives them the tapes, but he has no answer about Singleton's knee. He suspects the worst.

CHAPTER

6

The bus ride home from Elgin seemed to take forever. The team stopped for dinner and then rode through the night for five hours. Shannon stayed late in his office, making sure all the players had rides home. He got to bed in the middle of the night, and then rose early to watch the videotapes that the Downers Grove North coaches gave him. He spent most of Sunday playing them back and forth. What he saw worried him.

"They run that veer option," he said. "We haven't seen much of that. They got a good little quarterback and a couple of pretty good backs: We've got a lot of work to do."

In the veer, the quarterback takes the ball from center and then moves laterally along the line of scrimmage. If the defensive end drops off the line of scrimmage, the quarterback ducks through a hole in the line. If the end crashes toward the middle of the line, the quarterback keeps the ball and slides outside, looking for the outside linebacker. If the linebacker stays outside, the quarterback can dart inside of him. If the linebacker comes at the quarterback, he can pitch the ball outside to a trailing running back. Downers Grove North's quarterback is excellent at reading defensive coverage, and he has a good enough arm to fake the veer, stand up, and drill his tight end on short pass patterns.

Running the veer calls for discipline and good instincts. So does defending against it. The ends and the linebackers must fight the normal tendency to chase the ball. They must hold their ground, contain their zones and react instantaneously. "We haven't seen a veer team this good in a long time," Shannon said. "I don't know if we can play defense against the veer. But after the Larkin game, I don't know if we can play any kind of defense. The worst part about it is that, if we're going to win this game, we're going to have to do it with defense."

Shannon learns on the Tuesday after the Larkin game that Deondre Singleton's knee injury is going to require arthroscopic surgery. As he walks out of his office for practice that afternoon, trainer George Walsh pulls up in the parking lot with Singleton in the front seat of his van. "No go for Saturday, Bob," Walsh says. "The ligament's got a tear in it. The doctor said if he works on it for a couple of weeks, he might be able to strap him up for the championship, but he wouldn't recommend it."

"Uh-huh," Shannon says. He turns to Singleton, who is moving slowly on crutches that are new and unfamiliar. "How you feeling, son?"

"Better today, coach," Singleton says. "I'm going to be all right."

"I know you are, son. You work on it, but don't be thinking about playing. Stick'll do the job. You go talk to him."

Shannon desperately wants Singleton to play. He even talked to an Eastside booster who works at Fairmount Park, the nearby thoroughbred horse-racing track. "Guy's name is Pete. He says he's got some liniment that works on horses," says Shannon. "I told him to go to Deondre's mama. If she says it's OK, and it's safe, we'll think about it. Ol' Pete says he guarantees it'll work."

Privately, Shannon doesn't believe in miracles or horse liniment either. He is resigned to trying to win the game with Stick Eubanks at quarterback. "There ain't no use in getting Deondre hurt," he says. "He can have a future in this game and it ain't next week. Stick'll be all right."

But as he stands on his mound of dirt on the practice field, watching Eubanks work out with the receivers, Shannon knows differently. He's simplified his offense for Eubanks, sticking with four basic pass plays, all of them designed to get the ball into Homer Bush's hands. "That's what this whole offense is designed for, getting the ball to Homer," he says. "He can get us six points from anywhere on the field. We might even let him play in the slot and let him run the ball."

But Eubanks doesn't throw the ball with Singleton's timing and authority, particularly on the bread-and-butter 95 route to Bush that is so difficult to defend. Eubanks is hesitant and tentative, even in practice, and Shannon lets him know about it.

"I've been telling you for two years that you can't cock your wrist and you're still doing it," he screams. "The ball is going to float. Guy's going to be in your face, man. You got to throw the ball! You're going to get hit, quarterback. You think you can take that hit and get back up?"

Eubanks says nothing. He's used to Shannon's relentless

criticism. He just shrugs and continues throwing the ball the way he always has. "Guy's stubborn," Shannon says. "I asked him one time if he was a college recruiter, would he recruit Stick Eubanks. He said, yeah, he would. He's got that confidence, but I don't."

On this afternoon, Shannon has some unwanted coaching help. A small, scrawny man in a filthy green jacket staggers across the street next to the field and takes it upon himself to start yelling instructions to Eubanks and his receivers. The man looks like he hasn't bathed in a week and smells the same. His hair is matted and straggly, his eyes yellow and watering, his skin pocked with acne. His speech is so slurred that he can barely be understood as he walks across Shannon's weed-killer yardstripes and onto the field. He walks up and down field for ten minutes or so, screaming gibberish at the players. Finally Shannon stops him.

"Howyadoin' Coach Shannon?" he says. "Gotta get Eastside another championship."

"What are you doing here, man?" Shannon asks.

"Big Eastside fan," the man says. "Gotta win. I played a lot of ball myself. Coulda went pro. Gotta go talk to my man."

He walks out onto the field, waving his arms and screaming like a member of the coaching staff. Shannon just glares at him. A guy with Shannon offers to run him off.

"Nah, you got to be careful with that. Guys like that, you never know when they'll come back here with a gun."

Shannon lets the man rant and rave for a while, and then speaks to him gently. "What you want to be around these guys for, man?"

"Gotta win the game," he says. "Eastside is my team."

"You been drinking?"

"Yeah. I been drinking wine. Got into that wine. Got into them drugs, too."

"What you want to be around here for then? Let them guys see you like that? They're trying to do a job, man. Why don't you run on along."

"Can't do that," the man says. He reaches into his pocket and pulls out a battered pack of Newport cigarettes. He breaks off the filter and puts it behind his ear. He puts the other end of the cigarette into his mouth and pats his pockets. "You gotta match, Coach Shannon?"

"No."

"Gotta light?" the man asks the guy with Shannon.

The guy starts to reach into his pocket for a lighter. Then he catches Shannon's eye and the full force of his famous glare. "No, I forgot my lighter today," he lies.

The man staggers off. "I'll be back," he says.

"No, don't come back," Shannon responds. He watches as the man weaves his way right through the huddle of players, across the street, and up to the corner of State Street. He doesn't come back.

"I hate that," Shannon said. "You think they have guys like that down in Texas or Georgia? It's just the environment down here. I don't want guys like that around this team. They see enough of that when they leave high school."

As Eubanks continued throwing—his wrist was still cocked and Shannon finally gave up screaming about it—the talk on Shannon's little hill turned to the big news of the day. Mayor

Officer's office had announced that Phil Donahue was going to bring his television talk show to East St. Louis. The mayor was going to go one-on-one with Donahue, live from the East St. Louis High School gym. The title of the show was to be "Can this dying city be saved?"

"You know the mayor's got to be loving this," Shannon said. "He's going to control the tickets, so he'll have all his friends in there, cheering everything he says. I know what he's going to say. He's going to blame everything on the whites. That's what he's been saying for years.

"It kind of reminds me of when I was growing up. Back then in the South, everything was always put in racial terms. Back then it was the whites blaming everything on the blacks. Now you got the blacks blaming everything on the whites. I see a lot of George Wallace in the mayor. No matter what happens, they say it's race. They make it racial in order to perpetuate themselves."

The subject of race is never far away in East St. Louis or, for that matter, in the entire metropolitan St. Louis area. Very few of its neighborhoods are well integrated. Whites live in south St. Louis and in its western and southern suburbs. Blacks live in north St. Louis and its near-northern suburbs, and along the river in the Illinois suburbs. Public policy questions often are cast in racial terms, with separate white and black political structures meeting infrequently, and then only suspiciously. In many ways it is a southern city plunked down into the lower Midwest.

Bob Shannon, a black man who grew up in the segregated

South, went to an all-black college, has been employed in an all-black city his entire career, lives in the suburb of Ferguson, one of St. Louis's few integrated communities. Shannon doesn't live there because it is integrated; he lives there because it's safe. His approach to racial questions is practical, not political.

"Yeah, I was angry growing up, because my mama had to work so hard," he said. "But I never became bitter like a lot of people did. I always figured it was up to me. I was trying to move forward. I figured if I worked hard enough, I could make it. A lot of people now don't see it like that.

"People are all the time trying to get me to use what status I have in the community to perpetuate the system they've got there, which is basically racial prejudice. I don't see it that way. My job is to prepare those guys to do the best they can while they're here, and to survive once they get out of here. I tell them that this is basically the last all-black situation they'll ever have to deal with. When they move out of here, they've got to be prepared to deal with an integrated environment and not be intimidated by it. You've got to be able to function in it.

"My job is to teach them to judge a person by the kind of person he is. I wouldn't be doing my job if I told them to judge someone by the color of his skin, that all white guys are out to get you. I'm preparing them to leave this environment and to succeed when they get out. If they want to stay, that's OK. But if I do my job, they don't have to stay. They can deal with the outside environment. If I've got a negative, polarizing attitude about the whole thing, I'd be defeating my entire purpose."

Growing up in Natchez in the 1950s, Shannon says, he never

questioned the racial system. It was just the way it was. A little later, when he was in high school, he came as close as he ever came to racial activism. Charles Evers, the brother of the martyred civil rights leader, Medgar Evers, came to town to give a speech on the courthouse steps.

"This was right after his brother had been shot," Shannon recalled. "There he was, standing on the courthouse steps, talking tough with all these white policemen and sheriff's deputies standing there. There was electricity in the air, because folks in Natchez just usually tended to their own business. But he had them fired up. They didn't care that the police were all around. I felt it, I felt this great sense of pride in what was taking place. We were all fearful, standing there, but nobody moved, and nothing happened to us. I think that one day gave a lot of people the courage to continue the struggle. You know, we could be out there. We could stand our ground. After that, I think we all got caught up in the struggle in one way or another. We were all looking toward a brighter day. The older folks, they were fearful, but others had the courage and the conviction to make it happen. You know, just make it happen. For me, it made me think. I knew I just had to get away from there."

Shannon is not a joiner—not of the civil rights movement, not of political parties, not of civic associations. At Tennessee State one year, some of his football teammates decided to call an impromptu strike against the merciless practice sessions. Shannon listened to the strike talk and then buckled on his helmet. He didn't have time to strike. He had work to do.

That's still his standard reasoning for not joining causes: he doesn't have time. Even if he did, he doesn't have the inclination. He prefers situations he can control, and that limits him to his own football program. That way, there are fewer people he has to trust. His experience in East St. Louis sometimes makes him nostalgic for Mississippi in the 1960s.

"Bad as those times were," he said, "there was an innocence about it. There was a closeness of the people. The fun was legitimate, good, clean fun. I met so many good people, and they meant so much to me along the way. Good people. I never had an enemy until I came to East St. Louis. People just didn't dislike you for no reason. And even though there was cruelty in all its forms, we still got a lot out of it. We learned about ourselves. What it would take in life. Some of us were rejuvenated to carry on, and others of us fell by the wayside. Some felt it was just easier to stay there and do nothing.

"But let's face it. You've got to be smart. There's a lot of people alive today that didn't have anything to do with the hardships I went through growing up. I can't be too bitter about it, because it was a way of life there. That's all those people knew. You have to look at things from both sides. I'm just grateful I had the chance to survive it. It made me stronger. It gave me a chance to succeed in life. I didn't use it as a scapegoat, saying that the reason I didn't succeed was because of that.

"That's what I'm trying to teach these guys here. Yeah, we don't have what other guys have, but it's not a big thing. It's just an obstacle we have to overcome. You can't go through life figuring someone owes you something. I've always felt that if you work hard and you're dedicated, and you do things the right way, it's going to work out. I just believe that. I'm pretty much an optimist, and my situation attests to that. A lot of people have come forward to help our program, and 90 percent of them are white people. That's been good for the kids to see that, to learn there are good people who are willing to help. You see a guy like Tom Holley come in here, and ask for nothing, and give us the kind of help he gives, it's good for these guys. People around town tell 'em, 'You can't trust the whites,' but here's a guy like Holley doing all he does. It makes them think."

Tom Holley is a young white businessman who runs a chain of discount and sporting goods stores in St. Louis. In late 1988 he read a newspaper column about Shannon. That same day he drove to East St. Louis to introduce himself. A rabid and knowledgeable sports fan, he quickly became Shannon's biggest booster and closest friend. He's helped arrange for new uniforms and equipment. He chips in his own money to fill in many of the little needs that come up. Holley is in awe of the hold Shannon has on his team. "He is able to get players and supporters alike to run through walls with him," he says.

Before Holley came along, Shannon had had financial help from a number of St. Louis businessmen, but nobody had ever taken the personal interest in the program that Holley has. He has found jobs for Flyer alumni. He attends all of the team's games, traveling on the team bus to many of them and flying to the games in Chicago and Muskogee. Often he brings his wife and his children with him. Holley's young son acts as one of the Flyers' ballboys during games while his father prowls the sideline like a coach. He and Shannon speak almost daily, worrying about depth charts and injuries. His annual "Bird Dinner" is a sight to behold. He and Shannon decide on a date, and when practice is over that day, Holley hauls in a carload of fried chicken and side dishes, has ten cases of soft drinks delivered, and brings his children to dance away the evening with the players.

Holley's friendship has affirmed Shannon's belief in his own deeply conservative philosophy: Hard work is the greatest virtue, and virtue is its own reward. But sometimes it yields other rewards as well.

"Sure there are things in this country you don't like to see," Shannon said. "I remember something Dr. King said: 'Privileged people will never give up those privileges voluntarily.' That was the way it was in the South when I was growing up, but in America today, I see a lot of people who have been privileged doing a lot of things to help those who haven't been. There are people who care. Now, maybe there aren't enough of them. I'm not saying this is a Utopia. It won't ever be a perfect society. But we have had some great black leaders and some great black accomplishments, and it's important for people to know that.

"The thing that makes me most angry is the situation we're in now. We see guys in East St. Louis, instead of trying to live up to the example of the great black leaders, they're making excuses about why we can't get things done. You do that, and you're just making sure you won't get helped. There are corporations and foundations in America who would step in and help East St. Louis if they felt we were doing things the right way, if they felt they were putting their money into a legitimate situation where it would help the people of this community bring it back."

Shannon does not often speak of race and politics in so direct a way. "It's like I tell the players," he said, "you can't do nothing about it, so just move on."

But goaded on the subject, reminded of past and present indignities, his jaw clenches, and he begins speaking slowly and angrily, biting off each word.

"It makes me sad, but it's almost funny," he said, not smiling a bit. "We struggled down there in the South, and the struggle was with the whites who wanted to keep blacks down. But now, here, my struggle is with blacks who want to keep us down. So the struggle goes on, only this time with a different set of people who don't want to see you succeed. I guess life is nothing but a struggle, but I wouldn't have expected to see this, black folks trying to keep these black kids from succeeding. So many of the politicians we deal with, they lie to us. At least in the South, people told the truth. You might not have wanted to hear it, but at least if they told you something, you knew it was the way it was going to be. Here all we get is promises. History offered these people, these politicians, the opportunity to do so much, and they threw it away. This was their chance to show America that we could make a difference, and we didn't get it done."

To Shannon, the lesson is clear—stay clear of organizations that promise to do things for you. Rely only on yourself. Be careful whom you trust.

"So that's what I try to teach these kids," he said, waving an arm toward the practice field. The arm stays up, his voice rises, the lesson is almost complete. "I tell them we're responsible for what we do. Sure, there are people who would like to see us going the other way. I tell them if they go the other way, deal with drugs and other negative things, then you're playing into those people's hands, the ones who say blacks can't succeed, that drugs and poverty are their lot in life. I tell them they can succeed, but they're going to have to believe in themselves, and they're going to have to work hard at it. My message is the same in all ways— we're going to do the best we can do, and we're not going to accept anything less than the best. We are going to achieve excellence, drive them to a higher level, do whatever we can to get the point across.

"I tell them we don't blame other people, white people, for the problems we've got. Maybe that was true at some point in time, but not for the last twelve or fifteen years, because we've had the power, and we haven't gotten it done. I'm not talking about what happened thirty years ago, because I don't look back. People ask me all the time about players who've come through here, and I say I don't look back. It's counterproductive to look back. I'm looking ahead, and I'm looking at right now, and I'm saying, 'What do I need to get the job done?'"

Anyone looking for a racial angle in the Flyers' semifinal game against North High School of Downers Grove wouldn't have far to look. The Chicago suburb of Downers Grove is 97 percent white. North High School is huge and well funded, its athletic facilities top-notch. The trip to Parsons Field will be like an excursion to the Third World.

But the North High Trojans have a savvy head coach named

Pete Ventrelli, and he knows what to expect. He's seen Parsons Field, and he's seen the Flyers, and he spends the week before the game coaching not only football, but sociology. He will later recall that he knew East St. Louis would be a "culture shock" for his players, so he brought the team in the Friday night before the game and bedded them down in Collinsville. On Saturday morning, four hours before kickoff, he took the team to Parsons Field to let them loosen up and walk the field, to absorb its atmosphere.

"There's such an intimidation factor playing East St. Louis," Ventrelli said later. "Not only because of their great reputation, but because of the surroundings. They've got such great speed and their kids hit hard, and I wanted to make sure we weren't overwhelmed. I told our kids, and the student body, all week long that they were going to have the experience of their lives. Yeah, they were going to see some poverty, but they were going to play against, and meet, the students of East St. Louis High, and they were going to be impressed."

On game day Ventrelli doesn't bring his Trojans back to Parsons Field until thirty minutes before the 1:00 P.M. kickoff. By that time Parsons Field is filling up. The Flyers are used to playing before intimate crowds of family and friends, but not today. There are several thousand fans from Downers Grove in the rickety visitors' bleachers next to the railroad tracks and thousands more on the home side and on the cinder track around the field. Not only is this a semifinal playoff game, this will be the last game ever at Parsons Field. The weatherman has cooperated with a strangely warm day. The crowd is huge.

Shannon brings his players over from the high school an hour before game time. The Flyers are wearing their blue jerseys over white pants. Most of the players have chosen to customize their uniforms today with the number "11" scrawled in Magic Marker on their socks, or fashioned of adhesive tape and applied to their pants. This is in honor of Deondre Singleton, who usually wears number 11 but today wears a red San Francisco 49ers parka and a knee brace. He hobbles out to midfield on his crutches to talk with Stick Eubanks as the offense loosens up. Eubanks is bouncing around, relishing his role, satisfied that his moment of glory finally has arrived.

"He says he's ready," Shannon mutters, "but I don't know. We'll have to get it done somehow. I just hope we can figure out a way to stop them, score a few points, and maybe get Deondre back for next week."

In the press box, Irl Solomon—who has managed to get the public address system to work in time for Parsons Field's swan song—reads his usual welcome to the "ancient but venerable Parsons Field, the stadium that will not die." Next year Parsons will live on for junior high games. The Eastside Band plays its usual flat rendition of the national anthem. Shannon sends all of his senior players, in their last game at home, to midfield as honorary captains. The Flyers win the toss and take the ball. Downers Grove, dressed in white uniforms with purple numerals and silver and purple helmets, kicks off.

Chris Moore takes the ball back to the twenty-six-yard line. Eubanks hands the ball to Jerry Creer, who gets five yards behind Junior Green's block. On second down, Green pulls out of his right-guard slot, moves quickly across to trap the right tackle, and

Moore blasts through on 23 bandit for twenty-five yards. Moore adds seven more yards on the next play, another handoff. Shannon is determined to run the ball until Downers Grove forces him to let Eubanks throw one of his cocked-wrist passes. The fourth play is another run, with Creer going fourteen yards on another quick trap behind Junior Green. Eastside has gone fifty-three yards on four plays and has a first down on the Trojan 26. On the bench the Flyers are celebrating. On the field, Junior Green is having trouble standing.

A trainer trots onto the field and comes off supporting Green, who has badly sprained his right ankle. The Flyers' problems have just become considerably more complicated. Without Green anchoring the offensive line, blocking straight ahead on the right, pulling and trapping on the left, the big holes that Moore and Creer are used to may close down. Without Green's pass blocking, Stick Eubanks—who hardly needs more problems—will face a fearsome rush. And without Green's steadying influence on the defensive line, the discipline needed to contain the veer offense may evaporate. Junior Green, so quiet and steady he got taken for granted, is a very big loss.

Now that he's gone, it begins to show. Moore is piled up for no gain. Eubanks tries his first pass, hurries it to avoid the rush, and it falls incomplete. Moore is slammed again, looking for a hole that doesn't exist, and he fumbles. Downers Grove recovers and quickly runs two trap plays right over the top of Green's replacement. The first play is good for fifty-eight yards. The second goes for twenty-three and a touchdown. With four minutes gone in the first quarter, Eastside trails 7–0. It's the first time all year an opponent has scored first, and only the second time all year the Flyers have been behind. Shannon looks furious. His bench looks shocked.

But kick returner Cory Dent breathes life into the Flyers by taking the kickoff back fifty-six yards to the Trojans' twenty-nine-yard line. Moore finds a crack in the line and squeezes through for three yards. Shannon decides it's now or never. He must get the ball to Homer Bush or the game will be over. He calls two straight pass plays to Bush, but Eubanks hesitates both times, pulling the ball down and scrambling. He lacks the timing to throw the quick out pass, but he's a better runner than Singleton. His scrambling picks up thirteen yards and a first down. Shannon is torn; Eubanks is clearly more of a threat running than passing, but if he gets hurt on a tackle, the backup quarterback will be Creer, the fullback, and Creer hasn't taken a snap all year.

Shannon goes back to the running game, calling Chris Moore's number twice, and on the second play, Moore runs over two Trojan defenders for a touchdown. Roderick Fisher, a defensive back who has painstakingly been taught to placekick—head down, leg locked—kicks the extra point and the game is tied.

But not for long. The Trojans' veer offense grinds the ball up the field, six and seven and nine yards a crack. Downers Grove has a first and goal on the Eastside eight-yard line when the first quarter ends. The entire Trojan offensive team trots over to the sideline. Ventrelli told them before the game that he wanted a "gut-check." "I told them we were going to check with them at the end of the first quarter to see if they still wanted to play the game," he said later. "It was a motivation thing, and it worked."

Indeed, the Trojans' quick little quarterback, Dan Moreno, darts through the Flyers' line untouched on the first play of the second quarter to give Downers Grove a 14–7 lead. The Flyers' bench is silent again. Many of the players are huddled around trainer George Walsh, who is wrapping layer after layer of tape around Green's right ankle, trying to brace it. Green reenters the game on the next play after the kickoff, but he quickly limps back off. He can barely stand on the ankle, much less drive block off of it. He is through for the day.

With Green out of the game, Ventrelli stacks eight men at the line of scrimmage, daring Shannon to throw the ball. Shannon sees no one assigned to cover tight end Dennis Stallings, and sends in a play called 81 switch. The play calls for sending three men deep into the pattern, with the quarterback obliged to find the one drawing single coverage. It is Stick Eubanks's finest moment; he throws a perfect pass, laying the ball over Dennis Stallings's left shoulder and hitting him in full stride. The play covers fifty-six yards for a touchdown. Fisher kicks the point, and Eubanks trots off the field, a smile of redemption on his face.

Stallings is grinning wide, too, slapping hands and yelling. He is still celebrating when he reenters the game on defense. Trojan tailback Jeremy Sample runs right over him and goes sixty-five yards before Dent cuts him off at the four-yard line. Moreno slides in from there for the score, but Eastside blocks the point-after attempt. The Flyers are behind 20–14.

The game is taking on a desperate quality. The teams exchange fumbles, and then Eubanks, full of confidence now, hits Bush for two first downs and scrambles for another. The Flyers are on the

Downers Grove twenty-yard line with 1:18 left and a chance to take the lead into the locker room at halftime. Then they break down. A clipping penalty shoves them back fifteen yards, and then Eubanks is sacked for another big loss. The half ends on might-have-beens.

The Flyers find several cases of raspberry-flavored mineral water waiting for them in their cavelike locker room under the Parsons Field grandstand. Walsh has gotten a special deal on the water, an incongruous drink for an incongruous situation. Normally Shannon spends the halftime break deciding which of his reserves will play in the second half. Today he knows he has to come up with something fast, but he's baffled. Downers Grove is showing him nothing he hasn't anticipated, but he doesn't have the personnel to stop what they're doing. His whole program is devoted to creating situations he can control. Right now he's out of options.

His voice is calm, but the frustration is clear. "Fellas," he says, "we were doing all right there, but then we had that clip down deep. We can't make mistakes like that against these guys. They are playing a hell of a game. So what should we do?"

He likes to challenge his players like that, trying to see how much they have absorbed, to check their confidence levels. Today it's not a drill. He's looking for ideas. Nobody has any. The room is like a mausoleum.

"We're not in dire straits yet," he says, "but we're getting there. We might have to grind it out. I don't like to do that, but that may be all we can do. Stick, you're going to have to show more poise out there. You've got to stand in there longer before you start running. You've got to deliver the football.

"We ain't been in this situation much, fellas. You've got to dig down, tighten those chin straps. You linemen are going to have to come off that ball and beat your man, every down. They're coming harder than we are. We're going to see what you're made of this half."

He turns things over to John Davis, the defensive coordinator, who seems as confused with Downers Grove's veer offense as the players. Davis, the Eastside track coach, is a quiet and dignified man, but he is not consumed by football as Shannon is. His solution is to assign the safeties the responsibility of containing the pitch on the veer. The linebackers and the defensive ends will concentrate on the inside options. He diagrams the new defense on the blackboard as Shannon watches, arms folded over his chest. Shannon sees the flaw immediately—if the cornerbacks come up too early, it will leave gaping holes in the pass defense.

"You've got to disguise it better than that, man," Shannon says in exasperation. "If they get an idea of what you're doing, that quarterback is going to stand up and throw the ball. That's a good football coach over there. You can't let them know what you're doing. You've got to make it look like you're playing that pass."

The players' faces are blank. They are used to endless rounds of repetition in practice before anything new is tried in a game. Now they are being asked to disguise a zone pass coverage as man-to-man run defense. They don't have the slightest idea of how to go about it.

Sure enough. On the first play after the second half kickoff, Downers Grove runs the outside option for a short gain. Ventrelli sees immediately that a safety has made the tackle and sends in a pass play. Moreno breaks off the option, stands up, and drills his tight end for thirty-four yards. He does the same thing on the next play, this time for twenty-three yards and a first down at the Flyers' eleven. Sample takes it in from there, and Moreno passes off the option for the two-point conversion and a 28–14 lead.

The Flyers' offense can go nowhere, and the Trojans begin thinking the unthinkable: they're going to beat East St. Louis at Parsons Field. The thought makes them nervous—they fumble away one possession and take silly penalties on their next possession. Then they make a huge mistake. Early in the fourth quarter, Downers Grove forces the Flyers to punt, but the Trojans' return man drops the ball. Eastside recovers deep in Trojan territory. Two quick passes to Bush set up first and goal at the three-yard line, and Moore dances for the touchdown.

Down 28–20, Shannon knows he needs eight points to force a tie and force an overtime period. The question is whether to go for the two-point conversion now, or to kick the single point, hope to score again, and make the win-or-tie decision later. Shannon decides to play it safe and kick the extra point. But center Lamont Stith snaps the ball low and wide, and the conversion is blocked. Now Eastside needs a touchdown and a two-point conversion to force overtime.

Kickoff specialist Nate Robinson does his part, hitting his best kickoff of the year and pinning the Trojans deep. Clawing and scrambling, their chin straps buckled tight, the Flyers' defense plays like desperate men, forcing Downers Grove to punt. And then Stick Eubanks, already redeemed, undergoes a transfiguration. He is magnificent on this last, frantic drive. He hits Bush twice for a total of twenty-six yards. He scrambles for thirteen more. He hits Frank Spraggins for another first down, and then finds Bush again for eleven more. Less than two minutes remain, and Eastside has a first and goal at the Downers Grove three-yard line. Shannon calls a 23 power, a dive to Chris Moore, his biggest back. He gets two yards but is thrown back at the one. Shannon calls the same play, but Stick Eubanks wants this for himself. He takes the snap and knifes across for the score with 1:33 left.

Parsons Field, in its last gasp, is rocking. The Harcross chemical plant across the street is belching smoke, tire fires are burning in an adjacent field, a freight train is rumbling slowly by. But nobody seems to notice. Eastside needs two points for a miracle, and nobody doubts that Parsons Field holds one more miracle.

Shannon calls time out and walks slowly onto the field to talk to his team. All season long, they have ripped off yardage in huge gulps, fifteen, twenty, and thirty yards at a whack. Now they need just three. He talks to the team and walks back to the sideline. He is thinking point-counterpoint. He figures Ventrelli will be looking for Chris Moore, his big back, on 23 bandit, his bread-and-butter play. Instead he will show them 23 bandit and throw the ball off it. He will hand the season over to Stick Eubanks. "We're going with 1–23 bandit," he tells his assistant coaches.

Eubanks takes the snap, takes two steps, and fakes the ball to Moore. Homer Bush drives his man back five yards and then turns and hooks. Moore slides into the area Bush vacated. Eubanks rolls toward him, looks at Bush, and then cocks his arm.

Moore has a step on his defender, and Bush shoves the ball toward him. But instead of looping it, he tosses it flat. The frantic Trojan defensive back leaps and gets a finger on it.

The pass falls incomplete.

The Downers Grove bench explodes. Shannon grimaces and then turns around. He still has ninety-three seconds. "Kickoff team," he screams. "Nate, c'mere."

He tells Nate Robinson not to kick the ball deep, but just to nudge it ten yards. He wants an onsides kick, a long-shot ploy used only by desperate teams. The Flyers haven't been this desperate in years; the 1990 team has never practiced onsides kicks. Robinson gets too much foot into it, and the ball bounces all the way downfield into the end zone, his deepest kick of the year. The Trojans bleed the clock and punt with nine seconds left. Shannon has no more time-outs. His season is over.

Shannon pastes a smile on his face and strides across the field to shake Pete Ventrelli's hand. He walks along the line of jubilant Trojan players, shaking hands and patting backs. They all want to shake his hand. He is a legend in Illinois football, and Ventrelli has taught them to respect what he has accomplished. "Y'all get 'em for us next week," Shannon tells the victors. "We want to lose to the state champions."

Behind him, dogging his steps, is a crowd of reporters. Shannon turns to face them. "We did the best we could," Shannon says. "That's the way it goes. I'm proud of the guys. They made tremendous progress. We just came up a foot short.

Give 'em credit. They came into the lion's den and came away with the prize."

Someone suggests that a healthy Deondre Singleton might have made a difference. Shannon will hear nothing of it. He defends Stick Eubanks, the kid he spent all fall berating. "I thought Eubanks played pretty good for us in the second half," he says. "We don't make excuses around here. We either get it done or we don't. They came in here and got it done. We didn't get it done."

The reporters drift away. There is always more interest in the winning side. Shannon is left to the comfort of a few friends and supporters. He hugs his wife, Jeanette, who has tears in her eyes. The Shannons have no children, and Jeanette Shannon is the only person in the world Bob Shannon completely trusts. Football is their life, and Jeanette knows that the next few days are going to be strained.

There are handshakes and thank-you's from a few of the players' parents. There is a handshake from Art May, the athletic director, and from Sam Morgan, the principal. "Win or lose, I'm with you," Morgan says. "You know that."

"I know that," Shannon says, moving along. But he suspects otherwise. Morgan is not one of the people he trusts.

There are handshakes from Tom Holley and a few other businessmen who have helped out along the way. Finally he turns again to his own players, who are sitting in groups of two or three on the bench or scattered on the grass. Their heads are down, their eyes staring blankly. Two or three of the Flyers have torn off their equipment and thrown pads and helmets and jerseys in anger, or maybe bewilderment. They really don't know how to react. Most of them have never lost before. "Let's get on the bus, fellas," the coach says. "Let's go home."

There is no welcoming committee back at the school, just a handful of parents and girlfriends. The players file into the gym and take seats on the bleachers. This corner of the battered gymnasium, adjacent to the locker room, is where Shannon conducts his team meetings, his voice echoing off the rafters.

"All right boys, it's over," he begins. "We don't cry. We don't shed no tears. We work hard to get it done, and if we don't, we come back and work harder. When I send for you this winter, you make sure you come. Remember this. Remember how this feels. Remember how this tastes. It don't taste too sweet.

"Yeah, we're a little disappointed. But you have to try to learn a lesson from everything in life, and I want you to remember this. When you're in here lifting those weights this winter, you remember this. You know Deondre was hurt and Clarence got hurt, and Downers Grove took advantage of that. And we lost our confidence. Those coaches over there told me before the game they were confident they could beat us. You have to work hard to be confident, fellas.

"But I'm proud of you guys. You could have rolled over and played dead, but you did a heck of a job in coming back and playing tough. I told those guys we'd see 'em next year. The only thing is, I know we'll be back. I don't know about them. But there'll be someone tough out there. You'd better learn that lesson—when you get down to these last two games, the teams are there because they do what they do very well. They outplayed us, fellas. We wouldn't even have been in it if they hadn't messed up that punt."

He takes a deep breath. He's said all he wanted to say about this game. Don't look back, he always says, look ahead. It is time to look ahead. He smiles now and speaks very softly:

"Right now, I want you to take some time off. Catch up on your lessons. Rest up. And then come back in here and fix it so this doesn't happen again. We had a great year—for other people. But for us to go out in the semis, that's not so great. But we're going to get there again. But you've got to make it happen. What I like about you guys is that you like each other. You've got to like each other enough to make sure this don't happen again.

"But you've got to be prepared, fellas. Next time, we're going to be prepared for anything. If King Kong walks down the street, we'll be ready for him. I'm going to be dedicated. I'm going to be relentless. I'll be talking to everyone I can to make myself a better coach. We're going to get better, but you won't get better unless you work hard in the off-season."

He folds his arms across his chest and stares at the floor, trying to think if there's anything else he should say. Then he asks the assistant coaches if they have anything to add. John Davis and Ken Goss, the line coach, add a few more words about hard work. Davis, who is also track coach, suggests that running track is a great way to prepare for football. Then the room goes silent again.

Shannon, arms still folded, walks back and forth, trying to look every player in the eye. He begins speaking, very slowly. "One thing ol' Bear Bryant used to say," he says, "is that once a football season is over, he starts looking for the leaders for next season. I'll be looking. I'll be watching your schoolwork. I'll be seeing who you're hanging with.''

He stops in front of Chris Moore and says, "Chris, you want to be in that captain's circle, don't you? You lead by example, son.''

He pauses again, searching for something else to say. In the next few days, he'll see most of these players around the school and have personal words for all of them, but for today, he has said all there is to say. "Let's get our prayer,'' he says.

The Supreme Court would not approve, but the last thing the Flyers do after every game is say the Lord's Prayer. They kneel or stand in a huddle and hold hands, and a team captain—today it is Junior Green—leads the prayer. Line by line, the players repeat the familiar words that conclude, "For thine is the kingdom and the power and the glory.'' And together they say, "Amen.''

Then they quickly head to the locker room. They dress quietly and turn in their equipment and head for home. The assistant coaches drift away, too, back to families they've been away from for too long. Only Shannon and a couple of friends remain in the gym.

As the last players straggle out, Shannon starts replaying the game. He stands and walks through handoffs and pass patterns and linebacker responsibilities against the veer offense that has beaten his team. For forty-five minutes for an audience of two in an empty gym on the ragged edge of a town on the brink of oblivion, he is coaching football in a game of might-have-beens. "Time to go home,'' he says at last.

The coach is the last man out of the gymnasium. He slams the heavy metal door and double-locks it. He scans the glass-strewn parking lot and the weed lot behind it. He is looking to see if any of his players still need a ride home. Twilight is turning into darkness, and this is not a place to be waiting alone.

The place is deserted, as safe as it ever gets. He zips up his royal blue parka and starts walking across the weed lot to his Toyota. He shakes his head once and says, "Damn."

His next season has just begun.

CHAPTER

7

One mile east of East St. Louis High School, State Street crosses Interstate Highway 255, part of a ring highway system that encircles metropolitan St. Louis. If you pick up 255 at State Street and head north, and then turn west on Interstate 270, you cross the Mississippi just below its confluence with the Missouri. Seven miles from the Chain of Rocks Bridge is a long, winding street near a pleasant college campus. It is twenty-six miles from East St. Louis High School, but it might as well be in another world.

This is where Bob Shannon lives.

Most of his neighbors are white-collar professionals: a former airline pilot, a retired FBI agent, a college professor. The houses on his street are brick ranches, large and comfortable. The yards are nicely groomed, the shrubs well trimmed, the trees full-grown and shady. On Bob Shannon's street it is quiet and peaceful. Few people from the public part of his life are ever invited to this private place. The street number of his house is not posted on his garage or his front door or his mailbox. He is not a very sociable man. This house is his refuge.

The house is furnished in a style that might be called "eclectic comfortable." His trophies are everywhere—state championship footballs in a bookcase, trophies on the shelves, coach-of-the-year plaques standing on the hearth, citations and photographs hung on the walls. There is a television set in nearly every room of the house. The home is as meticulous and well ordered as his office at the high school is chaotic, but the dominant theme in both places is football.

"Football," Jeanette Shannon says matter-of-factly when asked what her husband's hobbies are.

And what does he like to read about?

"Football."

And what about his social life? What does he like to do?

"Football, mostly. It's all related to football."

She was not happy to be answering these questions. She was doing it only because her husband had asked her to. "We have these power struggles," she said. "I lost this one. This is the last interview I'm going to do. I did *People* magazine and *USA Today*. I did *Reader's Digest*, and I hated that one. This is the last one. I'm going to get it in writing."

She says this politely and with good humor, but she is quite serious about it. Jeanette Ridley Shannon is almost reclusive. Shannon says, "The only difference between her and Howard Hughes is that Howard had more money."

Many people would find Shannon himself reclusive. Though he is a moving and dynamic public speaker, he shuns most speaking invitations, particularly during football season. His hobbies are solitary—exercising, watching westerns on television. His only known vices are expensive athletic shoes and

Chapstick. He has no close circle of friends. Only rarely does he return to Natchez to visit his family. And yet his wife regards him as a regular social butterfly.

"We're two different people," she said. "He's more outgoing. He enjoys being around other people. I like to stay to myself. He always wanted to be an entertainer. I think football is his substitute."

The first time Jeanette Ridley laid eyes on Robert Shannon, he was sitting beneath a tree outside the women's dormitory at Tennessee State University. "He was singing," she remembered. "He likes to sing, plays the guitar a little bit. He's got a pretty good voice, or at least he thinks he does. He thinks he's James Brown. He even did James Brown at a talent show in school."

It is hard to imagine how the East St. Louis Flyers might react if Coach Shannon were to stop glaring and break into "Papa's Got a Brand New Bag" by the godfather of soul.

Jeanette Ridley grew up in Birmingham, Alabama. Her father was a mill worker, her mother reared six children. She went to church every Sunday and dreamed of going to college. She wanted to go to the Hampton Institute but wound up at Tennessee State. "It was my last choice," she said.

She was in no particular hurry to get married, but along came the tall, good-looking football player with the great singing voice. She didn't want to live in East St. Louis, but that's where Bob took a job. She didn't want to be a teacher, but she ended up teaching math in the East St. Louis school district. She wanted to move to a college town, but Bob wouldn't leave high school football. She didn't want to be interviewed, but here she was, answering questions. She saw it as a marital duty.

"You know what they say," she explained. "'For better or for worse.'"

Jeanette Shannon reads; her bookshelves are crammed with modern fiction. She experiments on her home computer, developing ways to help tutor her students. She attends nearly all of the Flyers' games, even those as far away as Chicago. She drives by herself and sits by herself. She likes to travel, he likes to stay home—unless there's a coaches convention or a sporting event at the end of the road. When he goes to a convention or a clinic, she will go with him if she's interested in the city where he's speaking. She liked California when they went to the Rose Bowl; she liked New Orleans when the National Coaches Convention was there.

She used to try to persuade him to move, somewhere back down South, or maybe to a college job. She's given up on that. "He'll never move," she said. "He'll be there until he dies. A man came up to us on the street corner, in the French Quarter in New Orleans, and offered him a job. He said, well, he didn't know. I knew."

Jeanette Shannon is a tough and independent woman, but she is devoted to her husband. Or maybe resigned to her husband. Even if she is the only person in the world he completely trusts, even she can sometimes feel his aloofness. "He is a fair man, and he does what he does because he likes those kids," she said. "But I think he could turn around and walk away from them tomorrow. I think so."

When he comes home from a tough game, such as the loss to Downers Grove, Shannon will be quiet for a few days. "It's only real bad when they don't play well," she said. "But there wasn't much they could do then. He talked about it some, but he didn't even get around to watching the tape of that game until the spring. He watched other tapes. He doesn't pay much attention to football, except his own team. He might watch the pro games on Sunday, but he might not. He's not caught up in all football, just Eastside football."

While she was saying these things, under duress, on a warm spring afternoon in the middle of the off-season, her husband was sitting in a lawn chair under a shade tree in his yard. He had a yellow legal pad in his lap along with a copy of a coaching manual by former Michigan State coach Duffy Daugherty. The book was opened to a series of offensive formations. It was a lovely Sunday afternoon in the middle of May, and he was trying to decide on his basic offensive plays for the next season.

Jeanette Shannon had tried to get him to mount a new mailbox on the post near the curb. He had declined, saying he had work to do. "Football," she said, "is what he does."

The mistakes and misfortunes of his twelve years as mayor began to catch up with Carl Officer in the winter of 1990–91. Shannon had given him an "F" the year before, and over the winter, much of the rest of the city adopted Shannon's grading system.

Nothing went right for the mayor. Phil Donahue came to town and skewered him on live television. Donahue's crew had turned the Eastside gym into a makeshift television studio, and Officer had confidently taken the single chair in the center of the spotlights. Donahue introduced him by listing the city's worst problems—the current debt, estimated at more than $40 million; the loss of the court battle with Walter DeBow, who suffered permanent brain damage from a beating that took place in the city jail; the debacle of the waterfront development plan. He asked the mayor if he saw good news anywhere.

Officer held his own for a while. His nickname among his boyhood friends is "Smooth," and he was. His city hall staffers and patronage network system had been in charge of tickets to the "Donahue" show, and most of the four hundred people in the audience were on his side. He easily parried questions about his own pay (he'd just proposed a city budget that called for doubling his salary; he said he was worth it) and about his social life, asking the woman who posed the question to see him in private. He turned his answers into long soliloquies about racism in America, and in particular, about racism in the courts in Belleville. He lambasted white politicians for caring more about sending aid to Eastern Europe than to "people of color," both at home and abroad. He said white businessmen in St. Louis were trying to grab the East St. Louis riverfront without guaranteeing the 25 percent local ownership that he said was necessary.

But Donahue bounced around the gym with his microphone until he found a few negative questioners. One woman shouted at Officer that she hadn't seen one problem taken care of in the twelve years he had been mayor. She suggested to him that if he was so rich that he didn't need his mayoral salary, he should use it to get the trash picked up.

The key question came from a man who wanted to know if the

mayor planned to run for a fourth term in the February 1991 primary election. Officer was disingenuous; he said he would base that decision "on my conversations every morning with God."

The reviews of Officer's performance on the "Donahue" show were, at least in East St. Louis, mostly positive. Sure, Phil had gotten his shots in, but he'd given the people a chance to talk, and Carl had been his usual smooth self in answering the questions. The bigger question was whether smooth was going to be enough anymore. Already politicians were lining up to challenge Officer in the February 26 primary. The primary would be the election that counted; in heavily Democratic East St. Louis, the general election in April would merely ratify matters.

As Thanksgiving approached, at least ten politicians were considering challenges to Officer, and many of them had substantial political clout. Three members of the Board of Aldermen were considering filing for mayor. So were two members of the St. Clair County Board of Review, the county's tax adjustment body, which had strong links to the old Democratic machine. So was Johnny Scott, the local head of the National Association for the Advancement of Colored People. So was Wyvetter Younge, the city's longtime representative in the Illinois House. Officer's contumacious style had alienated many who had once been his supporters. Worst of all for the mayor, the city's financial plight, with its series of payless paydays, had antagonized the one group that should have been most solidly in his camp—the city workers.

In late November, Officer's plan to bail the city out by running casino gambling boats from the riverfront took a heavy hit. The

Illinois Gaming Board denied a gaming license to Joe Terrell of Baton Rouge, Louisiana. Officer had designated Terrell as the city's preferred license applicant. The gaming board said Officer had deceived the Illinois Terminal Railroad, in the process of persuading it to grant Terrell exclusive access to the riverfront property adjacent to the casino boat's docking. In addition, the board found Terrell had acted as a go-between in an illegal political payoff scam in Louisiana, making his background, in the board's words, "less than impeccable." The result was that when Illinois passed out its first gambling licenses, East St. Louis missed the boat.

Despite these setbacks, Officer decided to file for a fourth term. He ran a curious campaign, spurning newspaper interviews and relying on a heavy schedule of meetings with small groups. In those meetings he continued portraying his administration, and by extension, the city, as victims of racism. His campaign was based on symbols, with himself as the champion of the underdog black citizens of East St. Louis, standing firm against the outsiders who were trying to take over their city.

Most of his would-be challengers eventually backed out of the race. The message had gone out through the machine's grapevine that the "boys in Belleville" and their surrogates in East St. Louis had decided that forty-eight-year-old Gordon Bush would be the unity candidate to run against Officer. Bush was a former East St. Louis city commissioner and city treasurer, a low-key black politician whose cooperation with the St. Clair County machine had earned him the reward of a job as chairman of the County Board of Review.

And though Representative Younge stayed in the race, as did a maverick newcomer named Darnell Thompson, the race quickly crystallized into an Officer-Bush contest—Officer's charm and contentiousness against Bush's low-key coalition-building. And as the campaign season hit high gear in February, Officer seemed to be ahead. But then the mayor took a couple of big new blows.

The first was self-inflicted. On Thursday, February 7, Officer was stopped by the Illinois Highway Patrol on Interstate 57 and issued a ticket for driving 105 miles an hour in a 65-mile-an-hour zone near Champaign. Officer said he was on the way to a fundraiser in Chicago. He was driving a gold 1990 Jaguar Vanden-Plas, a $48,000 luxury car that he said belonged to Edith Moore, a passenger in the car and a candidate for city clerk in East St. Louis. According to the state police, Officer cheerfully surrendered his driver's license as bond and was not arrested. Questioned about the incident two days later, he readily admitted he'd been speeding but confided that he hadn't really been going 105. He'd been doing 140.

The larger question was not how fast Officer had been driving, but who owned the car he was driving. Moore at first claimed the car belonged to her but changed her story a few days later. She said she was keeping the car, and maintaining payments on it, for a nephew who was on duty with U.S. forces then stationed in the Persian Gulf. Ten days later, the *Belleville News-Democrat* reported that Moore's nephew was not in Saudi Arabia, but in Arkansas, where he was doing ten years in jail for selling marijuana. The *News-Democrat* also reported that Moore and her husband, who owned a trucking firm, had been given thousands of dollars in city contracts over the years, including one for removing snow that never got removed.

Even for a city that had grown used to Officer's shenanigans, this one was hard to swallow. Complicating matters was that Moore's nephew, one Frank Cheers, had run his marijuana business out of a place called Earle, Arkansas, which also turned out to be the family home of the Rev. Joe Davis, the drug-dealing preacher Officer had embraced for years. The Earle connection brought back unpleasant memories for voters.

Officer, who seemed immune to embarrassment, shrugged off the controversy. He had a little more trouble shrugging off the other blow that hit him in the final weeks before the election. The federal judge handling the penalty phase of the great Matthews & Wright riverfront bond scandal took $7 million out of Officer's control.

The $7 million ($1 million a year over seven years) was the fine imposed on the Wall Street firm on its conviction for what the firm agreed amounted to conspiracy to commit fraud—the bonds sold to underwrite the waterfront development. Officer and Eric Vickers, the city attorney, had argued that the city's elected officials should control the money.

Vickers was more than a city attorney. He was a friend of the mayor's and a private attorney who had billed the city for more than $100,000 for his various services the previous year. He was particularly adamant about the handling of the fine money. "Elected officials were elected by the people to look after their basic public health and welfare needs," he said. "That's what government is all about."

But the U.S. attorney's office argued that city officials had withheld crucial data—the fact, in particular, that they owed Walter DeBow $3.4 million—and would never have gotten clear title to the land that was to be used for the riverfront development. In short, the government argued that Officer's administration was partly to blame for the whole mess and didn't deserve to be entrusted with $7 million.

Judge William Stiehl agreed. He set up a not-for-profit community foundation to spend the $7 million in fine money. He appointed seven community leaders to one-year terms as foundation board members. To add insult to Officer's injury, among the people Judge Stiehl appointed to the board was Bob Shannon.

The mayoral campaign season was highlighted by one mortification after another. The city missed its first payroll of the year when the Firefighter's Union garnisheed $70,000 in back dues. Then a citizens' group dumped trash at City Hall to protest the lack of trash pickup. About that time, the police department admitted it had been feeding its prisoners leftover prepackaged sandwiches because it could no longer pay for the McDonald's hamburgers it usually fed the prisoners. The sandwiches had come from a wholesaler that had first donated its leftovers to a homeless shelter. The shelter donated the leftover leftovers to the prisoners when the city couldn't pay its $40,000 tab at McDonald's. East St. Louis had thus become the only city in the country to be taking handouts from the homeless.

It was also about that time that trucks from one of the city's three fire stations were late responding to a fire because the doors to the fire station wouldn't open. The electronically operated doors had to be jimmied open by a fireman who happened to have a crowbar in the trunk of his car. And soon after that, the city's $46,000 voice-logging emergency telephone device was repossessed, leaving East St. Louis without a 911 emergency dialing system. On April 4, the *New York Times* summed up the troubles in a front-page story outlining the city's devastation. The headline was "Ravaged City on Mississippi Floundering at Rock Bottom."

In all it was a gloomy winter. And on February 26, the voters decided it was all Carl Officer's fault. Gordon Bush routed Officer by a nearly three-to-one margin, 6,730 to 2,470. Officer was stunned, but gracious. He dropped by Bush's campaign headquarters, hugged the new mayor-elect and said, "When I looked at some of the numbers, I was a little surprised ... and somewhat relieved."

He wasn't the only one. Bob Shannon took Officer's defeat as a sign of hope for East St. Louis, though he refused to get very excited about Gordon Bush. "He did go to Eastside," Shannon said. "He'll be the first mayor we ever had who went to this school, so maybe he won't play the games for the Lincoln crowd. If the city has some summer jobs, maybe Eastside guys can get a few for a change. Officer and Clyde Jordan always steered them to Lincoln kids."

Though Shannon's feelings about Officer were well known in

town, and even though he has a keen interest in public affairs, he stayed clear of any electioneering. The closest he came to getting involved in the East St. Louis election was to make a rare appearance at a Teachers Union meeting to vote against a proposal that the union donate twelve thousand dollars to Officer's campaign. "We didn't need to get involved in anything like that," Shannon said later. The proposal was defeated.

Shannon's preferred position in East St. Louis politics is above it all, which is why he surprised even himself when he accepted Judge Stiehl's appointment to the board of the community fund. "I had to think about it for a couple of days," he said. "I decided it was kind of nice that the judge recognized that there's some of us here in this community who've been working for a living, trying to do the right thing. I've tried to do the right thing here for twenty years, but I guess everyone wants to do something concrete for the community when he has a chance.

"The good thing is we're only on the panel for one year, and after that, they'll get seven new guys. I wouldn't want to be dealing with all these people coming and asking for money, for seven years. Some of them are liable to shoot me if I say no. There's always going to be guys in this town trying to lay their hands on any money that's floating around. I've always been out of the political arena, though, so they didn't feel like it was worth knowing me. I just hope they feel the same way now."

Shortly after his appointment to the board was announced, Shannon was amused to get a visit from Dr. Lillian Parks, the school superintendent. "She said she just wanted to get to know me a little bit," he said. "She said they had some projects they'd be bringing to the community fund. I told her I was glad to see her, but I thought it was funny she'd come to see me now after all the times I'd been to the school district and they didn't do anything for us.''

"She said, 'Oh, you're not going to hold that against us, are you?' I said, 'Oh, no,' and I won't. But I just thought it was kind of a funny coincidence when she showed up. There's been other guys who had members of the school board call me up and ask me to see them. I don't think that kind of stuff is appropriate, trying to use a guy's job as pressure on him. And I'm not going to put up with it.''

Shannon paused and grinned. "I will admit, though," he added, "that there's a certain kind of satisfaction in having guys be nice to you who've been giving you hell for twenty years.''

The appointment to the community fund board, coupled with Officer's defeat at the polls, helped brighten Shannon's outlook over the winter. So did Tom Holley's decision to spend $20,000 to refurbish the Flyers' miserable weight-training room. The two men had been fretting in their daily phone calls about what the Flyers needed to become a better football team and had decided that the two most urgently needed items were a defensive coordinator and better strength facilities. Holley told Shannon to find the coach and he'd take care of the weight room.

So without notifying anyone at the school district (who might only make problems), Holley hired a plumber to fix the broken water pipes that threatened to flood the weight room. Then he hired an electrical contractor who installed a fan and a ventilation system and rewired the dark and dismal room with enough lights to land a 747. Another contractor stripped the paint from the walls, repainted two of the walls in a brilliant white streaked with orange and blue stripes, and installed floor-to-ceiling mirrors on two other walls. Rubber floor mats were laid. The broken and rusted barbells and weight machines were hauled out to be sold for scrap. Shannon bought two weight machines from a bankrupt health club, and Holley ordered several more weight machines, tons of iron weights and barbells, racks and benches. The final result was a weight room the players couldn't wait to get into and didn't want to leave once they got there.

Another result was that Shannon stopped talking about making 1991 his last season at Eastside. "There's been some good things happening this winter," he said. "For me, the biggest thing has been Tom. He's made it possible for us to have some of the things that other teams take for granted. You want to give these guys something, let them see some reward for their hard work. Now we can do some of those things."

Shannon's search for a defensive coordinator took a lot longer than rehabbing the weight room. Week after week, month after month, he labored over his decision. It was almost as if he was glad to have something important to decide, something to help fill the empty spaces between playing seasons. He usually spends those long hours making up depth charts, assigning kids to one position or another, rating them and doing mental gymnastics. He watches the kids closely as they come in for after-school work-outs. Which ones are working hard? Which ones are putting on size and weight? Which ones seem to be taking leadership roles? He adjusts his depth charts accordingly.

But this off-season he was blessed with a lot of returning players and a good crop of sophomores. The depth charts were easy. By March he already had decided on most of his tentative lineup. The real problem was who would coach them.

He'd already decided not to rehire Wendell Smith, who'd coached the defensive backs the previous season. Smith had coached with him for three seasons, but Shannon had never been happy with him. Smith had balked at some of the coverage techniques Shannon had wanted taught to his defensive backfield. And besides, his personality was difficult. "Wendell is a loner," Shannon said. "We might all be sitting here and he'd be sitting over there. The kids see that, and they know something ain't right. We're teaching teamwork here, and he wasn't part of the team."

Shannon was considering asking John Davis to coach the defensive backs, downgrading his role from that of defensive coordinator. In Shannon's mind, Davis had lost his coordinator's job the day Elgin Larkin laid forty-two points on the Flyers.

"Coach D is a fine man, but coaching track like he does, he's not able to put in the time he needs to," Shannon said. "The level of ball we're playing now, a guy has to get out to clinics, go to the spring practices at the colleges and learn what we have to do to put a championship defense on the field."

Shannon had several candidates in mind for the defensive coordinator's job. One week he'd consider Coach X the leading candidate. The next week, Coach Y would surge ahead. The following week, Coach Z would have moved up on the outside. Shannon was especially intrigued by one candidate, John Hotfelder, the former head coach at Hazelwood Central High in suburban St. Louis. As a head coach, Hotfelder had developed power-house teams, but he'd given up coaching to take an administrative job in the Hazelwood School District. Missouri has a rule that administrators who choose to moonlight across the Mississippi in Illinois.

"John's a good man and a good a coach," Shannon said. "The question with John is, can he get over here in time for practice? He says he can leave work at 3:00 and be here by 3:30 or 4:00, but I don't know if he can be here in August for two-a-days. That's so important for a new guy coming in. Plus at Hazelwood, he ran the 4–0 defense, four down linemen, and we're used to running a five-man line. He'd want to coach the system he knows. Can he put it in if he can't make two-a-days, or would we be better off staying with what we know and letting him learn our system? Better him being confused than all of these kids. I don't know if we can work it out with John. He's a good man, and a good coach, but there's a lot of problems."

The ever-helpful Tom Holley had put forth another candidate, Jack Jones. Like Hotfelder, Jones had been a successful head coach in suburban St. Louis—at Webster Groves High School. Jones wanted to keep his hand in the game after retiring, but Shannon didn't know how serious he was. "I think he's some-body Tom put up to this," he said. "Tom really wants to be the coach himself, but he doesn't know how."

Shannon's biggest concern with both Hotfelder and Jones was that both men had coached in relatively affluent school districts.

Now it was Shannon who was worrying about the culture shock of East St. Louis. "This environment is different, man," he said. "They're used to saying, 'I need this and I need that,' and it happens. Here you say it, and nothing happens. There's things we need that we don't even ask for, because we know it's not going to happen so we don't bother. They're good guys and would do a good job, but you need to learn how to deal with guys in this environment. It's nothing for a guy to come up to you, high on drugs or wine, and want to hold a conversation with you. You've got to know how to deal with them."

What Shannon was really looking for was a top-notch defensive coach who was used to working in an impoverished environment with tough black kids. Luckily he had such a candidate. His name was Marion Stallings.

"Yeah, he wants to come back," he said. "He's a good coach, a super coach. He wants it bad. The question is, is he clean? He told me he'd be willing to be tested, but I said if I hired him, I wouldn't do that. Either I can trust a guy or I can't, and if he ain't clean, I'll know. Same way I knew it before. Who's he hanging with? What are his habits like? Is he on time? What's his attitude and his moods? It's not hard.

"I don't mind giving a guy a second chance, especially if he's a good guy. Some of these guys, they got involved because they didn't know the consequences. They know now. I've got another guy who used to coach with me who's floated a trial balloon about coming back, but everybody in town knows he's not clean. Stallings, I think, he's all right. The question now is is he the right guy for the job? He knows the situation here, but he's been away from the game a while. He *can* motivate people, though. He went up the ladder with me. We all found out together what it took to beat the best teams in Illinois. We taught the little things. And the thing about Stallings, he's the only guy who ever coached with me who bothered to learn both sides of the ball. He knows almost as much about the offense as I do.

"What I've got to do this winter is figure out what's best for the program. Whatever I do, whichever way I go, is going to be the best way for the team. Yeah, I'd like to give Stallings a break, because in a way, I owe a lot to him. But if he's not the best guy for the program, I won't do it. His schedule might be touch, getting off work. Same with Hotfelder and those guys. John might put in that 4–0 defense and take us to another level. I've got to weigh all that. I'm trying to figure it out."

Shannon's status in the high school coaching fraternity is exalted enough that he is often invited to lecture at coaching clinics in the off-season. College athletic departments sponsor these clinics, inviting high school coaches from their recruiting areas in for a weekend of shop talk and camaraderie, establishing relationships that can be crucial. You never know who the next blue-chip athlete is going to be and where he's going to go to high school.

Shannon loves these clinics; it gives him a chance to learn more football. As a lecturer, his travel expenses are paid. He delivers his lecture, most often on the subject of "developing the quarterback," and then immerses himself in the rest of the clinic. In the winter of 1990–91, he spoke at the Universities of Nebraska, Michigan, and Missouri, as well as to local clinics in St. Louis and to the National Coaches Convention in New Orleans. The Shannons also flew to California for the Rose Bowl, courtesy of Tom Holley, who'd won the trip in a contest.

When Shannon wasn't traveling, he was prowling his gym, supervising his off-season workouts and helping his seniors deal with college recruiters. Homer Bush was the busiest of the Flyer seniors, getting scholarship offers from a half dozen major universities before finally settling on the University of Missouri. Bush signed a letter of intent to attend Missouri, but later in the year, he changed his mind. He was selected in the seventh round of the June baseball draft by the San Diego Padres, who offered him forty thousand dollars to skip football and play minor league baseball instead. Under pressure from his family and from Art May, the Eastside baseball coach, Bush chose baseball.

Shannon was disappointed, but he'd come close to doing the same thing in 1965, so he understood. He wasn't nearly so disappointed as was a Missouri assistant coach named Kevin Faulkner. Faulkner had diligently recruited both Bush and Jerry Creer, but Creer had had trouble making the minimum grade of 18 on the American College Test required of incoming scholarship athletes. Missouri had thus backed away from Creer, who accepted an offer from Illinois State University. But later in the year, Creer too was selected by San Diego in the baseball draft and opted to play baseball rather than try college football.

Clarence Green, recovered from his ankle injury, won a scholarship to Northwest Missouri State, a small college willing to gamble on a fireplug-sized lineman. And to Shannon's great surprise, Stick Eubanks got a college football scholarship, to Millikin University.

"I didn't think it would happen," Shannon said. "But I'm glad for him. It'll show some of these younger guys what can happen if you stick around when you're not starting."

Bush, Green, Creer, and Eubanks were the only seniors whose grades were remotely good enough to attract college recruiters. Three others—Vaughn (Ubay) Johnson, center Lamont Stith, and defensive end Robert Perkins—were being recruited by a junior college in Joliet, Illinois. With a little luck and a lot of hard work, they might parlay two years of junior college into a major college scholarship. "The odds are against them, I know," Shannon said. "But you'd like to see them go on and try."

It was an impressive recruiting season for the Flyers. Counting the three would-be junior college players, all seven of the seniors who'd played in 1990 got college offers. And already recruiters were asking questions about the kids who'd be seniors in 1991.

Deondre Singleton was getting a lot of attention. Doctors had removed a piece of torn cartilage from his knee, and he had worked hard to rebuild the strength in his leg. Singleton, even on two healthy knees, had never been very mobile. Nor was he, at six-foot-one and 170 pounds, an overwhelming physical specimen, the kind of six-foot-four-inch, 220-pound quarterback who makes recruiters drool. But he could throw a football hard and long and straight, and he was the hardest-working quarterback Shannon had ever had. Shannon nominated him as a preseason All-American when *Street & Smith*'s football magazine sent out its annual research questionnaire.

Singleton never stopped learning. In mid-January, he was riding in a car with five other members of the Flyers' baseball team, coming back from a workout. He was in the back seat when the kid riding in the middle of the front seat playfully grabbed the steering wheel. The driver lost control and slammed into a light pole.

"I hadn't been worrying at all about coming back from the knee injury until then," Singleton said, "I was just taking it for granted. But when I had the car accident, it ran through my mind, all the things that Coach tells us about being with the right kind of people. That dude could have killed me right out on State Street."

Shannon also nominated Dennis Stallings for All-American honors. Stallings had the combination of size and speed that could make him a fearsome college tight end, but Shannon worried that he still wasn't taking his grades seriously enough, and his off-season training habits weren't so grimly purposeful as the coach would have wanted. Shannon wants his players in the gym after school at least three days a week, lifting weights and running. He makes an exception for those playing other sports. Frank Spraggins, for example, played basketball, and a dozen others ran track, played baseball, or wrestled. "I want them doing something," Shannon said. "If they ain't in here with me, I want to know that they're getting their work in somewhere."

Stallings went out for the baseball team, mostly so he could hang out with Singleton and Bush, his best friends. Shannon had wanted him to run track instead, but there was a little too much serious running involved in that to suit Stallings. "Dennis is still young," Shannon said. "He's a little bit lazy, too, but he'll be all right if you stay on him. He's not like Chris Moore. Chris isn't just lazy. He's got more chicanery in him than any kid I've ever coached."

In the off-season, Shannon had become preoccupied with Chris Moore, almost obsessed with him. For a brief time, in early January, Shannon thought he'd finally gotten through to Moore. He'd noticed Moore around school, acting more businesslike. He hadn't had complaints from Moore's teachers. Chris had told him he was going out for the track team to work on his speed and keep his weight down. Shannon had seen him studying in the cafeteria, instead of goofing around. "I went up to him and congratulated him," Shannon said. "I told him that last year at this time, he wouldn't have been doing that. But this year, he was about the business of getting ahead academically. He's a guy I really feel has changed."

Shannon had been excited. He'd gone back to his playbooks and started drawing up plays that featured Moore in a one-back offense. The year before, with a senior fullback in Jerry Creer who deserved to carry the ball, Shannon had played a two-back offense. But this year, with a gifted quarterback and a powerful tailback, he could do what he's always wanted to do, play one back and three wide receivers. "Just let 'em try to defend three wide guys and Chris Moore, too," he said. "We'll spread the field and run draws to Chris Moore, and he'll get some yards. I told him that, too. I want him to know that I appreciate what he's doing. He's maturing, realizing that if he's going to play on the next level, he's going to have to prepare."

But that was in January. By March Shannon was back to being

angry with Chris Moore, maybe even angrier than before, because Moore had fooled him. He'd gone out for track, but hadn't stayed long. Art May had told him he wasn't welcome on the baseball team because he was undependable. Moore either didn't show up at all to lift weights, or bugged out early when Shannon wasn't watching.

"I take back everything I said about him changing," Shannon said. "He ain't changed a bit. He's the complete opposite of Deondre. Deondre is playing baseball, but he still comes in to work out for football. Chris ebbs and flows. I told him he was going to have to split time at tailback with a few other guys. I told him we've had some great tailbacks, guys like Marvin Lampkin, who went to Iowa, and Kerwin Price, who went to Arkansas, but he's not going to be in that group unless he works hard."

For his part, Chris said he was spending some time letting his battered body heal—he'd gone out for track, but his legs had been tired. He said he planned to start lifting weights very soon and to supplement his workouts by mowing lawns for spending money.

"Mowing lawns, huh?" Shannon said when informed of Moore's training plans. "I'll believe that when I see it. Chris just tells you one thing and does another. He's a shyster. I hope he changes, but I got my doubts."

On a hot and muggy evening in late May, Clyde C. Jordan Memorial Stadium finally was opened, several years late and considerably over budget. The first events held there were the commencement ceremonies, first for Lincoln High, and the next night, for East St. Louis. "They tell me the Lincoln folks weren't too happy about coming out here," Shannon said. "They're saying it's our stadium and they shouldn't have to graduate in it. But things went pretty well, so they couldn't complain too much."

Shannon didn't attend the commencement exercise for his seniors. Instead, he went to the state track meet, where Coach John Davis's team won its first state track championship. That was another blow for the Lincoln partisans. The Tigers usually dominate the Flyers in track. It was a blow for Shannon, too. An Eastside junior named Camara Tucker, whom Shannon had been counting on to play a lot of football for him, won the four-hundred-meter race in the stunning time of forty-seven seconds. Tucker promptly decided his future was in track and that he wasn't going to play football anymore.

"He said we work 'em too hard at football and he's going to concentrate on track instead," Shannon said. "I said, well, that's all right. I don't want 'em out here if they don't want to be here. I'm stubborn enough to think I can take some other kid and work with him and still get the work done. I'm about commitment. If a guy isn't going to make the commitment, then he's not going to be as good as he can be at anything."

Shannon's judgment about a player usually boils down to the single word "commitment." He is harsh with those who don't commit and bubbles with pride over those who do. May and June are crucial months for Shannon's decisions about who is committed and who isn't. School is winding up, and he sees by exam scores who worked hard on grades and who didn't. He also wants to see who is committed enough to come into the gym on lazy spring afternoons to lift weights and work out. Late May and early June are when Shannon "fires" players. He seeks out those whose grades and work habits don't meet his standards and tells them not to bother to come to his summer camp, which begins in mid-June after school is out.

"I tell you what it's all about," he said in early May. "Did you see in the paper about Bryan Cox?"

The news was that Bryan Cox, who'd played for Shannon's state championship team in 1985 and then played linebacker at Western Illinois University, had been drafted in the fifth round of the National Football League draft by the Miami Dolphins. "It's funny about Bryan Cox," Shannon said. "When he was here, he was only about the fifth or sixth best player on the team. But he went up to Western Illinois, worked hard, played well. Now he's got a chance to go on to the next level. And he's going to graduate on time, too.

"You take a guy like Bryan and you compare him with another guy on that 1985 team, Arthur Sargent. When people talked about that team that year, Cox's name never came up, but Arthur Sargent's always came up. He was one of the best players we ever had, a split end and defensive back. He made all-state and All-American. He was fast, man. He came within an eyelash of setting the national record in the 330-yard low hurdles.

"He really wanted to go to Missouri, but he couldn't make the grades, so he went on down to Southeast Missouri State and wound up flunking out. The year before I had another guy, a kid who'd grown up across the street from here and was always hanging around when he was a little guy. He came out and played for us and was a star, got himself a college scholarship. He played for three years, had a chance to get himself drafted by the pros, but he wound up selling drugs to an undercover police officer. He couldn't sacrifice for one more year. He had to have those warm-up suits and those one-hundred-dollar tennis shoes. He could've done so much for his mom and his family. He came back to see me. He said it was the hardest thing he had to do, come back and face me afterwards."

He carefully clipped an article about Bryan Cox and the Dolphins out of a newspaper and taped it onto the bulletin board in the football locker room. He walked out into the gym to check on off-season workouts. "I don't understand the things people do to themselves," he said, biting his lip. "You know, they might not fail here, but they might fail later on. They don't learn the lessons. It's about commitment. They squander those opportunities, and it's frustrating, because not everybody in this town gets an opportunity like that. That's what makes a guy like Bryan Cox so special. He worked hard and took advantage of his opportunities."

For those who aren't like Bryan Cox, Shannon can be ruthless. The clock on his patience runs out in a boy's senior year. On the third day of June, the clock ran out on Chris Moore.

"He came into the weight room Monday, first time I'd seen him there in months, and I told him, 'Hey, don't bother, you're fired,'" Shannon said. "I said I didn't want to go into any long speeches. He knew, I knew, everybody else knew."

In two years at Eastside, Chris Moore had carried the ball 290 times for 2,958 yards and forty-nine touchdowns. He had averaged better than 10 yards a carry. He had begun getting letters from college recruiters when he was a sophomore. Heading into his senior year, he was rated as one of the top running backs in Illinois and among the best in the Midwest. But Shannon was fed up with him.

"I always say we stay away from just using a kid in order to win," Shannon said. "That's what I believe, and if I believe that, then this is what I had to do. With Chris, it wasn't even close."

Shannon said that in late spring Moore had begun dropping hints that he was thinking about transferring to another school, just as he had the year before. Moore had told Sam Morgan, and in mid-May Morgan had come to Shannon asking him to hold off on any decision about Chris's future. Morgan told Shannon that he would talk to Chris and his parents.

"I started thinking hard about it then," Shannon said. "It was like Chris was going to hold this thing about leaving over my head. I was supposed to forget about everything he'd done and welcome him back with open arms. He was going to use pressure tactics from the principal."

Chris Moore had cultivated Sam Morgan as a friend and confidant. The principal had even sold Moore's mother a used car for Chris to use to get to and from school. "That was the worst thing anybody could have done," Shannon said. "Not only did it make Chris mobile, but what kind of message did it give to the other kids? You know, screw around and break the rules and I'll get you a car."

Shannon began checking with Moore's teachers, all of whom told him that he'd been cutting class regularly and was either flunking or just getting by. Under Illinois's less than onerous academic eligibility rules, a student must pass four classes that meet every day in order to be eligible for sports. Theoretically, a student could make four D's and two F's in his six classes—a grade point average of .075—and still be eligible. By Shannon's reckoning, Moore was going to have trouble making even that minimal requirement.

"I know what he'll do," Shannon said. "He'll go back in there and try to get Morgan, his ace in the hole, to get him back in. At this point, Morgan would have to force me to take him back before I'd do it. Over the years, I've worked hard. I hope he'll trust me on this one. Black teachers, white teachers, male teachers, female teachers, they all feel the same way about Chris Moore. He's a guy who takes shortcuts, a guy who'll try to finagle a grade, but won't work for it."

Moore had gotten under Shannon's skin, made him angry. Whenever the coach talked about Moore, his jaw would set and his eyes would take on his famous glare. What made him angriest was that Moore threatened his absolute control over his team. Some of his seniors, including Singleton and Stallings, had come to Shannon to plead Moore's case instead of going to Moore to reinforce Shannon's rules. Though he wouldn't admit it, Shannon had begun taking it personally.

"It ain't about me, it's about the team," Shannon said the day after he fired Moore. He was standing in the gym, watching a physical education class go through a desultory game of volleyball. "Chris is the most negative influence on our team. I give a guy a chance as a sophomore because he doesn't know our system. I give him a little slack as a junior, too. But once he's a senior, it's too late. Chris just doesn't set the tone the way a senior is supposed to. He's got to go."

The coach's arms were folded across his chest, his jaw was set, and his eyes were staring into the distance. "Number one, we can get along without him," he said. "Number two, it ain't how good you are, it's what kind of guy you are, and Chris is a user. He knows how to use people. Morgan is the guy he uses when he gets into trouble. Morgan thinks he's got this rapport with him, but Chris has got him fooled. I look at it this way—I'm just helping him make that decision about transferring somewhere else. He can go ahead and do it now and not worry about me. Maybe it will be a good thing for him, because if he wants to play somewhere else, he's going to have to work harder than he's ever worked before. If he's going to succeed in life, he's got to change, man. But I'm tired of dealing with him. You can't save them all."

CHAPTER

8

For an optimist, Bob Shannon can go into some pretty serious funks. By the third week of the 1991 season, his attitude has become truly foul. His face is locked in a scowl. He's treating his players mercilessly, withering them with sarcasm, pounding them through long and relentless practice sessions, screaming at them, belittling them, and even cursing at them occasionally.

"Nice catch," he tells players who've just dropped passes. Or, "That's the way," to players who've jumped offsides. Or, "Good throw, quarterback" when passes bounce in front of wide-open receivers. For the most part he's kept his temper under control, but not always.

"What the fuck are you trying to do in there?" he bellows at a sophomore defensive end toward the end of a brutally hot and humid afternoon scrimmage. The sophomore had grabbed an opponent's face mask and yanked him forward. The kid hasn't been around long enough to know better, so he starts to answer back: "Motherfucker took a cheap shot. . . ."

"Shut the fuck up!" Shannon screams, stalking through the scrimmage to put his face three inches from the kid's face. "You don't tell me shit! You ain't been around long enough to know shit."

The older players, the juniors and the seniors, turn away. They've seldom heard the coach use language like that. He doesn't accept it from them and he's never accepted it from himself either. "They talk like that on the streets to sound tough," he's always said before. "We're about being tough, not sounding tough."

The players have seen the coach angry before, angry with mistakes, angry with dumb plays, but this season, his anger has turned personal. "People tell me you'll punk out on us, son," he tells a player one afternoon. "They say you're just a punk."

"I ain't no punk, coach," the player mutters.

"We'll see about that," Shannon says. He's smiling when he says it, but he isn't joking.

He uses his big voice, his gifts of mimicry, to humiliate players. "Don't be dancing in there!" he screams at a running back who's failed to hit a hole hard enough to suit him. "Here's the way you're doing," he says, prancing across the field like a ballerina auditioning for "The Nutcracker." "You're too big to dance like that. If I want a dancer, I'll go get that little guy over there. You're big, but ain't nobody said you're tough. You got to be tough."

To another kid, a would-be running back, he yells: "Get on out of there. Don't be telling people you're a running back here. I don't want to be embarrassed. I don't want them to think we're that hard up."

To Kenvir Dixon, a junior quarterback and wide receiver, the last in a line of Dixon brothers who've played for the Flyers: "Why don't you stop masquerading as a football player, Dixon? All them Dixons we've had have been pretty good players. All but one. I'll let you figure out which one."

To Deondre Singleton, who makes the mistake not only of throwing a curl when his receiver runs a hook, but of laughing about it: "What kind of dumbass quarterback we got out here? That shit ain't funny, man."

His mood will rise and fall from day to day, but by mid-September, it hasn't risen much above gloomy. One day in week three of the season, he stands with his coaches after a particularly droopy practice and gazes across the practice field to the spanking new Clyde C. Jordan Stadium. "You know," he says. "It's kind of funny. We finally got us a stadium. We're finally getting some of the things we need around here. Things are looking a little better. And now this program seems to be on the downhill slide. Work all these years to make things better, and when we get there, we can't get the job done."

Things *have* been looking better. Shannon opened fall practice bright and early at 8:30 A.M. on August 19 with a surprisingly large turnout of forty-five players. He longs for the days when ninety to one hundred players would come out for football, but he's given up complaining about it. Too many kids have other priorities. In 1991, he figured, what with a national recession adding to the city's crushing poverty, with high drop-out rates, with the easy money to be made with crack cocaine, forty-five was a pretty good turnout.

Tom Holley's weight room has made a big difference. Incoming sophomores are eager to get access to the clean, high-tech workout facilities, even if the plumbing and showers still don't work and they have to go home sweaty. Shannon has received cash donations from some St. Louis businessmen, and he's spent more than five thousand dollars on new uniforms. The school district has paid its bill to equipment suppliers, so there are clean, refurbished helmets and pads. Last year's game uniforms have been turned into practice uniforms. Practice sessions don't look so much like a refugee camp anymore. A construction contractor named Ralph Korte has arranged for a bulldozer to grade the rutted practice field. Shannon has persuaded Eastside's horticulture club to adopt the growing of grass on the field as its class project for the year. Eastside's facilities still aren't much, but they are getting better.

Shannon has bought a new video camera to use for taping practice sessions. He still runs the offensive drills himself, but when the defense scrimmages against his scout team, he can climb the fire escape and tape practices himself.

That luxury is permitted because he again has a defensive coordinator he trusts. He's rehired Marion Stallings. The school superintendent was leery about it, but Shannon told her, "If a guy wants to come back, and he's done everything else to turn his life around, and you don't hire him, then you're not offering him any kind of hope at all."

Stallings has made his presence felt immediately. He is a

dominating presence, loud and fiery, a gifted coach and teacher. He explains and he demonstrates, he wheedles and exhorts. His deep voice carries a hundred yards, even when he is face-to-face mask with an offending player. He and Shannon play off one another, carrying on a continuing dialogue, trying to one-up each other:

Shannon: "Block him! Put your hands up and block him!"

Stallings: "Aww, you hurt your wrist? I thought you were tough. We're still looking for tough people. Hit with your shoulder and you won't get hurt!"

Shannon: "It's a tough game. We need tough people."

Stallings: "Ice it down and get ready."

Shannon: "We got lots of ice. What we ain't got is tough people."

Stallings: "How can you let that guy get by you like that?"

Shannon: "I saw his grades, coach. You'd understand if you'd seen his grades."

Stallings: "You think we don't see that? We see everything, man. We see it when you walk on the field. We see it when you're dogging it."

Shannon: "We see it when you play hurt, too. We can respect that."

Stallings: "That's right. Show me some courage, we can respect that. We can work with that."

Shannon: "Take a little talent, some courage, we can parlay that into something good."

Stallings: "We can take that right on down the yellow brick road."

The players aren't sure how to react to the Shannon-and-Stallings Show, but it cracks up the other coaches. Ken Goss, the offensive line coach, is Stallings's biggest fan. "Even if we didn't get better any other way, that loud-mouthed little guy out there is going to make a difference," he said one day at practice. "The man's got something to prove."

With Stallings around to lean on and with a large crop of experienced seniors and juniors returning, led by an all-metro quarterback, Shannon has started fall practice well ahead of where he was a year ago. As usual, the Flyers have been ranked in preseason polls as the top team in Illinois and one of the top teams in the country. Shannon's "summer camp" was well attended, and he's been pleased at the talent displayed by the new batch of sophomores.

"There's a reason for the way we do things around here," Shannon told the summer campers on the first day of drills. "People who don't line up the right way will get you beat. People who don't play hard will get you beat. People who make mental errors will get you beat. People who don't make big plays will get you beat. We will be fair with you, but we want it done the way we want it done. You ask the juniors and seniors, they'll tell you. We're here this summer looking for leaders, guys we can depend on."

He worked with them daily from the first week of June to the end of July, getting them into shape, coaching them on technique, running them into the new weight room. A V-shaped young man named Frank Spriggs, a former instructor at a health club, has volunteered as the Flyers' strength coach. Under Spriggs, the weight training got deadly serious.

"We're older, we're stronger, we're more experienced, we ought to be better," Shannon said. "The polls say we ought to be number one, but those polls don't know Chris Moore ain't a part of this anymore."

Shannon was hopeful that somewhere among the kids working out at summer camp, Moore's successor at tailback would appear. His plan was to try juniors David James and Darron Suggs in the backfield. Both were six feet tall and weighed 205 pounds, and each had excelled as sprinters on the track team. Neither had carried the football before; they were linemen and linebackers last year. The new backs were very raw, unable to read the blocking in front of them and make the correct cuts.

"You guys are reading those blocks like you're reading Chinese," he yelled at them one day early in the summer camp. "You're looking at it, but you don't understand it. We've had some great tailbacks around here. We got Marvin Lampkin who's playing at Iowa and Kerwin Price who's playing at Arkansas. You might be the next one, but you've got to be smart."

The "who's going to play tailback?" question dogged Shannon all summer. Each time it was asked, Shannon took it as a personal affront. "In our offense, with the kind of athletes we have, it won't make that much difference," he said. "We have to have a great quarterback, a great split end, and a great tailback. Or if two of those three are great, and the other guy is only good, we'll still get by. We've got a great quarterback. Dennis Stallings is a great tight end, but I can move him to split end and he'll be great there, too. We can get by without a great back like Chris because we've got good guys to replace him. Whoever I put there is going to get twelve hundred or thirteen hundred yards and score twenty-four to twenty-five touchdowns, because the defenses have to worry about the passing game."

At least that was the plan. But as summer camp wore on, Shannon began to have doubts. He would scowl, watching Singleton throw passes in the gym to would-be receivers who weren't catching the ball. It didn't look like a high-powered passing game at that point. Still he was confident in his system.

"You have to understand the system," Shannon said. "I've got all these guys coming to me, asking about Chris, like the whole system depended on one guy. I tell them, 'Hey, I replace good players every year. I replaced Rollie Nevilles with Deondre Singleton, and I replaced Kenny Dunn with Homer Bush. We're going to treat Chris like he just graduated, find somebody new.

"That's the thing," he said, clenching his teeth. "These so-called fans of ours, they think this thing, this program, just happens to work out because we've got good players. They think anybody can coach these guys. It's hard for them to believe that anyone around this town is doing a job he's qualified for, because so many of them aren't qualified. They say I'm lucky, because I've always got such good players."

One day in early August, Shannon pulled a rickety plastic chair to a spot in front of the open gym door, the better to catch a stray breeze or two while he watched the endless repetition of the passing drills. The conversation turned briefly to Judge Clarence Thomas, who had just been nominated to the United States Supreme Court. Shannon heartily approved of the nomination. Like himself, Thomas was a black man who'd been raised in poverty in the rural South. Like Shannon, Thomas was deeply conservative.

"I understand what he's saying, because it's similar to what I say," Shannon said. "He doesn't believe in giving people anything, because he believes in self-help. What bothers me is the way people like the NAACP are dumping on him. If he doesn't think the way they say he should think, then they dump on him. They say he doesn't believe in helping the poor, but maybe he believes in the poor helping themselves.

"Hey, it's just like this Chris Moore thing," Shannon said, turning the talk back to the subject he couldn't let go. "You have to determine what's important to you—and to me, discipline is the most important thing. You either pay the price or you pay the consequences. You don't lower your standards to benefit one person. You keep them high to benefit the whole group. It's one guy against sixty. People come to me and say, 'You could lower your standards this one time,' and I say, 'Yeah, I could. But it'd be something new for me, and I don't like to change.'"

As word spread that Moore had been kicked off the team, Shannon began getting more and more pressure to reinstate him. One by one, various emissaries began showing up to plead Moore's case. Singleton led a group of seniors who asked that he reconsider Moore's case. "They said I should give Chris another chance," Shannon said. "I asked them, 'Where were you last February and March when I was trying to get him to do his work?' They said Chris didn't believe I would do what I said. I said, 'Well, if I take him back, that'd mean he was right.'"

He refused their plea, just as he refused pleas from team

boosters, from teachers, and from some of his assistant coaches. "They're telling me we might be passing up a chance to win a national championship," he said. "I figure we might want to win a few more down the road, and the way we do that is to run this program the right way."

But the pressure continued. The emissaries kept coming. Each would approach Shannon, tell him how well the team was shaping up, ask whom he planned to use at tailback, and then plead Moore's case. Shannon was certain the source of the pressure was Sam Morgan, Moore's biggest backer. "It's him that's been sending these guys to see me," he said. "He doesn't have the nerve to do it himself."

By early August, ten days before fall practice began, Shannon decided he'd had enough. "It's come down to the point where I may either have to take Chris back or resign," Shannon said. "And I will *never* take him back. Chris has been telling people all along that Morgan would fix it for him, and sure enough, he's trying to do just that."

Shannon spoke bitterly that evening. People he'd trusted, including some of his own coaches, were carrying messages for Sam Morgan instead of standing up for the program he had labored sixteen years to build. "I've tried to create a situation for Chris where he can maximize what he is about," Shannon said. "But now everyone is concerned about what we're going to do without him. There are guys who are trying to dictate what I do who have never put a damned thing into this program.

"I figure I work for free around here, considering the time I put into this," he said. "And now I have these guys jerking me around like this. There's a way to do it, and there's a way to do it wrong. I enjoy it, but not if I do it wrong.

"You've heard me. You've heard me talk about academic integrity and what kind of guy a kid is. Hell, academic integrity doesn't seem to mean a damned thing to these people. This thing is all backwards. *Sam* should be telling *me* not to play guys like this!"

Shannon was told that Morgan had adopted Moore as one of his "projects." Sam Morgan annually identifies two or three kids he sees as having great potential, but who need special help to stay in school. Morgan believes that students need to stay in school no matter what, that sooner or later lightning may strike and turn their lives around. If athletics is the only thing keeping a student in school, Morgan believes, then by all means athletics should be emphasized.

"That's not what I'm about," Shannon said. "I'm determined not to let Chris back. If I have to resign, that's the way it is."

Shannon decided, finally, to confront Morgan directly. He did so the next day. Principle met principal, and Sam Morgan backed down. "Whatever you want to do, coach," Morgan had said.

Shannon was grimly pleased. "That's the end of that story," he said. He was wrong about that.

On the afternoon of Wednesday, August 14, as Shannon and James Rucker were preparing equipment for the start of practice the following Monday, Chris Moore's father came by to see the coach. Lawrence Moore, Sr., was apologetic. He was also desperate. His son had come to see Shannon two days earlier to beg for reinstatement. Shannon had sent him home.

But Lawrence Moore explained that his son was out of options. He had tried to transfer to Belleville West and to Althoff, the Catholic high school in Belleville. Both schools had told him they weren't interested. Chris had then approached the coaches at Lincoln who'd wooed him the year before. Like jilted lovers, they'd told him they didn't want him anymore.

Lawrence Moore said he was afraid that if his son couldn't play football, he would probably drop out of school. Lawrence Moore said Chris was shattered, that he had been moping around the house for days. Lawrence Moore said he would back Shannon in whatever the coach wanted to do, but asked him if there was any way Chris could earn another chance.

"I've talked to everyone in that family, but the old man was the first one ever made any sense," Shannon said. And then he did something he doesn't like to do: he compromised.

Chris would serve a four-game suspension, meaning he wouldn't be eligible to play until October. In the meantime, he would work out with the team and concentrate on his grades. If his work habits and grades were good enough, and if Shannon got approval from his teachers, then Chris would get his uniform. "I hate to do it," Shannon said. "But if he don't have this, he don't have nothing. I have my doubts if he'll do everything I've told him to do, but he has nowhere else to go. We'll see what happens."

What happens is the team doesn't play very well. The offense Shannon has been designing for six months sputters. The players he'd been counting on, the ones who fill the slots in the depth charts he fiddles with constantly, don't perform the way he's envisioned. He finds himself moving players in and out of positions, tinkering with his offense every day, trying to find combinations that work. His biggest disappointment is Deondre Singleton. For six months, Shannon has been designing a complicated passing offense that would take advantage of not only Singleton's strong arm, but his experience. At long last, Shannon has a senior quarterback with size—Singleton has filled out to six feet, three inches tall, 191 pounds—and the ability to throw every pass in Shannon's playbook. Shannon has even talked about teaching Singleton to call "audibles," letting him recognize defenses at the line of scrimmage and change plays on the spot. Shannon prides himself in coaching quarterbacks, and in Deondre Singleton, the master teacher would have a master student.

But as the long days of three-a-day practices draw to a close, it's apparent that something is missing. Singleton has put in long hours in the gym over the spring and summer, but with the graduation of his friend and workout partner, Homer Bush, he hasn't been quite so diligent as he was last year. Shannon has watched him closely and thinks he's detected a change in his throwing motion. Gone is the easy straight overhand flick of the wrist, replaced by a labored three-quarters overhand motion. "He hurt his arm playing baseball," Shannon muttered. "He don't want to tell anybody, but I know. He was the only pitcher we had who was any good, and he threw too much."

Singleton is nursing his arm, confident there is no one who could beat him out of his quarterbacking job. Stick Eubanks has graduated and juniors Ben Williams and Kenvir Dixon are no threat. Singleton has found he likes the attention that an All-American quarterback prospect receives and spends a lot of time reveling in being a star. And, too, there seems to be some lingering effects from his knee injury.

"He's afraid he's going to get hurt again," Shannon said one afternoon, watching Singleton flinch in the face of a pass rush. "He doesn't have the confidence in these new receivers that he had in Homer. He knew if he threw it, Homer would catch it. With these new guys, he knows he has to put it on their numbers or they'll drop it."

For sure, none of the players Shannon has envisioned as Bush's replacement as the "go-to" receiver is working out. Frank Spraggins, Richard Jenkins, Roderick Fisher, and a flock of sophomores are tried and found wanting. They have speed to burn, but they can't hold onto the ball, at least not consistently. Shannon briefly toys with the notion of moving Dennis Stallings, an All-American candidate at tight end, out to split end, but Stallings prefers to play tight end. "I have to let him play there if that's where he wants to play," Shannon said. "He might have a future at tight end in college, with his size and speed, and I want to give him the best chance possible to play at the next level."

Not only is the passing game beginning to look suspect, but the running game—at least until Chris Moore's return—looks shaky, too. Neither David James or Darron Suggs looks like the answer at running back. They look great at linebacker, but on offense, they play like linebackers, too, dropping their heads and running into people instead of running away from them. To make things worse, the offensive line isn't shaping up very well. The defense, under the lash administered by Marion Stallings, is coming along well, but still Shannon is unhappy; he planned all winter for an offensive juggernaut, and the Flyers can't even move the ball in practice.

Compounding his problems is the fact that Eastside finally has managed to arrange a tough nonconference schedule to open the season. "Seems like every year we can't find anyone to play us who's any good," Shannon said. "This year, when we could use a few easy games, we open with three nasty ones."

The Flyers will open on the road with Larry Walls and the Sumner Bulldogs, who are returning most of the players who won the Missouri 4-A championship last year. The Flyers will then come home to open the new Clyde Jordan Stadium with the Muskogee Roughers, who gave them such a scare in Oklahoma in 1990. And then they travel to the Missouri capital to play the Jefferson City High School Jays. Jeff City is to high school football in Missouri what Eastside is to Illinois. The two power-houses have never played before. In Jefferson City, they're already printing T-shirts that read, "Flyers vs. Jays, the War to End All Wars."

"We could very easily be 0–3 by the time the conference schedule starts," Shannon said one rainy afternoon the week before the Sumner game. "Everybody is talking about Jeff City, but Sumner could beat us, and so could Muskogee. Both of them have got most of their players back from last year. Of course, we do, too, but ours aren't playing very well."

He stood in the doorway to the gym and looked outside, where the weather matched his mood. It was dark and gloomy, with thunder rumbling and lightning flashing in the distance. Shannon doesn't mind practicing in the rain, but he won't send the players outside when lightning threatens. He ordered the players to dress for practice and then to assemble on the bleachers in the gym. He rolled a TV set and a VCR out of his office, set it up on the gym floor, and then discovered the nearest electrical outlet wasn't working. "It's always something around here," he muttered.

Assistant coach Terry Hill scrambled to find a long extension cord, then climbed a flight of stairs, negotiated a balcony railing, unlocked a door, and finally found a working outlet. Shannon then showed the Flyers a tape of their previous day's practice session. Then he showed them a tape of a television interview a St. Louis sportscaster had done with a running back at Sumner. The Sumner back boasted that his goal for the year was to gain two thousand yards.

"How's he going to do that when he has to play us?" Marion Stallings screamed. "That's an insult. He's going to have to get two hundred yards a game to make two thousand, and he ain't going to get fifty against us!"

The players were outraged, just as Shannon and Stallings had planned. Outside the thunderstorm had moved on. "Put your helmets on, fellas," Shannon said. "Let's go to work."

There would be one more interruption this day, this one political, not meteorological. Shannon had invited the new mayor, Gordon Bush, to drop by to talk to the players. It was the first time in his career he'd ever invited a politician to his field. Gordon Bush, a member of the class of 1960, was the first

Eastside graduate ever to be mayor of the city, and Shannon approved of some of the steps he had taken since taking over at City Hall in May. Shannon had ordered a blue-and-orange Eastside coach's jacket with "Mayor Bush" embroidered on it, and he planned to present it to the mayor at halftime of the opening game at the new stadium. It would be a shot across the bows of the Lincoln fans—a new stadium located in Eastside's backyard, and a new mayor who didn't play games the way the old one had.

"We've got a new attitude around town, and it's the most hopeful people have been around here in a long time," Shannon explained as he introduced the mayor to the Flyers. "We want you to know we appreciate what you're doing."

Bush, a big, graceful man who usually wears an embarrassed smile, beamed in gratitude.

"We not only have the greatest football team in the country," the mayor told the Flyers. "We have some of the greatest young people, people who are as good as anyone in the world. You need to hear that."

Standing on the muddy field, light drizzle pooling on the brim of his trademark Panama hat, Gordon Bush gave the Flyers the same kind of speech that Shannon gives them. He spoke for only a few minutes, but not a player moved a muscle during his remarks. He concluded by saying:

"We believe that a miracle can happen in East St. Louis. We have people here who believe if they hang in there long enough, pay their dues, work hard, this can be a great city again. We can do anything we set our minds to doing. We can be the greatest football team in America. The greatest bricklayers. The greatest police officers. The greatest mechanics. Whatever we want to be, we can be the best. You have proven you can be the best football team in America. You have made us known, everybody in America knows about this football team. You are what we are about, and what we are about is making this a great place to live.''

The speech Gordon Bush gave the Flyers was, with only slight alterations, the same speech he'd given all over town the previous winter when he was running against Carl Officer. It was a political speech, full of platitudes and verities, but Bush believed every word. At forty-eight, he was a lifelong resident of East St. Louis, but he'd served a hitch in the army and still held a commission as a major in the Army Reserve. He believed in being a good soldier, obeying orders, following procedures. He didn't believe in making waves for the sake of making waves. He'd gotten a master's degree in urban planning and held public-sector jobs for twenty years. He'd been a good soldier for the St. Clair County Democratic Committee. Affable, cooperative, and slow to anger, he firmly believed that goodwill and hard work could make miracles happen.

It was only when he got to City Hall that he began to have some serious doubts. He got there two weeks late—Mayor Officer refused to leave office until the last possible minute. Officer had stayed in character by making time-consuming demands for severance pay and leftover vacation pay. Bush's inauguration day was pushed back, but finally Bush was sworn in. The next day the large color portrait of Carl Officer that had dominated the rotunda at City Hall for twelve years was removed. Officer renewed his mortician's license and went back to running his family's funeral business. For better or worse, East St. Louis was Gordon Bush's problem for the next four years.

Bush, who had won election in part by pointing out all the problems the city had, discovered he didn't know the half of it. Had someone called to offer to pay off the city's $40 million debt, the odds were that no one around City Hall would have bothered to answer the phone. Calls went unanswered; when they were answered, messages weren't passed on. Meetings were set up and then canceled without notice.

Bush decided that his first step was to rebuild City Hall's credibility. He fired the people who'd been Officer's department heads, including the chief of police. He eliminated half of the police department's administrative staff and put more cops back into patrol cars. He got the cars to put them in by making a deal with the state and federal government to fund a special antidrug task force.

Working with Bob Shannon and the other members of the community fund board appointed to spend the $7 million in Matthews & Wright fine money, Bush got the 911 emergency dialing system out of hock. The community fund made plans to begin cleaning up trash dumped all over the city. The first estimate for a citywide trash clean-up came to $7.5 million.

Bush submitted to the budget demands of the state-appointed oversight committee so that the city could qualify for the bailout funds the legislature had promised. He vowed that the first $3.5 million of state money would go to meet the city payroll. Assured of getting their paychecks on time, city workers began showing up for work on time.

To prove to the St. Louis business community that East St. Louis was again a place it could do business, Bush hired a man named H. C. Milford as his economic development director. Milford, a former insurance executive, lived across the river in an affluent St. Louis suburb. He had been chief executive officer of St. Louis County before losing a race for reelection the previous November. He was a white Republican in a black Democratic city, but he gave Bush the credibility he was seeking, at least in the business community.

It was a different story with some black politicians. They complained that Bush was turning power in the city over to "outsiders"—white developers and bankers who would not have the city's interests at heart. Black politicians complained that by putting Milford in charge of economic development and by submitting the city's budget for approval by the white-dominated state fiscal oversight committee, Bush was selling the city out.

Even as Bush and Milford hustled from meeting to meeting, trying to lure investment into the community, the entrenched political interests let it be known they weren't going to give up easily. The board of aldermen began voting down Bush's initiatives, demanding old-fashioned political tribute in the way of jobs and favors. The year before, in an attempt to curb Mayor Officer's power, city voters had passed a measure calling for a city manager form of government. In the face of the changes Bush was calling for, the aldermen decided to appoint a city manager to curb Bush instead. "It was like a bullet they'd meant to shoot at

Carl, but they're shooting it at Bush instead," one city cop explained.

By early September, when he came to Shannon's practice field to address the Flyers, Bush had been in office about one hundred days. He'd started with a bang and a flourish, but the problems of the city were too massive for bangs and flourishes. And for all of Bush's optimism, many things were clearly getting worse.

State Community College, the two-year junior college program that represented the best hope for higher education for many of the city's high school graduates, was threatened with a loss of its accreditation. Without accreditation by a national education association, the federal government would withdraw loans from the college's twelve hundred students.

The city's murder rate climbed at a record pace all summer long. The national rate was 9.4 homicides for every 100,000 in population; in East St. Louis in the summer of 1991, the rate was 117 per 100,000, nearly thirteen times the national rate. Across the river in St. Louis, where 1991 saw a record number of homicides, the rate was 50 homicides per 100,000.

The Flyers had come close to losing a player to the violence. In June, senior Roderick Fisher had been earning spending money by umpiring youth-league baseball games. When he made a call that enraged the coach of one of the teams, the coach had left the field and returned with a pistol, blasting away at Fisher in the midst of the players and fans. Fisher ran for his life and narrowly escaped. The players and fans dived for cover; no one was hurt. The coach was later convicted of assault to commit homicide, and Fisher found himself a celebrity; he also made the *New York Times*.

The new mayor had little success finding anyone to build and operate a casino gambling boat on the city's riverfront—at least not anyone the state gaming board would approve. A few miles upriver, the city of Alton already had found a developer and launched a gambling boat of its own. Just downriver from East St. Louis, the community of Sauget—a town best known for its topless nightclubs—was seeking a license for its gambling boat. Bush spent a lot of time before the gaming board, arguing that competitors already were squeezing his city out of the gambling market. Without casino boat gambling, the city would have no hope of paying off the bailout loans granted by the state.

The city already had drawn $1 million from the state loan pool to meet its operating budget, but the oversight committee in charge of the loan program wasn't happy with the city's management of the fund. The committee wanted a balanced budget, but Bush and the aldermen couldn't agree on where cuts would be made. Bush wanted to eliminate jobs. The aldermen, all of whom had constituents to protect, refused to go along. Instead they proposed a more creative solution: saving the $2.3 million spent on the police department each year by having the department become self-sustaining. East St. Louis would become a municipal speed trap. Cops would spend their days writing traffic tickets on the interstate highways that cut through the city. The cops pointed out that they didn't have the manpower to write that many tickets, unless they ignored everything else that went on in town, which they didn't think was a good idea.

Bush wanted to hire a professional city manager who could satisfy the state oversight committee by preparing a city budget with such niceties as accurate revenue projections. The aldermen were satisfied with their own city manager. The mayor and the aldermen feuded all fall before finally adopting a city budget that conformed to the state oversight committee's ideas of prudent management. The budget meant the layoff of fifty more city employees, but at least it kept the state bailout money flowing.

Privately, however, Bush and some of his advisers were beginning to wonder how long the wolf could be kept from the door. The city was so far in debt, and was so attuned to playing patronage politics with the money it did manage to raise, and was so far from any solution to finding new sources of revenue, that even an optimist like Gordon Bush was close to despair. It had taken him less than six months, but he was close to throwing up his hands.

For the record, though, the mayor was undaunted. "You can't be discouraged," he said. "You take small steps. The struggle continues."

Bob Shannon liked that attitude, but he was profoundly skeptical of Bush's chances of success. The mayor's situation sounded too much like his own, and the mayor couldn't build a bubble around City Hall the way Shannon had around his football team.

"I like to be hopeful," he said, "but most of those guys he's dealing with are right off the streets, man. I'm afraid the mayor might not be able to deal with them. Everybody who has something to lose is going to gang up on him. They play by the rules of the jungle—the biggest paws, the strongest jaws, and the sharpest claws. It's them that survive."

The Flyers open the 1991 season by beating the Sumner Bulldogs 26–0 on a broiling hot Saturday afternoon in midtown St. Louis. Stallings's defense had looked strong. Shannon's offense had looked pathetic. The defense held Sumner to a total of 190 yards in offense, but Eastside's offense managed only 105 yards, about a fourth of what it averaged a year ago. Singleton completed only five of seventeen passes, constantly flinching in the face of the Sumner pass rush. Chris Moore watched the game from the sidelines, dressed in jeans and a brand new Flyers jersey, standing apart from his teammates.

"The good news is we won a game with defense," Shannon said. "We couldn't do that last year. Of course, last year we had an offense. We couldn't have looked much worse."

He was wrong about that. The Flyers hit bottom in their next game, the long-awaited opener at their new stadium against the Muskogee Roughers. It was to have been a joyous celebration— the first game at Jordan Stadium and the first Friday night game played in East St. Louis in many years. The new stadium has bright lights, fenced-in parking, and is located in a part of East St. Louis that isn't quite so foreboding as the bombed-out environs of Parsons Field. The hope was that East St. Louis could be like the rest of America, where high school football on Friday night is cause for a community celebration.

A huge crowd turns out, standing in long lines for tickets, checking out the fancy brickwork and wrought-iron fencing around what was the first new building built in town in a decade. The evening has the feel of a giant party, and Shannon has dressed the players to kill in bright orange pants and jerseys. *USA Today* has ranked them number one in the country. They finally have uniforms, a stadium, and a crowd worthy of all they've achieved.

It's too much for them. They jog over to the field from the high school, looking around as if they've landed on another planet. They're confused and lackluster in pregame drills. "They're like zombies," Marion Stallings says. "They're not handling all this too well."

He and Shannon try to fire them up in the tiny little locker room under the grandstand, but they are too quiet and too fidgety. Suddenly Stallings begins screaming: "Did you look across at the other side of the field and see all those signs and banners those Oklahoma people brought? You see all that green paint, those signs saying 'Muskogee' and all those green flags? They've done turned our new stadium green!"

He rants and raves about the sheer effrontery of it all. The players begin to yell back. "Yeah! Why'd they do that?"

"How'd they come in here, taking over our new stadium?" Stallings screams, waving his arms and throwing his cap onto the floor. "Trying to take what's ours, that's what they're doing! Hell, we've done worked too hard for them to do that to us. We've got to kick their butts all the way back to Oklahoma!"

The players stand up, yelling and screaming, pounding each other on their shoulder pads, banging helmets against lockers. "Kick 'em out of here," they scream, storming out of the locker room and onto the field.

Shannon smiles as he watches them go. Stallings turns and winks. "Maybe that'll work," he says.

It doesn't. Muskogee is tough and well drilled. The Flyers

make critical mistakes. All of Shannon's endless repetitions, all of his ceaseless preaching about playing smart and avoiding mental errors go down the drain. Eastside is overwhelmed. The defense plays well, but not well enough to overcome the offense's mistakes. Singleton completes only five of twenty passes. He is sacked four times. He fumbles at the one-yard line. The Flyers take penalties for silly mistakes like having too many men on the field. The night has been planned to celebrate the new spirit of East St. Louis. It turns out to be another dose of bad news. Shannon is so angry he forgets about the halftime ceremony he's planned to present Mayor Bush with his new Flyers jacket.

As the clock ticks down, Shannon takes out his frustration on his quarterback. "We got no offense at all," he tells Singleton as he comes off the field. "I'm embarrassed for you, son. If there were any scouts here, thinking you were a big-time quarterback they might want to recruit, they're thinking different now. This is the game they'll remember. This is the kind of competition where you've got to excel."

Then he smiles at Singleton, who has said nothing at all. "But it's all right," the coach says. "If I've got to lose, this is the way I want it to happen. Maybe this will be your wake-up call. Maybe you'll go to work now and stop thinking how great you are. You're making junior high school mistakes."

Singleton sits down on the bench, putting his head in his hands. Shannon turns to the field and looks at the scoreboard that says Muskogee 22, Flyers 0, and the clock that is ticking relentlessly toward zero. "This is a nightmare," he says. "This is Friday the 13th, and this is a nightmare, and I don't mean on Elm Street."

This is Eastside's first regular-season loss since 1986, the first time they've been shut out since 1982. The big crowd files out of the stadium, grumbling. Shannon walks across the field to shake the hands of the Muskogee coach and players. He returns to his bench philosophical.

"We don't have a corner on success," he says. "Maybe some of our guys need to learn that. If we go away from here learning that, it won't be a bad lesson. We've been thinking we can come out and play bad and still win. But hey, it's still just a game. You can't get too upset; you have to remember it's a game and these are just kids. The sun's going to rise tomorrow."

The sun does rise, and shortly after that Shannon has the Flyers back on the practice field. He didn't sleep much. "My wife was in bed pretending to be asleep when I got home," he says with a smile. "I knew she was awake, but she didn't want any part of me."

He had tossed and turned, replaying the game in his mind, second-guessing himself. "I kept wondering, maybe there's something wrong with the system," he said. "Maybe there is something we should be doing that we ain't. But then I thought, hell, this system has been working for twenty years. We've been running this system, these plays, and they've been working. This is the same offense that scored forty-five points a game last year, so it ain't the system.

"We're just going to simplify the game and ask these guys to do a little more than they've been doing. We're going to move a few guys around, but we're going to stick with the system."

An Eastside alumnus named Derrick Johnson, who played for Shannon's 1979 state champion team and remains one of his biggest supporters, drops by the field. "I want you all to know," he tells the coaches, "that where I was sitting last night, there was a bunch of guys who decided that y'all have to go. All them coaches up there in the stands was calling for your heads. They say you're a fool for not playing Chris Moore."

"Yeah, I can understand why they'd want to get rid of us," Shannon says. "This program has been a doormat for a long time."

But he's been wondering about Chris Moore himself. He spent some time last week checking with Moore's teachers to see if Chris has been coming to class and getting his work done. The teachers passed him with flying colors. Shannon pulls a grade report sheet out of his pocket that shows Chris has three A's and two B's. One of the A's is in psychology. "The psychology part ain't no surprise," Shannon says.

Even before the Muskogee game, Shannon decided he'd seen enough. He told his assistant coaches that win or lose, he was going to reinstate Chris Moore in time for the Jeff City game. "In the old days, that never would have happened," Marion Stallings said. "Back then we didn't cut any slack. He would have been gone, period. And we would have replaced him with somebody just as good. Nowadays we don't have the kind of depth we had then."

The loss to Muskogee underscored that. Shannon wanted this team to be King Kong walking down the street. But King Kong doesn't get shut out. He doesn't like to admit it, but he's been wrong. His quarterback can't throw, his line can't block, his running backs can't move the ball on the ground. He needs a big-time running back to make the most of whatever holes the line opens up, to take the pressure off the passing game.

Shannon figures he's proved his point; his principles not only have gotten him beat, they've gotten him shut out. They've lost him a shot at the national championship. When the bruised and battered Flyers gather for practice the morning after the Musko-gee loss, he tells Chris Moore to put his helmet on.

"Yeah, it makes me mad, but this whole situation makes me mad," Shannon says. He frowns, watching Moore run agility drills, hopping back and forth over tackling dummies. Compared with the other backs in the drill, Moore is a man among boys. His steps are sure, his reflexes sharp, his motions fluid. He demands extra repetitions on all the drills, then walks over to the water coolers. He pours a cup of water over his head, towels himself off, and then walks over to Shannon.

"Can I have the key to the weight room, coach?" he asks.

"What for?"

"Do some lifting. Work on my legs."

"Last winter would have been a good time to lift. It's a little late now. Just go on back out there and watch the defense for a while."

Moore walks away, and Shannon scowls again. "Yeah, I'm pretty angry. Things have changed too doggone much around here and they ain't for the better. It's like if one of those old southern sheriffs from the 1940s came back in a time machine and landed in the 1990s. He'd see all those sophisticated criminals we got now and say, 'Whoa, I don't know if I want to deal with this situation anymore.' We got a lot of work to do, and I ain't even sure if I want to deal with it anymore.''

CHAPTER

9

"There's good stress and there's bad stress," Bob Shannon is saying. "We all know what bad stress is, but what about a guy walking through the jungle and sees a snake? A big ol' cobra? He jumps back out of the way and that ol' snake goes on his way. That's good stress, right? Makes him protect himself. The trick is, you got to know the difference between good stress and bad."

He is sitting behind a desk in a classroom, teaching a 1:30 sophomore health class. This is bad stress. He likes to have his 1:30 period free so he can go over his plans for afternoon football practice. Spending fifty precious minutes telling a group of bored fifteen-year-olds what they could read out of their books, assuming they bothered to read their books, is not his idea of a productive use of time. Bad stress comes from administrators who won't adjust his schedule, or his players' schedules either. Shannon would like to get his hands on his players at 2:30, but some of them are in class then instead of being out on the football field where he could subject them to some good stress.

Shannon teaches this 1:30 class perfunctorily, reading questions from a book, preparing the class for a test. He sits at a desk
in front of the room, long legs stretched out, fingers drumming
the pages of the book. He speaks slowly and loudly, trying to
make it uncomfortable for the kids who are dozing in the back of
the room. He throws in asides from time to time, little homilies
about teenage problems. "Everybody's got problems, right?" he
says. "You got to have somebody to talk to, your mamas or your
grandmas. Or your friends. Maybe your teachers. Don't come to
me, though. I ain't got time right now."

The kids sit up at that, and Shannon grins. "Nah, you can talk
to me. I'm just kidding."

No he isn't. This is Tuesday, September 24. Four days ago his
attitude about his football team underwent a 180-degree turn. The
Muskogee game had filled him with bad stress. The Jefferson
City game on Friday night changed all that. Suddenly he saw
possibilities that had escaped him before. All he has to do now is
spend twenty-four hours a day developing those possibilities. The
Flyers had gone into the jungle, seen the cobra, and chopped its
head off.

Jefferson City is a very tough place to win a high school
football game. The governor of Missouri may be the most
powerful man in the state, but in the little capital where high
school football is the only game in town, the governor has to ask
Pete Adkins for tickets. Adkins has been head coach of the Jeff
City Jays since 1958, and his rule is absolute. The Jays have
dominated high school football during his reign, capturing seven
state titles and winning 87 percent of all their games, including

seventy-one in a row at one point. He has eleven paid assistant coaches, two team doctors, and total control of the school district's athletic program. His school belongs to no conference. Adkins plays whom he wants, when he wants.

"Ol' Pete," Shannon said of him in the days before the game. "I wish I had a deal like he does. We've been trying to schedule him for years. I wonder why he finally agreed. He must think he's got a hell of a team this year. I saw him in the stands when we played Sumner. He must be licking his chops."

The one positive thing about losing to Muskogee is that it got the players' attention. They've been harangued all over town for their loss. Across town, the Lincoln Tigers have rolled to two big victories. "Those Lincoln guys been giving them fits," Shannon said. "I think they know what they're up against. It's hard to hold your head up in this town when you lose."

Practices are long and grueling, with Marion Stallings screaming and pushing and prodding his defense. Adkins's teams rely on the wishbone offense, very similar to the veer offense that Downers Grove used to befuddle the Flyers last year. Stallings, however, understands option offenses and how to defense them. He walks through every player's assignment, explaining, teaching, and at times putting his head down and making tackles by himself. By the end of the week, he is battered and bruised and so hoarse he can barely talk. But his defense is prepared.

"I think we're ready to play," Stallings says in the Flyers' locker room right before kickoff. "I think y'all are relaxed. I think y'all are confident. Don't see any of this nervous shit I saw last week."

"I think they understand why last week happened, coach," Shannon says. "I think they're ready to rectify the situation."

Outside in the cool, perfect fall evening, Jeff City's pretty little stadium is filled to overflowing. Vendors are hawking—with Adkins's authorization, of course—"Flyers vs. Jays" T-shirts. Latecomers are jamming their way onto the cinder track that runs around the football field. The Jeff City band, 160 strong, is filling the place with noise. Politicians are working the crowd. It is *the* place to be.

But inside the Flyers' locker room, Stallings is screaming. "Yeah, they're excited out there. But what they fail to realize is this is a game *we* want to play. It ain't just them and their fans. This is *our* game."

"This is like the old days, fellas," Shannon says. "This is big-time football. This is what Eastside football is all about. I want to see a trip down memory lane tonight, like that old song says, 'The Way We Were.'"

The players' faces look blank. Not a Barbra Streisand fan on the entire team.

"Well, maybe you don't know the song," Shannon says with a smile. "But I've got to tell you, the biggest thrill in football is to play on the road in front of a big and hostile crowd and take them right out of the game."

It takes a while, but that's just what happens. The Jays and the Flyers slug it out in a scoreless first quarter, and each team scores a touchdown in the second quarter. Stallings's defense bottles up Jeff City's wishbone running game, but the Jays get a touchdown through the air. The Flyers answer with a seventy-six-yard drive that features Chris Moore right and Chris Moore left and a great diving catch by Dennis Stallings.

The game turns late in the third quarter. Trying desperately to boost Singleton's confidence, Shannon calls the 95 pass play, the short sideline route, five times in a row. Singleton starts completing passes. On the fifth completion, Frank Spraggins slips a tackle and goes fifty yards before being knocked out of bounds at the Jeff City eleven-yard line. First and ten at the eleven. The big crowd begins to quiet down. But then the Jays sack Singleton twice, and the Flyers are whistled for a five-yard penalty. The Flyers have gone nineteen yards in reverse and face fourth down and twenty-nine yards to go at the Jeff City thirty. The crowd is back into it, louder than before.

"Pro-right basic, 81 switch," Shannon tells Spraggins on the sideline, and the split end trots in with the play. The split end and the flanker go deep and to the sidelines. The tight end runs a crossing pattern, and the tailback crosses in back of the tight end and runs right up the middle. Four men deep in the pattern means someone is left uncovered. The quarterback has to find him.

Singleton drops back and looks for Stallings, but the big tight end has drawn both safeties. Out of the corner of his eye he sees Moore open at the goal line. Singleton gooses the ball up the middle, an ugly floating pass that Moore circles under like a centerfielder waiting for a fly ball. He catches it at his waist and falls backward into the end zone. On fourth and twenty-nine, Singleton has thrown a thirty-yard touchdown pass.

You can almost hear the air whoosh out of the stadium. Whatever is left is sucked out on the Flyers' next possession.

Moore goes off tackle behind a devastating block by Stallings, cuts outside, sidesteps three tacklers and takes the ball seventy-seven yards for his third touchdown of the game. The Flyers' defense pounds Jeff City in the fourth quarter, and Eastside adds a fourth touchdown in the last minute of the game to make the final score 27–7.

"We grew up a little bit tonight," Shannon says after crossing the field to shake Pete Adkins's hand. "We needed this. This is as big a win as we've ever had. We proved some things to a lot of people. Hey, we proved some things to me."

Chris Moore, fifteen pounds overweight and aching in every muscle of his body, carried the ball eighteen times for 183 yards. His redemption has begun.

The Flyers' football season, like Caesar's Gaul, is divided into three parts: the nonconference schedule, which can be tough; the conference schedule, which is a cakewalk; and the playoffs, which is the purpose of the first two parts. With Jefferson City behind them, the Flyers get to the cakewalk with a 2–1 record. They lost their number one ranking in *USA Today*'s national poll, but the state championship is always the first goal.

"We've got to use these next six weeks to get ready for the playoffs," Shannon says. "I don't know what kind of a team we are. Are we the team that played Muskogee, or are we the team that played Jeff City?"

He is making some serious adjustments as the Flyers prepare to open the Southwestern Conference schedule with Belleville West.

David James, who opened the season at tailback, is moved to offensive guard. "David can be a dominating player," Shannon says. "And if we're going to depend on Chris Moore as much as we do, we're going to have to have someone in there who can open some holes. David James is going to be the next big-time player this program produces."

James is the complete package, six feet tall, 205 pounds, built like a Mr. America candidate, capable of running forty yards with sprinter's speed. He is a quiet, serious-minded kid, a straight-A student who is intent on winning a scholarship to the University of Illinois. He was a starting linebacker as a sophomore and is developing into an All-American linebacker as a junior. He likes the idea of carrying the ball, but is smart enough to look at the films of the Sumner game and realize he has no knack for it. When Shannon asks him to move to offensive guard, James quietly turns in jersey number 42 and asks for an offensive lineman's number. Rucker gives him 56, and David James begins studying offensive guard blocking patterns.

He becomes a force right away, tearing big holes in Belleville West's defense. The Flyers demolish the Maroons, scoring three first-quarter touchdowns and eight overall in a 53–7 rout. Chris Moore has four of those touchdowns, including a fifty-two-yard punt return and an eighty-five-yard run from scrimmage. He showboats on the punt return, prancing into the end zone with his finger held up to signal "Number One." Shannon climbs all over him when he gets back to bench.

"Where's ol' Pot Belly Chris?" the coach demands. "What'd you do that for? That guy almost caught you! That guy almost caught you! You ain't in good enough shape to do that, not for me anyhows."

Chris scowls and walks off to the water cooler. He gets a drink and then walks to the far end of the bench, out of Shannon's sight but in full view of the grandstands at Clyde Jordan Stadium. People are cheering for him and waving to him. He disdains them, a haughty look on his face. But he stands alone so they can drink him in. He has six touchdowns in two games. The Flyers are back in business.

Reporters keep bringing his name up after the game, and Shannon keeps trying to change the subject. He talks about David James's play at guard and about the ferocity of Marion Stallings's defense. But Chris has become the focus of the team. Shannon resents it, but he acknowledges it. "He adds a different dimension," he admits.

It worries Shannon to have to depend on Chris Moore, a kid he's tried to dump before and might have to again. "With him, you never know," he says. "We've got to get our passing game going so we don't have to depend on him to carry the whole load."

Singleton threw two touchdown passes against Belleville West, but neither was a thing of beauty. His timing was awful, he was missing open receivers, he was flinching in the face of the rush. Shannon decides to give him a security blanket. Homer Bush used to be his best friend, but Homer is gone. Now his best friend is Dennis Stallings. Maybe if Shannon moves Stallings from tight end to split end, where Homer has played, Singleton will find his confidence again.

It works well against the Granite City Warriors the next Friday evening. Stallings catches six passes, including two for touchdowns. The trouble is, he is the only receiver Singleton looks for. And at split end, he isn't available to block on running plays, so the ground game suffers. Moore has 118 yards on 26 carries, but 44 of them come on one touchdown run. The rest of the time he is averaging only 3 yards a pop. The Flyers win the game, 31–19, but Shannon is not happy.

"Dennis is going to have to go back to tight end," he says. "It's better for us that way, and better for him, too. He's got a chance to play at the next level, but not at split end. He'll play linebacker or tight end in college, so we have to get him ready. We're doing a kid wrong if we play him out of position just so we can win a few games."

Back to tight end he goes the next Saturday when the Flyers travel to Belleville East. Shannon is determined he'll find a split end somewhere else—Rod Fisher or Richard Jenkins or someone else. He is an equal opportunity employer, but none of his job-seekers can catch a pass. Singleton spends the first half bouncing passes off receivers' hands. He gets so flustered he starts forcing passes, and East intercepts him twice. The Flyers need a fumble and a blocked punt to take a 14–6 lead into the locker room at halftime.

Shannon is livid. "You guys are making too damned many dumb mistakes," he roars. "The trouble with you guys is you're not a cerebral ball club. You don't even know what that means, do you? It means you ain't smart!"

He stalks over to a chalkboard and diagrams a formation. "Let me show you again how this is supposed to work," he says, his voice dripping sarcasm. He pounds the chalk on the circle he's drawn to represent the split end. "This offense will work, but we need someone right here to catch a damn pass every once in a while."

He gives up on that concept in the second half and turns things over to Chris Moore. Time and again he calls Moore's number, and the tailback pounds it up the field for two touchdowns. Eastside escapes with a 28–14 victory, far too close for a cakewalk conference game. The Flyers run their record to 5–1, but things aren't working out as Shannon has planned.

"We can't throw the damned ball," he says at practice the next week. He is back on his little hill, watching passing drills. The kids aren't even catching the ball in practice. "Of all the things I wouldn't have believed, it would be that I had a team that couldn't throw the damned ball. I got a quarterback who throws a good pass about half the time, and when he does, some guy drops it. He's got no confidence in his line, and I don't blame him, but he's got to stand in there. We're going to have to run the damn ball."

Adjustments will have to be made. A fullback will have to be found, a kid or two who doesn't mind laying his body on the line for the greater glory of good old Eastside. The fullback would be the lead blocker on many of the tailback counter plays. He should also be able to run the ball a little bit, just to keep the defenses honest. Shannon takes Cory Dent, a tough little safety who's been running second-string tailback, and makes him a fullback. He takes Lamont Nicholson, a linebacker, and makes him a fullback, too.

He pulls out his playbook and starts working on plays from the wing-T formation. Old as the hills, the wing-T brings the flanker in from flanks and turns him into a wingback, lined up behind the tight end. There he can be an additional blocker and also run counters and reverses when defenses stack against the tailback. He makes Rod Fisher his wingback. "He can't catch the ball, but we know he can run because he outran that dude with the .38 pistol at the ballgame last summer," Shannon reasons.

The offensive line will need the most work. Run blocking is more complicated than pass protection. There are keys to read, angles to decipher. He has good linemen in David James and Derrick Eldridge, a senior cocaptain. He installs a huge junior named Wayne Stewart, just returned from a shoulder injury, at center, and lines up another big junior named Dwight Allen at left guard. He takes Chris Moore's best friend and most earnest booster, a senior named LaTosque Scott, and makes him a tackle. Scott carries 280 pounds on a five-foot, eight-inch frame. He is a human wine cask. He followed Chris on his unsuccessful quest to play at Althoff, Belleville West, and Lincoln, and got the same suspension. "Toskie will do anything Chris tells him to do," Shannon says. "Maybe Chris'll tell him to block."

With Stallings, a devastating blocker, back at tight end, the new-look offensive line averages 239 pounds a man, as big as some small-college teams. Ken Goss, who coaches the offensive line, goes to work with them. He gets some help when some boosters come up with a couple of hundred bucks for new blocking chutes, stockyard-like devices designed to force linemen to charge low and hard. Previously the Flyers have relied on a couple of two-by-twelve boards they laid on the ground. Charge straight along the board, keep your feet apart, try not to twist an ankle. The chutes are a big improvement.

The Flyers' new power offense gets its first test the following Friday night, a bitterly cold and windy evening, against the Alton Redbirds. Alton is a good place for a test; not only is it too windy to throw the football, but the Redbirds have won only one game. The Flyers can experiment as much as they want without much fear things will blow up in their face. Eastside blows them away, scoring forty-two points in the first half and sailing to a 62–25 victory.

"This is crazy," says one member of the Alton crew working the first down chains along the sideline. "We've got just as many good athletes as they do. You know what the difference is? We've got a coach who tells the kids to lift weights, and then there's nobody around to open the weight room. They've got a coach who works 365 days a year."

Of those 365, only the 30 days of November, playoff season, will mean more to Shannon than the next seven days. The next team on the schedule is them Lincoln guys.

"Them Lincoln guys are talking upset," Shannon said with a grin. "They've been giving Deondre and our guys fits around town. They say we can't throw anymore, and ol' Duby's having a pretty good season. They say this is their year. They're billing this as a battle of two 6–1 teams. They're forgetting that our 6–1 was a lot tougher than their 6–1."

He said this in the privacy of his office, watching a tape of one of Lincoln's earlier games. In private, he wasn't too concerned about the Tigers. Their quarterback, Duby Anderson, was having a good year, but the quality of their opposition was suspect. For public consumption, however, and particularly for the team's consumption, Shannon talked about the Tigers as the second coming of the 1972 Miami Dolphins. He and his assistant coaches, who had picked up his Lincoln paranoia, spent the week warning the players that they'd never be able to hold their heads up again if they lost to Lincoln.

Because both teams were 6–1 and it would be the first Lincoln-Eastside game played at Clyde Jordan Stadium, there was even more interest around town than usual. "Had a guy tell me last night this Lincoln guy bet him three hundred dollars they'd beat our ass this year," Ken Goss said one afternoon after practice.

"How many points did he want?" someone asked.

"No points. Straight up. Then that fool said he'd give fourteen points."

"We're getting fourteen points, huh?" Shannon said with a big smile. "Those people are crazier than I thought."

It *was* crazier this year. A school board election was in progress, with the usual charges, countercharges and deal-making. A lot of the economy of East St. Louis hinges on the school board election. Back the wrong slate and you're out of a job. "It used to be that City Hall was the employer of last resort here in town," one Eastside teacher said. "But now City Hall has the state looking over its shoulder. Down at the school board, it's business as usual. Every job in this district is for sale."

District No. 189 has about fifteen thousand students and an annual budget in excess of $7.5 million. The district spends about $5,000 a year educating each pupil, slightly more than other school districts in St. Clair County but less than half of what's spent in Illinois's most affluent communities. Still, the district's per-pupil spending is above the state average. Administrators argue that because so many of the East St. Louis students come from families living below the federal poverty level—80 percent—the district's needs are greater. Nearly 30 percent of its students are enrolled as "educationally disadvantaged." Administrators also argue that attracting teachers to such an environment is difficult, thus explaining why the average teacher in the district is paid more than $35,000 a year and the average administrator close to $50,000.

But that doesn't explain why the plumbing doesn't work and broken windows don't get fixed. It doesn't explain why kids have to pass textbooks back and forth because some classes have only one book for every three students. It doesn't explain why science labs don't have test tubes and why heat in the classroom is only a sometimes thing.

Candidates for the school board were arguing about these things, throwing blame and making impressive promises. "It doesn't make any difference," Shannon said with a shrug. "The only thing most guys are worried about is who gets to divide up the money."

He is angrier than usual about school politics today. It is a Saturday morning, the day of the Lincoln game, the seventh game of the year, and he's just received his entire equipment allocation for the season. "There it is," he says bitterly, waving toward a pile of boxes. "Thirty-two pairs of shoes and six footballs. And the shoes ain't no damned good."

Everything else he's needed, he's scrounged for himself. Pants, jerseys, mouthpieces, straps, ice machines, blocking chutes, neck rolls, knee braces. Football is an equipment-intensive sport. "Them Lincoln guys get all the equipment," he says. "Look at 'em."

Across the back yard of the school, you can see the Tigers filing into Clyde Jordan Stadium, dressed in black pants and white jerseys, bright orange helmets with a cat's paw emblem on the side. The Lincoln marching band is high-stepping into the stadium, too, nattily turned out in black and white and orange. The ragtag Marching Flyers band is wearing blue sweatsuits—their uniforms haven't arrived yet. "Now, our band ain't as good as theirs, I'll admit that," Shannon says. "But that ain't fair."

The battle of the bands turns out to be more interesting than the football game. On a cold, rainy day that turns the field sloppy, Eastside runs Lincoln right out of Clyde Jordan Stadium. Duby Anderson can't pass in the rain, and Deondre Singleton doesn't need to. He just keeps handing off to Chris Moore, who carries the ball twenty times for 254 yards.

"That Chris is a showman," Shannon mutters. "Last week he banged his knee into a concrete block in the gym. He had guys carry him out, he was moaning and whining. He limped around here all week. He wanted to make sure he was the center of things this week, with folks wondering if he was going to play. He don't look like it hurts very much today."

The only thing that can stop Chris is the Lincoln band. Every time the Flyers are in the Lincoln end of the field, the band pumps up the volume as loud as it can. The Eastside band, about a fifth of the size of the Tigers', responds with gusto. The referee tells Shannon and Jim Monken, the Lincoln coach, to make their bands knock it off. "You'll have to excuse our band, Mr. Official," Shannon says. "This is the only time all year they get to play, and they got kind of carried away."

Shannon calls off the dogs when the Flyers build a 43-0 lead late in the third quarter. Lincoln gets a consolation touchdown and two-point conversion in the fourth quarter to make the final score 43-8.

Somewhere in the press box, a statistician notes that Chris Moore has accumulated 1,110 yards in six games. He looks up the state record for most yards gained in a high school career: 5,079, set in 1979 by a back named Jeff Campbell at tiny Catlin High School. Campbell did that in four years; in three years, Chris Moore has 4,068. He needs 1,012 yards to break the record. With Collinsville left on the regular-season schedule and a possible five more games in the playoffs, he might have a shot at it. After the game, someone hands the numbers to Chris.

"You could almost see a light bulb go on over his head, like in the cartoons," Shannon said later.

Back in the gym after the game, Chris asks the coach's permission to address the team. He mumbles a little speech, thanking his line and the fullbacks for doing a good job of blocking. "I'm going to get the record," he says, "and we're going to state."

The next time he touches the ball, six days later on a cold and soggy Friday evening in Collinsville, he goes fifty-two yards for a touchdown. The Flyers quickly get the ball back, and on his second carry of the game he goes sixty-seven yards for another score. And he isn't even the most spectacular back in that game. Wingback Rod Fisher, running a play Shannon calls "wing right basic, 47 reverse," has touchdown runs of forty-seven and forty yards and runs a kickoff back ninety-five yards. With the Kahok defense sucking toward Chris Moore on every down, Fisher has a field day and the Flyers win 53-8. The Flyers finish the regular season 8-1. Part two of the season is over. The Flyers are ranked as the top team in Illinois. Now they have to prove it.

James Rucker's equipment room, small and cramped and stacked floor to ceiling with everything the Flyers own, doubles as a lounge for the assistant coaches. They gather there the morning after the Collinsville game, ready to begin the playoffs, wondering who they'll play in round one next Wednesday. Shannon has called a Saturday practice session, of course, but the players are slow in arriving. Some of the seniors are in tutoring classes, preparing for the ACT college entrance test. Other students, members of Junior Achievement classes, are on an outing. "Hey, I don't usually mind Junior Achievement," Shannon gripes. "I want them doing things like that. But not today. We got something else we've got to achieve."

The coaches kill time by speculating about playoff pairings, which are to be announced later in the day. Last night Shannon sent Art Robinson and another scout to check out the East Moline Maroons and the Pekin Dragons. Along with the Flyers and the Granite City Warriors, they are the only downstate teams to qualify. Shannon, who's switched from Lincoln paranoia to playoff paranoia, is convinced he'll draw Pekin. The Dragons, who have the top-ranked quarterback in the state, are the team he most fears.

"Those politicians at the IHSA always stack it against us," he complains. "It's getting harder and harder for us to compete against those big schools. They've got 2,000 or 2,200 and we're down to 1,468 this year. "Even when they count the ninth graders in junior high to make us a four-year school, it's getting harder to justify us being a 6-A school. Enrollment-wise, we ought to be 5-A. Our athletes and the politics keep us in 6-A."

"That's right," said Terry Hill, who's curled up on a wide shelf in Rucker's equipment room. He has a hat over his eyes and is using a parka as a blanket. In the middle of the room, Marion Stallings is stretched out on a workbench. Ken Goss sits at the end of the workbench, his long legs dangling. The other coaches are scattered throughout the room.

Shannon has been delighted with his coaching staff this year. Stallings has made the biggest difference; his enthusiasm has rubbed off on the others. Several volunteer coaches have turned in long hours, including Rod Fisher's dad, Roderick, Sr., known to everyone as "Bull" Fisher; and Johnnie Oakley, a tough, bowling ball–shaped former player. Frank Spriggs, the weight coach, has also turned out to be a statistics nut. He keeps voluminous charts on every player's performance. Derrick Johnson and Cliff Dancey, two of Eastside's biggest fans, have attached themselves to the coaching staff, pitching in whenever there are errands to be run. None of them understand the nuances of the game the way Stallings does, but Shannon is pleased. "They work hard, they're fair to the kids," he says. "And they're all good guys. That's the most important thing. Too many of these kids don't have their dad around the house. They need to see guys like this."

As the coaches wait for the players, sitting on boxes and crates, they fiddle with equipment and talk about the old days, bemoaning their fate. Their voices rise and fall.

"People are moving out of this town like rats from a sinking ship."

"What's left of the black middle class is all up in Fairview Heights or O'Fallon."

"Taxes in this town, who can blame 'em? Can't afford to keep a decent house in East St. Louis no more."

"Taxes and welfare. The thing that's destroyed East St. Louis is the welfare check. Got these people think that check is a right, man. They don't want to do nothing but cash that check. These women, man, they have their babies and get that check."

"They've run us men out of there, the government has. They don't get paid if the man is around."

"The kids grow up thinking that's the way it is. They're soft, man. Their mamas spoil 'em, wipe their noses for them every time they cry. Kid goes cryin' to his mama how he needs a $75 pair of tennis shoes."

"They got eight or ten pair of shoes layin' around the closet already. My whole life I didn't have eight pair of shoes."

"My kid came to me, said he needed a $95 coat before he could start school. I said, 'What happened to the coat you had last year?' He said, 'It's too small.' Small, hell. He just don't like the style no more."

"Kids are soft, man. Spoiled. By the time we get 'em, they're already spoiled. They don't want to work like they used to."

"We work 'em like we used to, they run off. Go tell their mamas the coach is picking on 'em. They're soft. Most of 'em won't even come out for football. They say we're too tough."

"We got fewer kids and a lot fewer tough kids."

"The only thing that might save us would be if they'd combine these high schools. That ain't going to happen. Those Lincoln guys would never go for that, send those kids over here to play for us."

"Ain't tough enough to play for us."

"What might happen is they'll make us a four-year school. That would save us. That way we could play freshman football, get these kids in here and start working with 'em. Teach them the system. That way we could get some use out of them as sophomores."

"Ain't gonna happen, gentlemen," Shannon says, turning away from the conversation. "They ain't ever going to do nothing to help us. We got to help ourselves."

He's spotted the seniors trudging into the gym. They are dragging, tired from last night. Outside a bitter north wind is blowing, putting a crust of ice on the muddy practice yard. No one wants to spend Saturday afternoon getting cold and muddy, even if it is playoff time. Shannon compromises; he tells them to put on helmets and shoulder pads, but to leave their tennis shoes on. They'll practice in the gym. Cold and tired or not, it is November. He hasn't been happy with the way his defensive line has been reading blocking angles. Before he turns the team loose, he wants to spend an hour working on line slants.

"Let's go, let's go, let's go!" he shouts. "Them Dragons are working, getting ready for us. The playoffs is the payoffs!"

It's not them Dragons. It will be them Warriors. The IHSA matches East Moline against Pekin and sends the Flyers ten miles up the road for a rematch against Granite City. The weatherman provides a late-fall snowstorm for atmosphere.

In Pekin, the snow and the wind nullify the Dragons' passing game. East Moline pulls an upset, winning 12–6 in overtime. In Granite City, snow doesn't start falling until halftime, by which time the Chris Moore Show is in full flower.

Shannon, who's been checking regularly with Moore's teachers, discovered that Chris not only has been going to class, but has made the honor roll. He rewards him by naming him a team captain. Beaming, Moore tapes his football shoes, one with orange tape and the other with blue. He walks out to the center of the field for the coin toss wearing a blue ski-mask over his face. Then he goes to work.

He carries the ball twenty-two times for 226 yards. On one play in the first quarter, he turns what should have been a 5-yard gain into a highlight-film 66-yard touchdown romp. He pops off tackle, bounces off three tacklers, takes two steps, and cuts left.

He's spun around by another tackler. He stops dead in his tracks, letting another Warrior fly by. He plants his right foot and takes off. Nobody touches him the rest of the way. As he runs, you can almost see his mind subtracting each yard from how many he needs for the rushing record. "How many yards I got now?" he gasps when he gets back to the bench. His honor-roll brain goes clickety-click: "I got to average 166 the rest of the way."

The lousy weather is perfect for the power offense. The Eastside line charges low and hard, and Moore erupts through holes so quickly that the Warriors begin stacking extra defenders to his side. Shannon counters with quick traps to Cory Dent, the fullback, or sends Fisher back across the flow on the wingback reverse. Marion Stallings's defense has begun to take on some of their coach's controlled frenzy. They bottle up poor Granite City, which finishes 8–2, unbeaten against everyone but the Flyers. Eastside rides home through the snow with a 26–6 victory.

The Flyers practice in the snow the next day, chewing up what is left of the grass on their practice field, bundling up in hooded sweatshirts, wearing the hoods under the helmets and pulling sweatpants over their football pants. "Playoff weather," Stallings shouts over and over. "It's a tough game. Takes tough people to play it."

Stallings isn't happy with the Flyers' level of intensity, nor with their level of appreciation for the legacy of Flyer football. "These guys take this all for granted," he complains. "They don't ever remember when Eastside wasn't in the playoffs."

So he careens around the gym and practice field, screaming: "PLAYOFFS. THE . . . PLAY . . . OFFS! Time to get the JOB DONE!"

Shannon takes a different tack. He tells the players to start showing up in the mornings before school starts. He walks them through drills and works them out lightly, and then tells them to come back in the afternoon. He also has decided that motivation is hanging from water pipes in his office. He breaks out the blue-and-orange wool award jackets that have been hanging there for more than a year. He hands one to each player. The kids finger them lightly, precious garments, and try them on gingerly.

"The guys who came before you won these," Shannon tells them. "They were state champions, and you're getting the rewards. You can wear them this weekend. If we win, you can keep them another week. If they win, I want 'em back on Monday morning."

"We're keeping them, coach," the players say. "Ain't giving them back."

Shannon smiles. "Well, we'll see about that."

The rewards of success continue. On Friday afternoon, wearing their motivation jackets, the players board two buses for a 280-mile trip to East Moline and the second round of the playoffs. The mood is relaxed and carefree. Art May has booked the Flyers into what Shannon calls "my favorite hotel in this state. They got a field right behind the hotel we can use to practice on."

The Holiday Inn Holidome in Moline also has a swimming pool, a pool table, a game room, a miniature golf course, a basketball court, and a gift shop full of Michael Jordan posters. The players think they've died and gone to heaven.

"We stay in nice places because it's important for these guys to know there's places like this if they work hard," Shannon says.

"Even if they're in there, four to a room, it's the nicest place most of them have ever stayed in. We've got to teach them about rewards."

Art May has worked out the usual group discount at the local smorgasbord restaurant, which in the Quad Cities area, happens to be located next door to a sporting goods store. Led by Chris Moore, the players charge into the store and spend every dime in their pockets, including buying out the entire inventory of blue and orange soccer socks.

"That guy who ran the store had this scared look on his face when we walked in," said Cliff Dancey, one of Shannon's volunteer assistants. "By the time we left, he was just punching those keys on the cash register, smiling and asking if there was anything else we needed."

When the buses leave for the game the next morning, the players are carrying their helmets and shoulder pads in blue equipment bags. They've already donned their orange game pants. All but one of them is wearing one blue sock and one orange sock. The Chris Moore look. "I like to look pretty when I play," Chris explains. "I can't play right if I'm not dressed right."

The only exception is a sophomore who is making his first overnight trip. "We got up here for practice and he came to me and said he didn't bring his uniform," Shannon says. "I asked him why not. He said he thought we were going to buy them when we got here. Just when you think you've seen everything, you get an all-time first."

Marion Stallings watches this fun and frivolity with a jaundiced eye. He isn't happy with the team's attitude. "They're joking around, they're having a good time, but they're flat," he complains. "They still haven't figured out what this is all about."

He blows up in the locker room at the Moline fieldhouse. "You guys think you're going to walk in here with your fancy socks and win this game, you'd better think differently," he explodes. "It wasn't no fluke these guys beat Pekin. They're a good team and they ain't afraid of you. This is the *play...offs,* man! We're going to have to play hard today, and you guys don't know that. Man, it gets tougher and tougher each week. Haven't you figured that out? You've got to go out there and *pound* those guys!"

He slams a fist against a locker to emphasize his point. "We don't want to be embarrassed out there. They're not out there, whooping and hollering. They're going about their business. They got one goal, and that's to beat our ass and send us back to East St. Louis. And if that happens, it's on the shoulders of everybody in this room."

Shannon, dressed in a black snowmobile suit and a blue Winnipeg Jets stocking cap, listens stoically to Stallings's diatribe. Stallings is the fire, he is the ice. "We've had a good trip, a loose trip," he says. "I've got no problem with that if we play good. If we play bad, I've got a problem, and the next trip will be different. Now let's get our prayer."

They kneel, as always, in a cluster on the locker room floor. The coaches remove their caps. Roderick Fisher leads the prayer that Shannon insists the Flyers say before every game. It is handed down from team to team, part of the Flyers' legacy:

Dear Lord, as we go through the battles of life
We ask for a chance that is fair,
A chance to compete with all in the strife,
The courage to do or to dare.
If we should win, let it be by the code
With our face and our honor held high.
If we should lose, let us stand by the road
And cheer as the winners go by.
Day by day, we get better and better.
The team that won't be beat, can't be beat.

With a cheer, they break out of the locker room and run out to the field. Shannon gathers them around him once again, right before kickoff. "OK, we want to play hard, don't take anything for granted," he says. "If we lose, I want those jackets back Monday. All right, one-two-three, Flyers. One, two, three. . . ."

"FLYERS!"

East Moline, playing in front of a big home crowd on another cold and windy Saturday, makes a game of it for a while. They blitz Singleton furiously, and Moore has trouble keeping his feet on the muddy turf. But Dennis Stallings is throttling the Maroon offense, stacking up running backs at the line of scrimmage and five times sacking the quarterback.

On the third play of the second quarter, with East Moline stacking their defense toward Chris Moore, Shannon sends in 47 reverse. Singleton turns to his right as if to hand the ball to Moore off tackle. Fisher cuts inside and Singleton slips him the ball. David James has pulled from his guard's position and levels the defensive end. Fisher cuts off his block and goes fifty-eight yards for the touchdown.

On the next series, Stallings blasts the East Moline quarter-back, and Lamont Nicholson recovers a fumble at the Maroons' 35. It takes the Flyers ten plays, but they punch the ball in for a 13–0 lead. Moline strikes back right before halftime to make it 13–7.

"They're outplaying us," Shannon says in the locker room. "You guys are all out there, worrying about being cold, and those guys are kicking your butts. We're ahead, but it feels like we're behind. We're going to have to rise up."

Dennis Stallings does the rising. Again he blasts the Maroon quarterback, and again the ball comes loose. Dwight Allen recovers the fumble. Chris Moore takes over after that. He stops dancing around, stops trying to chase the record 50 yards at a time, and begins lowering his head and plowing out 5 and 6 yards at a crack. He scores early in the fourth quarter on an 8-yard run, and then breaks loose for a 36-yard gain that sets up the last score of the game. He finishes with 159 yards on twenty-two carries, his orange and blue socks down around his ankles, covered with mud. The Flyers win 27–7.

"We ain't going to have as much fun next time," Shannon vows. "These guys are getting the rewards of this program, and they ain't paid the price yet."

Fifty-one weeks ago, after his team was eliminated from the 1990 playoffs by Downers Grove North, Shannon told Trojans coach Pete Ventrelli that he'd see him next year. He said it offhandedly, knowing that the odds against a rematch are pretty long. "I know we'll be back," he'd said. "I don't know about them."

They are back. The Trojans will play the Flyers next Saturday afternoon at Clyde Jordan Stadium in the quarter finals of playoffs. "Mo...tiv...a...tion," Marion Stallings says with a sly smile. "Sometimes you have to dream it up. Sometimes it comes easy."

Stallings relishes this chance. He knows Eastside's defense was bamboozled by the veer offense last year, when he was sick. He knows it won't happen again. His sister's laid-back son, Dennis, has turned into a fearsome defensive end under his uncle's ceaseless prodding. The other end is manned by senior Theotric Jackson, a little small at six-two, 189, but a fine pass rusher.

Coach Stallings inserted a gritty sophomore named Mitree Jenkins at nose guard. At six feet, 191 pounds, Mitree is lankier than nose guards usually are, but he is one of the toughest kids on the team. The more he gets banged around, the harder he plays. Derrick Eldridge, the senior cocaptain, plays one defensive tackle. He is a blocky young man who kills time on long bus rides by leading the team singing hymns from his church. The other tackle is manned by the euphoniously named Montsho Jones. He is six feet, three inches tall and weighs 220 pounds. He spent three seasons being lashed for not using his size and athletic ability. Finally, midway through his senior year, he's gotten the message. Montsho has turned macho. He is a terror.

Linebackers are critical in stopping the veer, and in David James and Lamont Nicholson, Stallings has two smart, hard-nosed kids who are punishing tacklers. The coach is satisfied. He intends to own Downers Grove. He pushes his defense relentlessly in the days before the game, driving them in the cold and the mud, hammering the scout team hours on end. By Thursday the players are so tired they don't want to come out of the locker room to practice. They linger inside, trading gossip, laughing about a rare strain of gonorrhea someone has picked up. Basketball star Magic Johnson has just shocked the rest of the country by announcing he's contracted the AIDS virus, but these guys are young and they live in East St. Louis. In East St. Louis, everybody knows someone who's about to die.

"That shit happens," says one.

"Doesn't bother me," says another.

"Got to be careful," says still another. "But if it's your time, it's your time."

Chris Moore bounces into the room, talking at the top of his lungs, breaking up the bull session. He is waving a piece of paper, an official East St. Louis Senior High School report card in the name of Moore, Christopher. "Check it out," he orders, taping the report card to the bulletin board.

Economics: B. Ecology: B. Psychology: B. Art: A. Grammar and Comprehension: C.

"Y'all go and get outside," Chris orders happily. "Coach's waiting."

He then goes off and slips into a warm whirlpool bath. His ankle and a knee are hurting, and besides, it is thirty-five degrees and raining. He needs 445 more yards to break the rushing record, but he figures he is a mortal lock. He is an honor roll student. Everybody loves him. College recruiters are coming to see him, and some of them are saying his grades won't be a problem. Reporters are writing about him. Photographers are taking his picture. Even Shannon has gotten off his case. His redemption is complete.

Shannon has indeed come to terms with Chris Moore. Yes, he compromised by letting him back on the team. And yes, he's compromised again by shortening the suspension. But Chris has done everything he asked him to, and has carried the team on his back in the bargain. Still, it bothers him. He said he didn't need Chris, but without him, the Flyers would have gone nowhere. They would have lost to Jefferson City for sure, and maybe to Granite City, and Belleville East, and who knows, maybe even to Lincoln. Deondre Singleton has been everything he ever wanted in a quarterback, but Deondre has regressed. Shannon never before has coached a quarterback who's regressed as a senior. It violates his whole philosophy of player development. But even if Deondre was able to throw effectively, and even if Shannon found a split end who could catch the ball regularly, the weather would have neutralized the passing game. It has been cold, windy, or rainy week after week, weather that demands slugging it out on the ground, weather that demands a great tailback. Chris Moore, with his bad habits, bad grades, and bad attitude, was everything Shannon's ever tried to avoid in a football player. But without him, the Flyers would have been lost.

He consoles himself with the hope that maybe Chris has turned his life around. Maybe, by giving him a second chance, Shannon has helped him see the light. Maybe the new Chris, the honor roll Chris, the team captain Chris, is the real Chris. Maybe these playoffs, this shot at a sixth state championship, is his reward for doing the right thing by Chris. Maybe. But if you ask him where he thinks Chris will be a year from now, he'll only stare into the distance and shake his head.

"I don't know," Bob Shannon says, as he watches the players trudge slowly onto the practice field. "I've stopped trying to figure it out."

There will be one more interruption today. Deborah Fields, a music teacher at Eastside, has begged him for ten minutes to rehearse a rap song that a student, Trevon Brock, has composed for a school assembly. The football team is going to get up on stage and sing the rap, an ode to Eastside's glory. "Go ahead," Shannon says. "But this is the last year I'm doing this. We've got business to attend to."

She climbs halfway up the fire escape at the back of the gym, holding a red umbrella over her head against the rain, and gathers the players below her. Mortally embarrassed, they mumble the words a couple of times, and then get into the spirit of it. Dennis Stallings nudges Ben Williams and they start singing at the tops of their voices. The other players pick up the volume. A few feet away, the coaches watch with big grins on their faces as the rappers get down to business:

Eastside is the side with pride,
So much pride we just can't hide.
Started it off in eighty-four,
These are the boys who opened the door.
Satisfied with an alarming grin,
Shannon's boys . . . Shannon's boys . . . Shannon's boys . . .
Can win!

They sing at the top of their lungs, laughing and looking over their shoulders at the coach. Shannon winces, and then turns on his heel and walks away quickly lest they see the smile on his face. The rap echoes across the muddy field:

Shannon's boys . . . Shannon's boys . . . Shannon's boys. . . .

Two days later, in the cold and mud at Clyde Jordan Stadium, the Flyers wreak revenge on Downers Grove North. Chris Moore carries the ball twenty-nine times, scores all four Flyers' touchdowns and gains 230 yards. The defense knows everything there is to know about shutting off a veer offense. The Trojans manage only 103 yards in offense. The Flyers give Coach Stallings a shutout, 26–0.

He primed them before the game, unleashing a torrent of motivational cliches that somehow sounded just right. "There's no tomorrow, no tomorrow," he began. "When we leave here today, we want to say, 'What I had, I gave. What I had left, I lost forever.' Don't leave anything out there, fellas."

"I think they're ready, coach," Shannon told him.

"If we ain't ready, we don't deserve to play in the *playoffs*. The quarterfinals. The quarter *finals*. Y'all know what that means? It means eight. Eight teams. After today, there'll be fo'. Not *four*, fo'. We are the East St. Louis *Flyers*! The *Final Fo'*!"

What they had, they gave. They are back in the semifinals. They will have to give a lot more next week, in a game that will test everything Shannon has ever taught them.

CHAPTER

10

Is this Eastside?
Yeahhuh.
Is this Eastside?
Yeahhuh.
Is this Eastside?
Yeahhuh.
What side?
Eastside!

It is the pregame ritual, the Flyers circling their captains for calisthenics, the captains calling out the questions, and the players roaring back the answers. They pop their hands on their thigh pads, rhythmically, ritually. Whap, whap, whap, whap.

Is this Eastside?
Yeahhuh.
What side?
Eastside.

You can see players on the other team, warming up at the other end of the field, glance up at the noise, trying not to notice. They have heard of the Flyers, way up here at Victor Andrew High School in far south Cook County, out here where the houses are huge and comfortable and so new that bulldozers are still parked on some of the lawns. Andrew High School was built in the middle of a cornfield in 1977 in the expectation that Chicago's population would eventually creep that far south. Now, fourteen years later, Andrew has twenty-two hundred students and an undefeated football team. The Victor Andrew Thunderbolts—T-Bolts, for short—have never been this far in the playoffs before, and now look what is awaiting them at the other end of their stadium.

What side?
Eastside!

The Flyers are all business today. They checked into another grandiose Holiday Inn yesterday afternoon, but this time Shannon told them to leave the blue-and-orange awards jackets at home. "You can wear them to state if we win," he said.

There were no shopping sprees in sporting goods stores, no laid-back evening goofing around the hotel game room. Shannon scrounged a hotel meeting room with a TV and a VCR. Friday night's entertainment consisted of a tape of the Downers Grove game. He told them to get to bed early. They had a 6:00 A.M. wake-up call and a 7:00 A.M. breakfast. Then trainer George Walsh and Coach Stallings taped the players' ankles. By 10:00 A.M. Saturday, the Flyers have their game pants and game faces on.

They gather at a side door of the hotel, peering through a set of glass double doors at the parking lot where their buses are warming up. They watch light poles in the parking lot swaying back and forth in the wind, and listen as the wind howls around the building. Rain is falling sideways. Whenever someone opens the outer door to run to the bus, the players huddle together and pull their coats a little tighter. Chris Moore strolls up, wearing a black and white plaid coat over his orange game pants, carrying his equipment bag, two suitcases, and a boom box. The voice on the radio says the wind is gusting up to forty miles an hour and the temperature is expected to fall into the mid-twenties by early afternoon.

"Let's just get on the bus, play the game, and get the hell out of town," grumbles LaTosque Scott. "I don't like it here. It's too cold."

"I like weather like this."

"Who said that?" demands Shannon, huddled in his black snowmobile suit and the blue Winnipeg Jets stocking cap he borrowed from Scott before the playoffs began. Shannon is not a superstitious man, but he isn't going to change hats at this point.

"I did," says Chris Moore. "I like to run in the mud."

"That's good," Shannon drawls. "You're going to get about thirty chances to prove that today."

At eleven o'clock the Flyers finally board the buses for the twenty-minute ride to Andrew's field. As the buses navigate the subdivision streets, the players stare in disbelief at the dozens of expensive new homes being built in the cornfields. There hasn't been a house built in East St. Louis in years. And there never have been any houses like these.

There's never been a school building like Andrew High either: a vast, four-story complex, impeccably maintained. The Flyers walk past a sign pointing toward the school's swimming pool to their dressing area in the girls' locker room. It is huge and antiseptically clean and features a shower bay as large as the football locker room at Eastside. A couple of Flyers run their hands over the shower heads and try the faucets. "Hey, they work," one says.

"Get dressed and you special teams guys get out to the field," Shannon snaps. "We've got to get used to this wind."

A polar bear couldn't get used to the wind. It is blowing from the southwest, ahead of a fierce storm sweeping across the Midwest out of the lower Rockies. The temperature is thirty degrees, the wind chill factor stands at zero. Snow is forecast for later in the day; flurries already have begun. Singleton and Kenvir Dixon, the two punters, try a dozen practice kicks apiece into the wind. Most are blown back over their heads.

Compounding the problem is the condition of the field. The center of the south end of the field is a quagmire, with standing water between the ten- and thirty-yard lines. The rest of the field is a quilt of mud and well-trod grass. "We're in for a defensive struggle," Shannon murmurs. "One touchdown may have to do it. And they've got a great defense."

The Thunderbolts have given up only twenty-seven points in twelve games. They haven't been scored upon in the first half all year. Their team captain, Mike McKibben, is a six-foot-two-inch, 192-pound defensive back who has a dozen big-time college offers waiting for him.

The rest of the Flyers trot out to the field to join the kicking units. Many of them are badly underdressed. They haven't brought enough clothes for this kind of weather. A few wear long johns under their game pants, but many are bare-legged. Most have gloves and sweatshirts of one sort or another, even if the sweatshirts are the ones they wore for the trip and will have to ride back home in. Derrick Eldridge, who habitually lets his bare belly hang over his belt, has condescended to wear a T-shirt under his pads. "You know it's cold when you can't see Eldridge's gut," one of the assistant coaches cracks.

Blowing on his hands and tugging at his T-shirt, Eldridge leads the captains in circling the team for pregame calisthenics. The cadence begins:

Is this Eastside?
Yeahhuh.

The Flyers win the coin toss, and Shannon elects to take the wind and defend the quagmire at the south end of the field. Andrew breaks a couple of running plays as the Eastside defenders try to find their footing, slipping and sliding, grabbing at the T-Bolt running backs instead of lowering their shoulders and popping them. Flyers cornerback Marceo Haywood stops their drive by intercepting a pass that skewed off into the wind.

Pinned deep in the mud, the Flyers' offense can do nothing. McKibben and the T-Bolt defense are primed for Chris Moore. They hammer him into the line of scrimmage, and Singleton drops back to punt from his end zone. At least the wind is at his back. But Matt Buford, who handles the deep snaps for the Flyers, can't get enough on the snap to drive it through the wind. The ball sails high to Singleton's right. He falls on it in the end zone, and Andrew takes a 2–0 lead on the safety.

Dennis Stallings has figured the footing out. He breaks through and slams the T-Bolt quarterback after the free kick, getting the ball back for Eastside. The Flyers begin driving but have to change ends of the field as the first quarter ends. They are stuffed on downs in the middle of the south end quagmire at the three-yard line. They failed to score, but now Andrew must try to drive the ball out of the swamp. The Flyers hold, and it's Andrew's turn to try to kick out of the south end zone. Their center, too, can't penetrate the wind, and this time the Flyers get the safety when the ball sails out of the end zone.

"I can't feel my hands, coach," Singleton tells Shannon. "I put my hands down for the ball, and I can't feel it."

"Gotta anticipate it, quarterback," Shannon says. "You've got to play smart."

Anticipating, feeling for the ball, Singleton begins leading the Flyers up the field, back into the swamp. The offensive line, Stallings and Eldridge, Toskie Scott and Wayne Stewart, Dwight Allen and David James, are now covered with mud. Each play they get a fresh coat of mud, each coat freezing as they go back to the huddle. But each play they drive ahead, crashing into the T-Bolt defenders, pushing them off the line, rolling them into the mud. Chris Moore follows them, muddy turf spitting off his cleats, lowering his shoulders and driving straight ahead.

On the sidelines, Shannon squints his eyes against the wind, sending Cory Dent and Lamont Nicholson back and forth with the plays. The two fullbacks are indistinguishable, swamp creatures shuttling to and from the gloom. "Thirty-three dive," Shannon says. "Twenty-eight sweep." "Twenty-six counter."

The Flyers are moving the ball. He has preached to them about discipline, about toughness, about strength, and about attitude. Out there in the mud, their arms and legs soaked and caked with mud and ice, they are doing everything he asked them to. They drive the ball to the one-yard line, where Chris Moore's face is ground into the goo. He comes up spitting mud and grass, his helmet covered with slime. On the next play, Singleton puts his numb hands under Wayne Stewart's butt, grabs for the ball, and surges forward. Bodies pile up, but he gets the ball across the goal line. Touchdown.

Nate Robinson has no chance on the extra point kick into the wind. The Flyers take an 8–2 lead back into the warmth of the locker room for halftime.

The players collapse in a muddy heap on the white tile floor of the room. Some are obviously in pain. None of them complain. A few gather around wall-mounted hair dryers, holding their faces to the hot air. Shannon marches to a portable blackboard, dragging it into the shower bay so everyone can see him. He starts diagramming a play. "We got to get us another touchdown, some way," he says. "One might do it, but I'd feel better with another one."

Three days ago he put another play into his game plan, a variation of 47 reverse, the wingback reverse that Rod Fisher has run with such amazing success since the middle of the season.

The variation is called 49 reverse. It changes blocking schemes slightly and is designed to go around the end instead of off-tackle. Shannon has run 47 reverse twice in the first half without much success. Now he means to spring his trap. One more time he diagrams the blocking scheme and then turns the blackboard over to Marion Stallings.

Eastside football means everything to Stallings. He found that out when he was away from it. Now the Flyers are so close to the championship game he can taste it. He is wrapped so tight he can barely control himself. He starts yelling, going over defensive assignments. His voice gets louder and louder. He pounds on the blackboard so hard the chalk crumbles.

"We're one half away from the state championship! And you guys are pussyfooting around out there!" he screams.

"Calm down, coach," someone tells him.

He stops dead, like Chris Moore waiting for a linebacker to slide by.

"*Calm down*?" he screams. "Calm down? You guys need to get fired up like me!"

But he stops himself. He takes a deep breath. "OK, I'm calm now. I'm calm. You guys need to get fired up like me," he repeats. "But I know, I know. I'm fired up, but I'm ready. I'm focused."

No one wants to go back outside, but they peel themselves off the floor and march through the door. "Bite down a little harder on those mouthpieces," Shannon says. "Take care of business."

Andrew kicks off to begin the half. The temperature seems to have dropped another five degrees during halftime, the brutal wind seems to howl louder. Chris Moore carries twice, pushing the ball out to the Flyers' thirty-five-yard line and getting a first down. Then he tries to sweep right end and loses four yards. Second and fourteen at their own thirty-one with the wind at their backs. Shannon knows Andrew expects a pass. "Wing right basic, 49 reverse," he tells split end Richard Jenkins, who carries the play into the huddle.

Andrew is blitzing, just as Shannon had hoped. Fisher takes the inside handoff from Singleton and follows David James around left end. Cory Dent blows off tackle and seals off the inside linebacker. James kicks the safetyman back three yards. Fisher goes sixty-nine yards down the sideline for the touchdown. It works just as it was diagrammed.

With a 14–2 lead, Shannon begins coaching against the weather. After the defense holds the T-Bolts and the Flyers come up short on third down deep in their own territory, he orders Singleton not to try to punt the ball into the wind. Instead he tells him to take the snap, turn, and run for the back of the end zone. It means giving up a safety but allows the luxury of a free kick that Andrew will have to handle in the swampy end of the field.

The defense holds again. Then the Flyers get lucky. Singleton loses his footing trying to pitch the ball to Moore. As he is falling forward, he scoops the ball toward Moore. The timing is off, but it confuses Andrew more than the Flyers. Chris takes it fifty yards before being driven out of bounds at the three-yard line. He goes in from there on the next play. The defense gives up nothing else. The scoreboard reads 20–4 when they flee for the warmth of the locker room.

The place is bedlam. Kids have tears in their eyes, from pain or joy, or maybe both. Muddy clothes are flying, high-fives are slapping. Chris Moore, his eyes glazed, his face caked with mud, leans against a wall, talking to reporters. He has carried the ball thirty-one times and gained 169 yards. He needs only 58 yards to break the rushing record. He says he's exhausted. He says he's dizzy.

"Dizzy, huh?" Shannon says when a reporter tells him. "Well, I'll go along with that. But he's a great player. I'm proud of him. I'm proud of all these guys. What you saw today was the Flyers of old. This is what it's all about, rising to the occasion and letting nothing get in the way."

As he is saying this, David James limps slowly into the room, the 56 on his jersey unreadable through the mud. He pulls off his helmet, shakes a divot of gooey turf from the face mask, pounds the helmet against the wall, and starts screaming:

What side? What side? What side?

E P I L O G U E

The Glenbard North High School Panthers never knew what hit
them. They'd never played in Normal at Hancock Stadium on the
last Saturday in November. They'd never been to the finals of the
Illinois 6-A football championships. The Flyers were there for the
eighth time in Bob Shannon's sixteen years as head coach. And
for the sixth time, he climbed the platform set up at the fifty-yard
line and claimed the championship trophy.

His black snowmobile suit was soaking wet when he claimed
this one. With two minutes left in the game, Derrick Eldridge had
sneaked up behind him and emptied a Gatorade cooler full of
water over his head. It was a calculated risk on Eldridge's part,
knowing how the coach takes nothing for granted. But it turned
out that not even Bob Shannon was worried about a 48-6 lead
with two minutes left to play. Three minutes to go, maybe it
would have been different.

The Flyers had spotted Glenbard North a 6-0 first quarter lead.
The Panthers were piling nine defenders at the line of scrimmage,

all of them looking for Chris Moore. They were daring the Flyers to throw the football. Shannon took the dare. So did his quarterback.

"Twenty-eight bootleg pass is there, coach," Singleton told him early in the second quarter.

"Run it," Shannon snapped.

He took two steps to his right and put his left hand in Moore's belly, just as he does to start 28 sweep. But the ball was in his right hand, behind his hip. Deondre Singleton suddenly found everything he'd lost. He threw the ball like he had all those long summer days with Homer Bush, standing in the pocket like his knee had never been hurt, looking, looking, looking, and then seeing Dennis Stallings streaking across the middle. Touchdown.

Then there was Dennis again, cutting across on a deep post. Deondre laid it out for him, and Dennis dove for it, juggled it just like in those long afternoons in passing drills, clutched it to his chest, and fell over the goal line. Touchdown.

Then there was Chris Moore, sliding off left tackle midway through the second quarter, picking up the 5,080th rushing yard of his career, becoming the state's all-time leading rusher. On the next play he added 30 more yards and got the seventy-eighth rushing touchdown of his career, also a new state record. He would add another touchdown in the second quarter on a 1-yard burst and another in the third on a 47-yard cutback that was a thing of beauty. In the fourth quarter, on his seventeenth carry of the day, he went 9 yards for his fourth touchdown of the day. It was the last time he touched the ball as an East St. Louis Flyer.

"This is Chris Moore," Bob Shannon said as he introduced his team captains to the postgame press conference. "He should be an All-American."

Happy chaos and pandemonium filled the locker room, of course. Players squirted one another with Pepsi-Cola and then dragged trash cans into the showers, filled them with water, and chased down assistant coaches. Terry Hill got caught and drenched. The others escaped.

Shannon dressed by himself in an adjacent gym. He put on a red warm-up suit and a new pair of basketball shoes. He packed his wet snowmobile suit and his lucky stocking cap into one side of a big brown suitcase. On the other side, on top of his dry clothes, he dropped his plastic-covered play sheet. He snapped the suitcase shut and put on a red ski jacket.

"We've had better teams," he said, picking up the walnut-and-bronze championship trophy. "But this one might be my favorite, the way they picked themselves up off the floor and got the job done. Six of these trophies now, but this one might be the sweetest. A lot of people gave up on us, but the kids never gave up on themselves. They just worked harder. They came in early in the mornings, before school, and they did what we asked them to do. This one is sweet."

He hoisted the trophy onto his hip. "You know, my wife told me I should take this one and quit. I said, 'Why should I do that? What am I going to do, sit home and watch you play solitaire on the computer?'"

They made the usual road-trip stop at the local smorgasbord, where the Flyers ate everything in sight and then took off to check out the adjacent shopping mall. Then Tom Holley rounded them up, one by one, and dragged them into the back room of the restaurant. There, his wife, Debbie, took a picture of each of them holding the championship trophy. "I know it seems dumb," she said. "But some of these guys don't have any pictures of themselves."

The buses pulled into the parking lot at the high school shortly after 11:00 P.M. Exactly eight persons were waiting, parents and friends there to pick up the troops. The players, exhausted smiles on their faces, walked into the gym. Many of them sprinted across the floor to the athletic director's office, where they used the telephone to call for rides home. Then Shannon gathered them around him for the last time.

"You guys did a great job," he began. "I want to emphasize that. A *great* job. We came a long way. We worked hard. We were convinced that what we were doing was right. You understand now what it takes to win. There are some things you have to do. You have to get mentally and physically prepared. You young guys, you don't understand that yet, some of you. But the sooner you learn, the better off you're going to be. This is a golden opportunity for you, and it ain't just about football."

He paused, putting the glare on one more time, and talked briefly about a few of the mistakes the team had made that afternoon. Then he caught himself.

"Hey, I'm not going to be negative here," he said, grinning and shrugging. "We did what we wanted to do. Enjoy that. Let the celebration begin. Some guys downtown at the school board want to have a parade for y'all tomorrow at two o'clock. Be down there at two if you want to ride in the parade. I ain't going to promise you that I'll be there. It's been a long year for the coach, and I need a little rest. I ain't much for parades. Let's get our prayer and get out of here. . . ."

He stopped himself. "Oh yeah, one more thing. Before we leave, I want all your equipment back. Just stack it on the floor, helmets in one pile, shoulder pads in another, and such as that. I want everything, even the locks for your locker room. It'll save me a lot of trouble chasing you guys down in the next couple of weeks. We need to be ready for next year. Now let's get our prayer."

Everyone in the gym knelt to recite the Lord's Prayer, arms linked, heads bowed. At the final amen, there was just a brief moment when no one moved and no one spoke. Then one by one, everyone got off his knees and moved away. The players began turning in their equipment. Blue helmets were lined up in neat, even rows. Shoulder pads were stacked in bundles of six, according to size. Shoes went into an old grocery cart, filling it to overflowing.

The old gym was quiet as a mausoleum. Dirty uniforms and practice uniforms were tossed into piles and trundled into laundry bags. Thigh pads were wrapped with blue-and-orange game belts. Shannon passed out three-by-five index cards and told each player to hook his combination padlock onto the card and write the combination on it. In the bleachers, two coaches accepted the return of the blue-and-orange wool jackets. "The seniors can keep theirs," Shannon said.

In a matter of fifteen minutes, the only visible sign of all those months of work were a few scraps of adhesive tape littering the gym floor. Everything else had been locked away. It was over. The next day, at a school assembly, each player would receive a gold-plated medallion hanging from a red, white, and blue ribbon. For a day or two, among those in East St. Louis who still care, they would be heroes.

Over the next few weeks and months, a few players would get other rewards: all-state honors for Moore and Stallings and Eldridge, all-metro honors for those three and Cory Dent, college scholarship offers for six of the senior players. In years to come, there would be another, less tangible, but far more important reward. Bob Shannon said it like this: "Some day they will look back on this and realize everything they achieved and everything they overcame. And they'll be awed."

But right now, the players were in too big of a hurry to realize it was all over. They fled for the door and their rides. They had celebrating to do.

When the last of the players had gone, Shannon met briefly with his assistants, thanking them for all they'd done. "If I had the money, I'd give you all a bonus," he said. "But I don't. You know how that goes."

The other men zipped up their coats and headed off, most of them to Rucker's house where the beer was on ice. Shannon locked the equipment room and padlocked a chain on the fire door of the gym. He double-locked his office door and checked to see if the door to the athletic director's office was locked. The trophy was stored there. He flipped off the lights to the gym, picked up his suitcase and walked out the back door. He pulled it tight behind him and checked to see if it was locked. He walked toward the parking lot, where Jeanette was waiting for him.

"You know," he said, "we might have a pretty decent team next year."

The next afternoon, a dingy yellow fire truck followed by two dozen cars crawled two miles from the school board building out State Street to East St. Louis High School. The weather was cold and windy. There was no one on the streets to watch. But Bob Shannon rode in the parade.

Appendices

1990 FLYERS ROSTER

No.	Name	Position	Year	Height	Weight
10	Roderick Fisher	SE / DB	Jr.	5-9	160
11	Deondre Singleton	QB	Jr.	6-1	170
12	Chris Moore	TB / SS	Jr.	5-8	175
14	Ben Williams	QB	Soph.	6-0	162
15	Kenvir Dixon	QB	Soph.	5-10	154
16	Homer Bush	FL / SE	Sr.	5-11	185
17	Darren Eubanks	QB	Sr.	6-1	165
21	Paris Johnson	CB / FL	Sr.	5-4	148
23	Lamont Nicholson	CB	Jr.	5-11	169
24	Jashane Staten	TB / DB	Jr.	5-11	180
25	Toby Isom	TB / DB	Jr.	5-8	165
26	Cory Dent	FL / DB	Jr.	5-9	176
27	Chris Cook	TB / LB	Soph.	5-5	148
28	Frank Spraggins	SS	Soph.	5-11	154
30	Rodney Craig	DB	Soph.	5-8	150
31	Antwon McNeese	FB	Soph.	5-8	168
32	Nathaniel Robinson	LB / RB	Soph.	6-6	186
33	Jerry Creer	RB / FS	Sr.	5-8	175
34	Rolando Cameron	RB / FS	Sr.	5-9	200
35	Corey Houston	FL / C	Sr.	5-10	171
36	Marcus Bester	CB	Sr.	5-9	175
37	Ronald Hull	SE / S	Jr.	5-8	168
38	Atlas Hopkins	DE	Soph.	6-1	198
39	Lorenzo Powell	SS	Jr.	5-7	145
40	Richard Jenkins	RB / CB	Soph.	5-9	170
42	David James	LB	Soph.	6-0	190
45	Jarvis Williams	LB	Soph.	6-0	190
50	Darron Suggs	T	Soph.	6-6	186
52	Gregory Millender	C / DE	Soph.	5-10	170
54	Nolan Welch	G	Soph.	5-9	145
55	Carl Mayes	LB	Jr.	6-0	205
62	Robert Perkins	G / DE	Sr.	6-2	215
64	Lamont Stith	C / T	Sr.	6-0	236
65	Chris Johnson	LG	Sr.	5-10	210
68	Derrick Eldridge	TE / G	Jr.	5-8	254
71	LaTosque Scott	G	Jr.	5-8	230
72	Dwight Allen	T	Soph.	6-0	206

No.	Name	Position	Year	Height	Weight
73	Kasen Isaac	T	Soph.	6-0	240
74	William Riney	T	Jr.	5-8	212
75	Clarence Green	G / T	Sr.	5-10	230
77	David Douglas	T	Soph.	5-10	247
78	Vaughn Johnson	G / NG	Sr.	5-9	238
82	Theotric Jackson	DE	Jr.	6-2	176
83	Marcus Malone	K / TE	Soph.	6-1	175
84	Fred Jones	DE	Soph.	5-11	169
85	Terence Charles	DE	Soph.	5-9	151
89	Dennis Stallings	TE / DE	Jr.	6-2	215

Coaching Staff: Bob Shannon, head coach. Assistants: John Davis, Ken Goss, Art Robinson, Lenzie Stewart, Wendell Smith, George Walsh, Terry Hill, James Rucker, Morris Hunt.

1991 FLYERS ROSTER

No.	Name	Position	Year	Height	Weight
10	Roderick Fisher	SE / DB	Sr.	5-9	180
11	Deondre Singleton	QB / P	Sr.	6-3	191
12	Chris Moore	TB / SS	Sr.	5-10	205
14	Ben Williams	QB	Jr.	6-0	182
15	Kenvir Dixon	QB / FL	Jr.	5-10	160
16	Jashane Staten	TB / DB	Sr.	5-11	190
17	Damon Gladney	SS	Jr.	5-11	170
21	Justin Garner	SS	Soph.	5-7	140
23	Lamont Nicholson	LB / TE	Sr.	6-0	180
25	Terence Charles	DB	Jr.	5-11	160
26	Cory Dent	FL / DB	Sr.	5-9	180
27	Chris Cook	TB / LB	Jr.	5-5	152
28	Frank Spraggins	SS	Jr.	5-11	155
32	Nathaniel Robinson	FB / K	Jr.	5-7	191
34	Marceo Haywood	C / TB	Soph.	5-7	180
35	Charnicholas Walker	DB	Soph.	5-11	168
36	Darron Suggs	RB	Jr.	6-0	205
37	Shawn Johnson	RC	Jr.	5-11	155
38	Anthony White	FB	Soph.	5-10	172
39	Lorenzo Powell	SS	Jr.	5-7	158
40	Richard Jenkins	TB / CB	Jr.	5-7	155
45	Jarvis Williams	LB	Jr.	6-0	190
48	Nolan Welch	LB	Jr.	5-11	155
50	Joe King	C / NG	Soph.	5-11	249
54	Theotric Jackson	DE	Sr.	6-2	189
55	Carl Mayes	LB / C	Sr.	6-0	210
56	David James	TB / LB	Jr.	6-0	205
58	Dushon Givens	G / T	Soph.	5-11	215
62	Montsho Jones	DT / OT	Sr.	6-3	220
64	Mack Buford	C / NG	Jr.	6-0	220
65	Richard Yerbough	G / T	Jr.	5-9	270
66	Wayne Stewart	G / DT	Jr.	6-2	260
68	Derrick Eldridge	TE / G	Sr.	5-8	254
69	Manfred McGee	NG	Jr.	5-9	295
71	LaTosque Scott	RT	Sr.	5-8	279
72	Dwight Allen	T	Jr.	6-0	220
73	Kasen Isaac	T	Jr.	6-0	240

No.	Name	Position	Year	Height	Weight
74	William Rainey	DT	Sr.	5-11	205
75	Byron Mitchell	NG	Sr.	5-8	205
77	David Douglas	T	Jr.	5-11	247
78	Christopher Ewing	DE / T	Jr.	6-5	233
80	Mitree Jenkins	DE	Soph.	6-0	191
82	David Searcy	SE	Soph.	6-3	185
83	Freddie Barber	FL	Soph.	5-9	141
89	Dennis Stallings	TE / DE	Sr.	6-2	215

Coaching Staff: Bob Shannon, head coach. Assistants: Marion Stallings, Ken Goss, Art Robinson, Lenzie Stewart, George Walsh, Terry Hill, James Rucker, Morris Hunt, Frank Spriggs, Roderick (Bull) Fisher, Johnnie Oakley, Clifford Dancey, Derrick Johnson.